NELSON ROCKEFELLER

James Desmond

NELSON ROCKEFELLER

A Political Biography

THE MACMILLAN COMPANY, NEW YORK
COLLIER–MACMILLAN LIMITED, LONDON

Second Printing, 1964

THE MACMILLAN COMPANY, NEW YORK
Collier-Macmillan Canada Ltd., Toronto, Ontario
Library of Congress catalog card number: 64-11758
Printed in the United States of America

To my wife.

SO MANY PEOPLE HAVE CONTRIBUTED IN SO MANY WAYS TO THIS
BOOK THAT IT WOULD BE UNFAIR TO ATTEMPT A LISTING BECAUSE
NONE SHOULD BE OVERLOOKED. I MUST MAKE MY SPECIAL THANKS,
HOWEVER, TO GOVERNOR ROCKEFELLER FOR THE LONG HOURS HE
MANAGED TO SPARE FOR INTERVIEWS; TO DON IRWIN FOR USE OF HIS
INVALUABLE NOTES ON MR. ROCKEFELLER'S EARLY WASHINGTON YEARS,
AND TO ROBERT MCMANUS AND MISS BETTY BUTTFIELD, OF THE GOVER-
NOR'S STAFF, FOR THEIR FORBEARANCE IN HELPING CHECK SCORES OF
DETAILS.

THE AUTHOR

Contents

THE PREMISE

1 THE FIRING LINE 1

2 A MAN OF OUR TIMES 6

3 THE ROCKEFELLER POWER 15

4 BOYHOOD 22

5 DARTMOUTH 32

6 APPRENTICESHIP AT THE TOP 46

7 MARRIAGE 65

8 WASHINGTON ASSIGNMENT 71

9 FIGHTS FOR SURVIVAL 86

10 THE WAR YEARS 92

11 MR. ASSISTANT SECRETARY 114

12 A SEMI-PRIVATE CITIZEN 133

13 THE MOVE TO POLITICS 154

14 WINNING A NOMINATION 170

15 AN ELECTION UPSET 178

16 THE GOVERNOR 195

17 NATIONAL SOUNDINGS 212

18 THE GAGE DECLINED 239

19 A TIME OF TROUBLES 247

20 PERSONAL CRISES 285

21 THE SECOND ELECTION 309

22 A POLITICAL CREDO 321

The very rich are different from us.

F. SCOTT FITZGERALD

The Premise

To BE BORN in the inner circle of great wealth in America is to be born unique: it is to be born to status without distinction, to privilege without legal standing, to security so great that a whim can become a way of life. It is to be born furthermore, into the straitjacket of a class so circumscribed by the vastness of its possessions and powers that it turns inward upon itself because it fears and only dimly comprehends the stresses lying beyond it.

One consequence is that the very rich, particularly of the third and later generations, find themselves living outside the mainstreams of American life while participating formally in its rites and aspirations. They subscribe, with notable and well-publicized

exceptions, to the mores of the middle classes without the need
for conformity that makes those mores meaningful. They strive,
according to their tastes, for excellence without the goad of necessity. They sometimes accomplish much, but their accomplishments must be very great to confer personal distinction.

In the field of politics all strivings by the very rich are suspect.
It is part of the American folklore that because there is corruption in politics all politics is corrupt. So it follows that when a
very rich man enters politics, the public assumption is that he
"bought" his way to nomination or election. Although the absolute power of money has been proved time and again to be declin-
ing in American politics, this belief persists even to the present
when Big Government, Big Labor and Big Philanthropy have
risen to share the national power with Big Money.

The very rich, sharing the mores of the country, share also in
its folklore. The very rich of the second and third generations—
the inner members of the hundred or so families at the top of the
financial pyramid—therefore have been chary about seeking elective office. They have preferred careers in government in administration or diplomacy, posts that could be obtained without the
risks of public campaigns. And those who have sought elective
office—the Tafts of Ohio, the Clarks of Philadelphia, the Du Ponts
of Delaware, for example—have made the grade only on regional
or state levels where family reputation and local power offered
the best assurances of support. The rolls of the U. S. Senate and
the lists of the governors of the states attest how such policies
have succeeded.

But where does a Rockefeller seek a limited field of influence?
How does the bearer of a name, once the most hated in the country and still the most-recognized symbol of uncountable wealth
around the world, select one area where family power and influence are greatest and where the ever-present American suspicion
of the very wealthy will do the least harm? How, in America, can
the test be made whether the third generation of great wealth
can compete for the votes of the electorate without inviting
retribution for sins or errors of a distant, but not quite forgotten
past?

These were questions long debated in the closed family circle of the Rockefellers. They were questions that Nelson Rockefeller long considered as, in and out of government, he came to the conclusion that the White House is the seat of true power. For make no mistake: the White House has been his goal from the day he entered politics. Whether he succeeds will depend on influences and factors that may be beyond his control. He set out aiming for the top.

1

The Firing Line

THE REPORTERS WHO ASSEMBLED in the airy offices of the Messrs. Rockefeller on the fifty-sixth floor of Rockefeller Center on that somewhat sticky afternoon of June 30, 1958, knew exactly why they were there. They had been summoned to witness the entry into politics of the second son of John D. Rockefeller, Jr., and to hear him announce that he would seek the Republican nomination for Governor. There would be little new at the press conference. For a year, the political reporters had been hearing rumors that Nelson A. Rockefeller was going to run for office; for six months they had been checking on polls and surveys, "secretly" leaked, that showed Rockefeller as the standout choice of the Republican rank and file. They also had been checking out other directly contradictory data that indicated the Rockefeller cause was hopeless.

What brought out the press on that June afternoon was not the news in prospect, but the chance of meeting and sizing up the man making the news. Few of the reporters present had ever seen Rockefeller; none knew him intimately. And most had come equipped with a high degree of skepticism that any Rockefeller could get anywhere politically in New York State, or in the nation. The casual conversation before Nelson appeared produced a consensus that the candidate-to-be was a "tame millionaire" of the Franklin D. Roosevelt age who was taking a fling at politics out of boredom. Advance estimates of his abilities ranged from "playboy" to simple "I-don't-know's."

Beneath the skepticism there was also a certain amount of understandable awe. Like all Americans, the reporters were impressed by the thought of money in huge, vulgar blocks—like $200 million, which was the minimum estimate of Rockefeller's net worth, or $1 billion which was advanced by the romantics. It was worth turning out to meet and talk with a man commanding such incomprehensible wealth, even if he hadn't been providing everyone present with a front-page story. With the story assured, the reporters could indulge their curiosity.

The surroundings were conducive to imaginative speculation. The quiet luxury of the Rockefeller offices was impressive even to reporters accustomed to impressive offices. The art hung on the walls was authentic. The furnishings were tasteful and the colors soothing. It was about as unlikely a place for a political announcement as could be chosen.

But it was a pleasant place to learn the first human fact that most of the reporters were to learn about Rockefeller: he was late. As usual he had crowded his schedule, as he was to crowd it seemingly daily in the coming years, with more chores than he could handle, and time slipped away from him. By twenty minutes past the hour for the press conference, the talk was getting desultory; speculation was shifting away from Rockefeller and back to other interests.

Then Rockefeller's closest confidant, Frank Jamieson, slender, soft-spoken as always, with his white hair and slight stoop, appeared to announce that the subject was on hand and ready to go. After greeting the reporters he knew, including a colleague from his distant days as an Associated Press reporter, Jamieson led the way to the press conference down a long, quiet corridor. It was quite a transition. The press went from the conventionally luxurious reception room to a frankly modern meeting room, furnished with the same luxury, but definitely reflecting a strong individual taste.

After the press settled itself and the usual handouts were distributed, Jamieson, the public relations chief for the Rockefellers, and Jamieson's newest staff aide, Dick Amper, recently a political reporter for *The New York Times,* brought in Rockefeller through a side door. No one got to his feet because rising is a press conference courtesy reserved for those who win.

The man the reporters met on that June afternoon was a broad-shouldered, strongly built 5 feet 10 inches, just a few days shy of his fiftieth birthday. His thick brown hair needed a trim and his complexion could best be called sallow-tan, lacking the glow of the golfer and without the burned-in deepness of the seaside sunbather. He wore a double-breasted suit with lapels somewhat wider than were favored that year in New York and somehow managed to create an impression that he was a man too busy with other things to be bothered thinking about clothes.

His manner was friendly, some thought overfriendly, open and faintly impatient as if, already fallen behind schedule, he was hoping to make up lost time. The trace of impatience vanished as he picked up the papers before him after the greetings and settled down to the business of announcing that he was becoming a politician—a word that he didn't apply to himself that day or for many months, but a label he was to adopt eventually with pride.

My notes of that first political press conference held by Nelson Rockefeller are skimpy. I had gone to it because I was covering state politics and I was curious to see Rockefeller, whom I had seen around Albany, in closeup action. I remember the usual silly questions—and, as anyone who has watched a Presidential press conference on TV knows, reporters can ask some pretty damn silly questions—but I find there is nothing in the notes to show any deep probing.

The strongest memory of the press conference is the way Rockefeller threw himself into it. Once the give-and-take began, he seemed to forget the clock and that he was behind schedule for the day. He was absorbed in the immediate business of dealing with the press to the apparent exclusion of all other concerns. He was patient. He was courteous. He dealt gravely and without any hint of irony with the most naïve questions. Never once did he interrupt or look at his watch. He laughed easily at the weak sallies that pass for humor at such meetings.

The session dragged on. The news was disposed of in the first five minutes, but no one wanted to be quite that abrupt about it. Half an hour later someone finally closed it out with the traditional "Thank you." The reporters clustered around Rockefeller to shake hands.

Then they filed out, descended to the street and dispersed into the sticky afternoon. Their consensus was they had met "a nice guy." If any of them realized that they had met, also, a newcomer who was to make the most spectacular splash in Republican politics since Wendell Willkie, it wasn't apparent in the stories in the papers the next day.

Upstairs, as the reporters left, Nelson Rockefeller was stuffing papers in an attaché case, preparing for a quick drive to Kinderhook, New York, to make his first public bid to line up delegates to the state convention behind his banner. Politically he was on his way.

Whether he realized it or not the press conference that June afternoon had changed Rockefeller for life. From the sidelines of appointive office and White House assignments, exciting though they were, he had moved into the mainstream of American politics. From bystander and party contributor, he had moved to the firing line. In the coming months, he would be drawn deeper and deeper into the fray by the endless fascination that some men find in the battle for votes and the manipulation of party machinery. He would find in himself new qualities. And he would find new challenges.

He was hooked.

2

A Man of Our Times

NELSON ALDRICH ROCKEFELLER, who became Governor of New York at the age of fifty on his first try for elective office, likes to look back and say he has always been interested in politics. He cites as an example his college electioneering when he ran for class office at Dartmouth (he was vice-president as a sophomore, but lost out when he made a bid for president as a junior). Whether that was his starting point, as he finds it in retrospect, is irrelevant. Certainly, at the time, Rockefeller never contemplated a political career. He had gone to Dartmouth to prepare himself—as the very wealthy young men of his generation almost uniformly were preparing themselves—for a career in finance and

6

industry. As he wrote in the Dartmouth alumni magazine, in 1930, he majored in "economics as being most likely to be most useful to me in business."

The piece was written during Nelson's senior year when, freed of classroom routine by a fellowship, he plunged into the study of the arts, particularly architecture, painting and sculpture, which were to become lifelong enthusiasms. At no time in this year was politics a basic consideration in his program.

Of course this was only to be expected. From boyhood to the present day, Nelson Rockefeller has had the priceless gift of enthusiasm, the ability to throw himself totally into what he is doing to the exclusion of everything else. And in his senior year at Dartmouth, the campus was his center, his interests were his studies, and very little from the outside penetrated this closed world. Even the stock market crash of 1929, which heralded the worldwide Depression that was to plague a generation of Americans, seems to have had little impact on Rockefeller, although it came only a few months after his twenty-first birthday. There was nothing in his letters home during this period to indicate any stimulation of his political interest. In his essay in the alumni magazine the following June, he showed no awareness of the Depression. He was concerned rather that his fellow graduates develop interests to occupy their leisure in the years ahead.

All this was in character. Rockefeller is preeminently a man of his times, reacting to the pressures of those times and sharing the aspirations of his contemporaries. In the 1920's, politics was held in low esteem by college students, and, for that matter, the electorate at large. The election campaign of 1928 was bitter, but the battle was waged far from the Dartmouth campus, and in the preceding years the scandals of the Harding Administration, with a Cabinet officer winding up in prison as a bribe-taker, and the virtual abdication of power by Calvin Coolidge in his Presidency, made government seem impotent. The high purpose and intellectualism that Woodrow Wilson had inspired in the White House had faded with victory in World War I and his humiliating rejection by the U. S. Senate on the League of Nations. The heroes of the decade—a decade that brought politics to its lowest point in this century—were the channel swimmers, the golfers, Charles A. Lindbergh with his solo flight to Paris, the world heavyweight champions, Jack Dempsey and Gene Tunney. College students everywhere were reacting to Henry L. Mencken's wholesale rejection of all politicians in his *American Mercury*. The Baltimore iconoclast had set out to be a gadfly on the body politic and succeeded so well that, although his readership was limited, his point of view was reflected profoundly in ways he never dreamed. His influence, in fact, was so great that when the world changed in the Depression, he found himself without a career.

On the more intellectual campuses of the period, of course, there was considerable political interest but among, it must be stressed, relatively small groups. The Communist Revolution in Russia was still an experiment to be examined and debated. Whittaker Chambers, for example, was to write a generation later that he was recruited into the Communist Party in the mid-1920's while at Columbia University where an active "cell" functioned even before the movement, which was driven underground during the first years of the decade, surfaced as a political entity.

There is no evidence that any of this ferment touched pre-Depression Dartmouth. It was a small school with a big football team and its intellectual pretensions were on the modest side. Its goals were to train young men, chiefly white Protestants from the upper classes, in the prevailing mores and to provide them with a certain polish before launching them on careers as the leaders and managers of business. Political science was for the specialists and grinds. Nelson Rockefeller was neither, although he worked hard enough in his own subjects to win a Phi Beta Kappa on graduation. It is true, however, that in this period, while taking economics under Stacy May, he first conceived his detestation of Communism. May, later to join the Rockefeller Foundation, remains the chief Rockefeller adviser on the Soviet.

But there were profounder reasons why young Rockefeller largely ignored the politics of his college years. From the Civil War through the 1920's, and for the early part of the 1930's, government had been dominated by business and finance. The

Rockefellers and the Morgans, the railroad barons and the oil, lumber and mining interests all had their "men" in Presidential cabinets, their "own" Senators and their highly placed administrators to steer government into the paths that served them best.

In American folklore this was the accepted, although often deplored, order of things, and to Nelson Rockefeller, the college student, the acceptance was complete. He had met Presidents and Senators and the mighty of the earth, both in his own home and in his wide travels. He was aware, as he has remained aware, of the deference paid the family name, and the respect accorded to any Rockefeller pronouncement. He believed in the genius of American business, and he had no misgivings about bigness as he was to demonstrate in his college economic thesis, which celebrated, somewhat more romantically than realistically, the achievements of his grandfather, the original John D., in building the greatest fortune the world has even seen. It was only natural that the young man, casting about for a career in which he could distinguish himself, should fasten upon business as the true seat of power.

The climate of the times encouraged this thinking. World War I and the long, speculative, postwar boom had produced a whole new crop of millionaires—among them Joseph P. Kennedy, father of the President. And what Thorstein Veblen called the "predatory" instinct got a shot in the arm, as the new money contended with the older wealth for position and power.

It is doubtful that Nelson Rockefeller ever saw the situation in terms as naked as these. As a boy, he had been put through an elaborate routine to teach him the value of money—a limited allowance, for example, with records to be kept meticulously (something at which he often failed)—but money qua money meant, and means, very little to him. Like the other Rockefellers, he finds it a tool to accomplish what he wants. And like the other Rockefellers, his strongest drive, perhaps, comes from pride of family. This pride required the family to hold its place in the national hierarchy.

Americans have always equated excellence with wealth, but in the 1920's it became an obsession. Prohibition had spawned lawlessness across the land. The guttersnipe gangsters of the bottle era were debasing municipal politics by becoming partners, and often the bosses, in the corrupt machines that ruled the leading cities. Money, and the more of it the better, was the password to the popular esteem. On almost every level of government—always excepting of course the diplomatic corps and the upper echelons of the State Department—there was little to attract a man of wealth to the public service. A pervading national cynicism seemed to counsel against it.

In these circumstances, it is scarcely strange that Nelson Rockefeller, a young man in a hurry to find a career, a young man soon to command one of the great personal fortunes in the nation, a young man allied to other fortunes with power far beyond the sum total of their dollar holdings, gave no thought to a political career. His professed interest in politics was passive. As he came into control of his fortune, he would become a steady and substantial contributor to the Republican Party, as his father and grandfather contributed, but he joined no political clubs and he took no part in trying to run party affairs.

Any other course would have been foreign to his nature. He was a Rockefeller and no Rockefeller in the direct line ever had held public or party office. The family exerted its influence at one remove, confident that its wishes, as set forth by associates, would be duly considered at the proper times. There was no need to get involved in the details.

The national ferment of the coming decade would profoundly alter this situation. In the excitement of the political revolution ushered in by President Franklin D. Roosevelt's New Deal, more and more men of wealth would be attracted to government service —usually on the administrative level—and to politics as the rise of Big Government and Big Labor set up counterforces to the long sway of Big Money in running the country.

But Nelson Rockefeller was no groundbreaker. His generation accorded its highest accolade to business as the most honorific of careers, and Nelson accepted this evaluation wholeheartedly. His acceptance was the more complete because his grandfather, John D. Rockefeller, Sr., was and is one of his heroes. "He certainly is

an extraordinary man, about the finest I know," young Nelson
wrote of his grandfather a couple of years after leaving Dartmouth. "There are few people that I really admire as being all-
round successes, but he leads the list."

To those familiar with the literature of the Rockefellers that
began with the muckrakers of the turn of the century, continued
through Ida M. Tarbell's carefully documented study of Standard
Oil and was revived in the 1930's in Matthew Josephson's *The
Robber Barons* and Ferdinand Lundberg's *America's 60 Families,*
this appraisal is naïve. Nelson Rockefeller considers the naïveté
to rest with the writers.

Although he admits he never read the muckrakers and their
spiritual descendants ("I lived it; why should I read about it," he
told me when I put the question to him pointblank), Rockefeller says that from cursory acquaintance with these works he
can't accept their premises.

"You can't take a man out of his times and judge him arbi-
trarily by the standards of a later age," Nelson says. "My grandfather was a great man."

Rockefeller's statement that he "lived" the family story is, of
course, a touch of hyperbole. His grandfather retired from business long before Nelson was born, and when the Rockefeller reputation touched its nadir at the time of the infamous Ludlow
Massacre in the Colorado Fuel and Iron strike of 1913–1914,
Nelson was little more than a toddler. By the time the 1920's
rolled around, Ivy Lee already had embarked on the public relations campaign that was to change the public image of the
Rockefellers. Emphasis on the very great Rockefeller philanthropies, and a changing perspective in a society that was beginning to realize the benefits of the American industrial revolution,
rehabilitated the family reputation. And as the Ludlow Massacre
receded into the past, the realization grew that Nelson's father,
John D. Rockefeller, Jr., who was made the villain of the piece in
the press and in popular opinion because he was the major stockholder in Colorado Fuel and Iron, had never been aware of the
methods and tactics by management executives that brought on
the bitter strike.

This is not to say that the old stories were forgotten. In the years of Nelson's growing awareness of the world, it was still popular for politicians and demagogues to drag in the name of Rockefeller in their periodic diatribes against the evil plotters of Wall Street. And even Nikita Khrushchev, when looking for a capitalist bogeyman for his fulminations against the Free World, uses the name Rockefeller—frequently centering his attack on Nelson personally—as the most readily acceptable world symbol of great private wealth.

By the time Nelson reached his majority in the summer of 1929, the portrait of the original John D. Rockefeller as an ogre had faded. A new generation, a generation that had heard only vaguely of the Ludlow Massacre, knew the founder of the family fortune only as a shriveled old man who distributed dimes to those who approached him on his infrequent public appearances and whose philanthropies were adding luster to the family name. Overt hostility to the Rockefellers had all but disappeared, except on the extreme fringes of the left wing, and even there the hostility was more a nostalgic clinging to an old slogan than an expression of active enmity. The cold fact was that damning the Rockefellers lost its value as a rallying cry for the discontented. In the coming generation popular opinion would swing around behind the Rockefellers as the spread of their philanthropies earned them the gratitude of minority groups, particularly the Negroes of the South.

The change in the popular opinion of the Rockefellers was not, of course, solely the result of the family's policies. The whole climate of America was radically altered in the 1920's, and, among the very wealthy, the Rockefellers were only the best known of those who turned from moneymaking to philanthropy. Andrew Carnegie already had distributed his millions, and most of the other families who made or solidified their fortunes in the post-Civil War period were turning to foundations to establish their reputations with posterity. With the institution of the Federal estates tax in 1928, followed by the gift tax of 1932, this trend was to be accelerated until by the 1960's the proliferation of huge foundations would bring Big Philanthropy into play as a force in national life.

But there were profounder reasons than philanthropy for the changing American attitudes in the 1920's. Although the literature of the second half of the century tends to picture the country in the twenties in terms of its lawlessness, its corruption, the rebellion of its "flaming youth" against Puritanism, its vigorous growth in literature and its Babbittry, it was also a decade of tremendous economic growth. The capital concentrations that followed naturally from patterns established by the senior John D. Rockefeller brought a great expansion in business enterprise. The middle and lower-middle classes grew at unheard-of speeds. There was still grinding poverty. Slums were spreading their blight over all our cities; in the countryside tenant farmers lived in what amounted to peonage, although the word was never acknowledged in respectable vocabularies. Far more than the one-third of the nation that Franklin D. Roosevelt was to find "ill-fed and ill-housed" in the next decade was living in squalor. Labor and management still fought each other with guns and goons. Yet living standards definitely were on the rise. The mass-produced automobile, which was changing the patterns of American living forever, also was bringing to the new recruits rising from the underprivileged classes to the limited privilege of the lower-middle class a sense of property they had never known. Electricity appeared in the tenements and slums. The telephone became a necessity rather than a luxury. The long run of the bull market through the "normalcy" of President Warren G. Harding and the passivity of his successor, Calvin Coolidge, encouraged a vision of an ever-increasing prosperity, a vision more apparent than real, but a vision strong enough to mute if not silence the attacks on great wealth.

The handful of economists who rose to challenge the vision were the loneliest men of their era. The press, the pulpit and the Presidency were dedicated to perpetual progress. To hint that the prosperity of the twenties was more speculative than real was heresy to the American dream. To inquire whether the prolonged boom was concentrating more and more wealth in fewer and fewer hands, even though basic living standards were rising, was to invite the taunt of Bolshevism. To criticize business in any substantive way was, in fact, to seek out obscurity because there was no widely distributed outlet for the expression of criticism.

It is not in the least surprising, therefore, that Nelson Rockefeller, studying orthodox economics at Dartmouth, accepted without question the popular view of his times, complete with its enthronement of business as the guardian of all things American. He could not foresee, no man then living could foresee, that out of the torments of the Great Depression and World War II there would come a world remade in which new forces would arise to share the national power with business, and government would be invested more and more with the guidance of the day-to-day life of the people.

Nor could he foresee that in the changed world, a world in which Sir Winston Churchill would proudly label himself a "politician," politics would become an honorific career that would attract some of the most brilliant members of the very wealthy class to its practice.

The change from passive to active politics was far in the future for the Nelson Rockefeller who was graduated from Dartmouth only a month before his twenty-second birthday. He had a lot of growing to do and a lot of maturing. But when he finally made the big jump from the sidelines to the campaign platform, he would vault in a single move to election as Governor of New York and a place in national politics within striking distance of a chance at a bid for the Presidency.

3

The Rockefeller Power

THE HISTORY OF the Rockefeller family, as the Rockefellers themselves trace it, is singularly brief. For practical purposes it goes back only to William Avery Rockefeller, father of the original John D.

A lusty, handsome man of Germanic antecedents, with a great gusto for life and little talent for domesticity, William A. Rockefeller was a part-time farmer outside Richford, New York, where John D. was born in 1839. A patent-medicine man, who quite naturally picked up the sobriquet, "Doc," William Rockefeller roamed widely in western New York, Pennsylvania and Ohio when not farming, and as his business interests grew, he gave less and less time to his farming. By the early 1850's, the family moved to Cleveland.

The burden of raising the children, as a consequence, fell on John D.'s mother, the pietistic, strong-willed Eliza Davidson Rockefeller, who shaped the character of her famous son. A strict disciplinarian, she inducted her family into the Baptist Church in Cleveland and that has remained the family religion, with some deviations, ever since. Her particular care was her son John, with whom she lived out her later years after he'd achieved his eminence as the smartest oil operator in the country.

William Rockefeller, for all his roving, seems to have been a solid, reasonably successful, businessman. There is, at least, no evidence that his family ever needed anything despite his frequent and prolonged absences. And he was unquestionably warmhearted. Family tradition assigns him an important part in the Underground Railroad—the system of smuggling fugitive slaves to Canada that flourished in Ohio just before the Civil War. This is a point his great-grandson, Nelson, frequently makes in his civil rights speeches. Documentation on just how important William was in the slave smuggling is lacking, but that, of course, is only to be expected. The entire operation was technically illegal and there are few records of any of the participants.

Raymond B. Fosdick in his biography of John D. Rockefeller, Jr., comments that the "incompatibility" of temperament between William and his wife widened in their later years, but that no allusion to the situation was ever made in the family. John D. himself always spoke highly of his father, Fosdick noted, quoting his remark: "To my father I owe a great debt in that he himself trained me to practical ways. He was engaged in different enterprises and he used to tell me about these things, explaining their significance; and he taught me the principles and methods of business."

And John D. Rockefeller, Jr., who saw his grandfather Rockefeller at the family's summer home in Forest Hill, Cleveland, from time to time when William dropped in for a visit, remembered him as "a most lovable person. . . . All the family loved him," John D., Jr., recalled. "He was a most entertaining man, coming and going when he felt like it. He lived a detached kind of life and I didn't know much about it."

But while the Rockefellers pay more or less routine homage to William and Eliza, they really look upon the enigmatic, complex John D. as the founder of the family and the inspirer of the very great pride they all take in their name. (It is a pride that extends beyond the Rockefellers themselves: Nelson's wife retained the Rockefeller name after their divorce as did his brother Winthrop's first wife, Bobo Sears.)

So many judgments have been passed on John D. Rockefeller, Sr., and the methods by which he built his fortune that it is unnecessary to attempt another here. Certain it is that the Standard Oil Company, which he founded in 1870 with Samuel Andrews and Harry M. Flagler, was monopolistic in purpose and ruthless in method. Standard crushed its smaller competitors and fought the bigger boys with goon squads and in the markets. It extorted rebates from railroads and, by controlling the flow of oil, controlled its price.

But this was the standard operating procedure of the era. In railroads, in finance, in mining, in cattle, and in lumber, similar wars were being waged. What distinguished Standard Oil was its almost frightening efficiency and the complex corporate structure that John D., Sr., developed around it to centralize huge aggregates of capital in his hands for further expansion and exploitation. Historians since, most notably Allan Nevins, whose monumental *John D. Rockefeller; the Heroic Age of American Enterprise* is considered the definitive work on the oil baron, have found in John D.'s Standard Oil the prototype of all the great capital accumulations that enabled the United States to become the foremost industrial country of the world. And, while deploring the "questionable"—the word is Nevins's—methods that Standard Oil used, the conclusion in wide circles has been that if John D. hadn't lived, it would have been necessary for American capitalism to invent him in order to fulfill its destiny.

John D. himself never had any misgivings on that point. Devout Baptist though he was, he had no excuses to offer when he looked back on the history of Standard Oil after his withdrawal from active business. "Every one of the steps taken was necessary if the business was to be properly developed," he wrote. "And only through such successive steps and by a great aggregation of capital is America today enabled to utilize the bounty which its land pours forth and to furnish the world with light."

We are concerned here more with the wealth that John D. Rockefeller accumulated than the methods by which he got it. For his aquisition is history; his fortune remains a potent factor in the present world. And since his second grandson in the direct line, Nelson Rockefeller, hopes to be President of the United States, the inquiry is germane to the purpose of this study because he is one of the third-generation controllers of this vast wealth.

Putting a dollar value on the so-called net worth of any man is a kind of exercise in imagination; putting such a value on the wealth that John D. Rockefeller piled up in his lifetime borders on fantasy. All authorities are agreed that he was the world's first billionaire, but whether he made one, two or three billions of dollars as various students of the Rockefellers have estimated at various times is a matter of debate. Allan Nevins, who had access to records denied some other investigators, places his estimate at something more than $1 billion before John D. retired and without considering the value accretions of later years. For practical purposes, it is a nice handy figure. It is, furthermore, useful, because it crops up rather consistently in discussions of the Rockefeller money. *Fortune* magazine in 1931 published a survey indicating that the Rockefeller holdings amounted to about $1.1 billion in 1929 and about half of that on paper after two years of the Depression. By 1960, the same magazine, in rating the world's richest men, put the individual holdings of the direct-line Rockefellers—the five Rockefeller brothers and their sister, Abby, now Mrs. Jean Mauzé—at more than $200 million each, again a total in the neighborhood of Nevins's nice round figure. The income of the current Rockefellers is estimated at $5 million a year each.

These figures really convey only a fragmentary picture of the

Rockefeller wealth. It must be remembered that the older John D. was not only the richest man the world had ever known up to his time, he was also the greatest giver-away of money in history.

Here again the vastness of the Rockefeller holdings defeats attempts at accuracy. And the malice of some Rockefeller critics, who have charged that bookkeeping gimmicks were used to inflate the philanthropic contributions, specifically by crediting transfers from one fund to another as new gifts, has further obscured the matter.

The best evidence, however, indicates that John D. and his only son, John D., Jr., who guided his father's philanthropies, gave away between $500 million and $775 million in their joint enterprises, and that John D., Jr., gave another $400 million on his own account. The third-generation Rockefellers handle their philanthropies through the Rockefeller Brothers Fund, and already their contributions have been substantial, although not of course approaching the scale of giving of their progenitors.

The family philanthropies bulk as large as the family holdings in fixing the unique place of the Rockefellers in American society. For their philanthropies have endured and grown. From the outset of their giving, the founder of Standard Oil and his son insisted on careful investigation of the causes they were putting their money into, and they insisted, with lasting benefit to all concerned, on expert and efficient management of the foundations, boards and trusts they set up. The consequence has been that the public esteem won by the gifts has multiplied many times down through the years.

In the total assessment of holdings-*cum*-philanthropies, the wealth of the Rockefellers emerges in sharper focus, but it does not even suggest the power wielded by the Rockefeller family. Stewart Alsop, a sophisticated and knowing investigator of great wealth, has estimated that the Rockefellers—he includes all branches of the family, not just the direct line—and those bound to them by ties of interest control more than $10 billion. Alsop's estimate, whatever its accuracy, is significant because it points up the widely held belief that merely trying to count the number of dollars John D., Sr., amassed and passed on to his heirs misses the whole point, which is that through the fortune, whatever its size, the Rockefellers hold a unique position of power in our national life.

Social critics deplore wealth and power of such magnitude. Even Raymond B. Fosdick, in general a wholehearted Rockefeller admirer, wrote: "So vast a fortune under single control runs the risk of being an unhealthy ingredient in any kind of economic order. It was one of history's felicitous deviations that Mr. Rockefeller [Jr.] turned out to be the kind of man he was."

But the Rockefeller power was never so absolute as the romanticists, critical or admiring, imagined it to be. The growth of the public sector of the national economy, spurred on by the fantastic expansion of government spending in the Depression and World War II years, diminished the influence of all millionaires. And the rise of new fortunes in the twentieth century created new millionaires to dilute the power of the Carnegies, Morgans, Harrimans, Dukes, Armours and other powerful families which competed so fiercely with John D. Rockefeller, Sr., and each other in establishing their own hegemonies in the economy.

In this grouping, the Rockefeller money was always somehow on the outside. John D. frequently made alliances for specific purposes, notably with Andrew Carnegie in a bid to control steel, but he preferred to operate alone. This was chiefly responsible for the unique place he occupied in American life. The Harrimans in railroads, the Morgans in finance, the Du Ponts in their various enterprises, the McCormicks in farm machinery, the Armours in meat-packing and the Dukes in tobacco were always connected with others. In oil, John D. stood alone. And when he moved from oil to finance, he ranked from the outset on a par with Morgan, the premier banker of the country.

The limitations of financial power, even in a free society, are few. They intrude, however, whenever the consent of the people at large is concerned. In an earlier day, the Big Money men of the country made and broke governments. The significant money interests had their own members of the Cabinet and the Congress to protect their interests. More recently, however, the spread of egalitarian thought in what John Galbraith has called the "afflu-ent society" has raised the bulwark of independent middle-class thinking against the exercise of this power. It is the kind of thought that has compelled even the wealthiest to submit their actions to the judgment of the people. It has influenced even the Rockefellers.

This is not to imply that great wealth, whatever its limits of power, doesn't have a mystique of its own that molds its posses-sors even when they are constrained, as the Rockefellers are peculiarly constrained by strict family upbringing and the con-stant stress on duty imposed on them in childhood, to conform with middle-class mores and ideals. It was in the interplay of these forces that the character of Nelson Rockefeller was formed —a character far more complex than appears on the surface, and a character that merits meaningful study because Nelson Rocke-feller is a force in American political life that, for better or worse, will affect national direction throughout this decade.

4

Boyhood

NELSON ROCKEFELLER was born on July 8, 1908, on his paternal grandfather's sixty-ninth birthday, in a rented cottage on Wayman Street in Bar Harbor, Maine, where the Rockefellers were spending the summer. The birth apparently was an easy one. Mrs. Rockefeller was attended by Dr. Allen Thomas, of New York, but there is no evidence that his duties were more than routine.

The boy, named for his maternal grandfather, Senator Nelson Aldrich, of Rhode Island, was husky even by the standards of the day when babies generally came in larger sizes than is now customary. Young Nelson weighed in at nine and a quarter pounds. He was well-formed, healthy—the good health was to stay with him—and he looked like any other baby, except perhaps to his parents. Some family historian has recorded that the infant bawled out his first greeting to the world at exactly 12:10 P.M.

Except for having imported a physician from New York to attend Mrs. Rockefeller, the family had made no great stir about the event. Most babies of the time, rich and poor alike, were born at home, and Mrs. Rockefeller, in bearing the future Governor of New York and possible candidate for the Presidency, only conformed to the custom of her generation. In view of her respect for the proprieties, it probably would have been impossible for her to do otherwise.

News of the birth was telegraphed to both grandfathers, and, dutifully, they sent the usual congratulations. But the original John D., although ostensibly retired from business, was busy in New York marshaling his resources to fight the antitrust suits against Standard Oil, and Senator Aldrich was helping the Republican Party get ready for the coming presidential election. Neither took time out to see the boy. After all he was the second son and third child of John D., Jr., and grandfathers engaged in important matters are rarely so doting as the American folklore would have them be.

The Bar Harbor of 1908 was one of the two cherished summering places of Society, with a capital *S*. Although Cleveland Amory, the social historian of America's first families, says the great days of the resort ended before the turn of the century, only a handful of experts is equipped to make such a fine distinction. Then, as now, Bar Harbor, which attracted over the years the Rockefellers and Fords, the Potter Palmers, Stotesburys and Kents, J. P. Morgan and distinguished writers and artists of several generations, was in the popular mind the top gathering place of Society, less splendid in its display than Newport, but somehow more exclusive.

It was not Society that drew John D. Rockefeller, Jr., to Bar Harbor. He and Mrs. Rockefeller, the former Abby Aldrich, daughter of Senator Aldrich, were looking for a permanent summer home for their growing family. And to Mrs. Rockefeller, who was born in Narragansett, that meant a place close to the ocean. Bar Harbor, lying on the northeast coast of Mount Desert Island, which is almost within reaching distance of the mainland, with its scenic splendor ("Unequaled by any other American resort," Amory wrote in *The Last Resorts*) was worthy of consideration.

Mrs. Rockefeller, always mindful of her family's health and particularly the health of John D., Jr., whose frailties sent him traveling a good part of his life, was "convinced," as she was to write many years later, "that there is no air in the world like the air of Maine."

Another charm of Mount Desert Island in the summer of Nelson's birth was its remoteness. That was a time when the Rockefellers were being pilloried daily in the press, when Congressional committees were uncovering one trust after another, and when labor leaders and agitators had chosen old John D. Rockefeller as the prime symbol of villainy. Little of this ferment penetrated to Mount Desert Island. The natives lived off fishing and the wealthy summer cottagers, whose cottages ran to twenty to thirty rooms and required a dozen or more servants to maintain, and they had little interest in or connection with what the courts and the papers were doing on the mainland.

It was in a typical Bar Harbor "cottage" that Nelson was born. John D., Jr., had rented it from Edward McLean, the Washington publisher, who with his wife, Evelyn Walsh McLean, famous as the owner of the Hope Diamond, were among the Society rulers at the resort. But there is no sign that the Rockefellers gave any thought to capital *S* Society. Family-centered from John D., Sr., to the present day, the Rockefellers simply did not and do not play the Society game. They move in Society as a matter of course, but they are neither overwhelmed by it nor ambitious to shine in its sometimes curious rituals. And there is nothing in the bygone Society pages to suggest they made a big splash in Bar Harbor in 1908.

But it was Mount Desert Island, not Bar Harbor, per se, that attracted the Rockefellers. When John D., Jr., decided to build

the family summer home, he chose Seal Harbor, down the coast
from Bar Harbor, which was Society's main stamping grounds,
and in those days with limited transportation available (automobiles were barred) this cut off any close association with the
Society crowd, except for special visitors. John D., Jr., named the
place "The Eyrie," but the family preferred to call it simply Seal
Harbor and does so to this day.

The Eyrie, first occupied in 1910, is a rambling building overlooking the sea and the fine protected beach and perfect boat
landing in Seal Harbor. Eventually, John D., Jr., a man whose
passion for building equaled that of a Roman emperor, was to
add a huge playhouse, with bowling alley and squash court, formal gardens, extensive stables and miles of trails and roads to
create a virtually separate world that no one had much cause to
leave, particularly, as Amory has noted, because Bar Harbor
Society was slightly on the dull side for all its exclusiveness.

It was here that Nelson Rockefeller would learn to sail, to
camp out with his brothers and to do the other things that a
growing boy must do. But, although born in Maine, Seal Harbor
would never be "home" to Nelson in the intimate sense. That
word was reserved for Pocantico Hills, outside Tarrytown, New
York, where Nelson and three of his brothers, John D. III,
Laurance and David would eventually build their own homes.
The fifth brother, Winthrop, after splashing through the headlines in his $5 million divorce settlement with Bobo Sears, his
first wife, would move his base to Arkansas, where he remains
today.

Yet Nelson did a lot of his growing up in Seal Harbor, and
he still returns there for sailing when he gets the chance, although
The Eyrie is gone now, torn down a couple of years ago because
it was too big. Nelson's Seal Harbor place these days is a 16-room
house at water level.

The children of John D. Rockefeller, Jr., grew up in surroundings of underplayed luxury. In the three fully staffed
homes the family maintained (there was no servant problem in
the first quarter of the century), they could find anything they
needed or wanted from ponies and horses at Seal Harbor and in

Pocantico Hills to a gymnasium and squash court in the nine-story town house at 10 West 54th Street, just a few doors away from John D., Sr.'s, own city residence.

Governesses and tutors were on hand to guide and instruct them through the early years (the children started school later than is customary, beginning their lessons at home), and their taste was shaped by music lessons and the constant association of art treasures, ranging from Greek statuary to paintings to the Japanese prints collected by Mrs. Abby Rockefeller to the exquisite porcelains prized by John D., Jr., himself. The collection of art, largely instigated by Mrs. Rockefeller, eventually became so big that the town house couldn't hold it, and Mr. Rockefeller acquired the building next door at 12 West 54th Street to handle the overflow. This early association with art had a profound effect on Nelson Rockefeller, who later would found the Museum of Primitive Art and play an important role in the affairs of the Museum of Modern Art.

The town house, which had a fully equipped infirmary in addition to its other fittings—all the Rockefellers are extremely health conscious—was the chief base of operations, as Seal Harbor was the summer home. But it was Pocantico Hills, which the children referred to as the "country," that was the happiest place. Nelson once remarked that he'd give three weeks at Seal Harbor for three days at Pocantico, and he still prefers Pocantico when he wants to rest and think.

Nothing perhaps so clearly demonstrates the Rockefeller passion for personal privacy as the Pocantico Hills estate. Lying east of Tarrytown, about thirty miles north of Grand Central Station, in the Washington Irving country, Pocantico is a world unto itself with miles of winding roads for driving, riding trails that seem to be never-ending, the homes of the Rockefellers, a $500,-000 playhouse, swimming pool and, as a recent addition, a lodge built by Nelson after his election as Governor of New York to be used for high-level conferences. Originally, the holding amounted to about 4,000 acres, but over the years the size fluctuated as new parcels of land were added here and there and others were sold off. The present estate is about 2,200 acres, but the Rockefellers own a couple of thousand adjacent acres as a hedge against unwelcome encroachment.

Walled in part and ringed for many years with barbed wire, which John D., Sr., insisted on over the protest of John D., Jr., who was fearful of public resentment, the estate is a haven where the Rockefellers can be safe from any intrusion. For many years the grounds were patroled carefully, and even today you must be identified before you are admitted through the main gate.

All this only suggests the grandeur of the estate. The Rockefellers always have forbidden photographing of their homes, and this has applied particularly to Pocantico. Even writers, who just want to walk around and report their impressions, are firmly and definitely discouraged. Nelson, after his election as Governor, permitted some family photographs to be made within his own home at Pocantico, a graceful white building about a hundred yards from the gate, but resisted the heaviest kinds of pressure from newspapers and picture magazines seeking to do special features on the whole estate. Unable to get in, some of the cameramen turned to aerial photography, but the estate is so sprawling that pictures taken from planes didn't tell the story.

Luxurious surroundings of this kind were not, of course, peculiar to the Rockefellers. Americans of great wealth in the early part of the century customarily lived in this style, some of them a lot more ostentatiously than the Rockefellers. To the growing Rockefeller children, whose opportunities to see how the rest of the world lived were strictly limited in their preschool years, it was only normal; there was no standard for comparison.

Normal, also, because they had no other guide to evaluate by, was their strict childhood.

Raymond D. Fosdick observed that "religion to Mr. Rockefeller, Sr., was more a way of life than a theology." In essence, this meant that the original John D. accepted the rather austere code of the Midwest Baptist Church of the 1850's, which he joined at the age of fifteen, and lived by it. It was a rigid code, celebrating the virtues of thrift and abstemiousness and frowning on frivolities such as dancing, theatergoing and cards.

John D. Rockefeller, Jr., was brought up in this code, with,

perhaps, a great deal more emphasis on the strictly church side
of his religion than his children were to know, because in his
boyhood days the Rockefeller Forest Hill estate in Cleveland,
which the elder John D. maintained as a summer home after he
moved to New York, frequently looked, as one family friend put
it, like a "home for superannuated Baptist ministers."

When Mr. Rockefeller, Jr., started raising his own family, he
accepted the code, but modified the rules. At Brown, John D., Jr.,
had learned the pleasures of theatergoing and dancing. Unlike
his father, of whom Allan Nevins wrote, "Always a narrow man,
he remained narrow," John D., Jr., broadened as he matured, and
his marriage to the gay and witty Abby Aldrich, who brought
an infectious love of life to the somewhat dour Rockefellers,
encouraged a tolerance that possibly would have repelled his
stern grandmother.

As in his father's house, John D., Jr., introduced to his family
the practice of communal prayers before breakfast—a custom that
Nelson carried on when he came to raise his own children—and
strict attendance at church. On Sunday nights there was hymn
singing, which Mr. Rockefeller enjoyed, although the youngsters
didn't exactly share the enthusiasm as Nelson revealed in a note
to his mother when he reported that one Sunday while she was
away his father was "luckily" called out during the singing and
it was cut short.

Additionally, it was stressed to the children that possessing
money entailed responsibilities. Even before they could possibly
have grasped what kind of money they would eventually come
into, they were taught not to throw money away. And, apparently,
they absorbed the lessons. With all the opportunities they had
to become wastrels, the Rockefellers on the whole used their
money with discretion, and they have continued the philanthropic tradition of the family.

Along with impressing on his sons the responsibility that
money involves, John D., Jr., undertook to teach them to handle
money. This was to be accomplished by giving each an allowance
—Nelson got twenty-five cents a week as a boy—and requiring him
to pay all expenses out of it, save something each week and give

something to charity. Accounts also were to be kept as John D., Jr., in his boyhood had kept meticulous records of his spending in imitation of his father. But in the third generation, the Rockefellers were inclined to be a little careless in matters of this sort, and their bookkeeping was frequently more confusing than enlightening. Whether the system really taught them anything is moot. But there is absolutely no record anywhere that any Rockefeller ever despised money.

John D. Rockefeller III prepared for college at the Browning School, which developed out of a tutoring class that his father attended in the 1890's. But Nelson and his younger brothers, Laurance, Winthrop and David, after they outgrew home tutoring, were enrolled in the unique Lincoln School, an experiment in progressive education that intrigued John D. Rockefeller, Jr., who was the principal contributor to its support for many years. The school finally foundered after it became a cat's-paw in a Communist power play in education—a fight that involved Nelson Rockefeller deeply and personally—as the shadow of World War II fell across Europe. Nelson fought the good fight with John Lockwood, an association that led to lifelong friendship.

The Lincoln School was founded under the auspices of Teachers College of Columbia University to test the theories of the educator-philosopher, John Dewey, who believed that teaching strictly by rote stultified the pupil and defeated the purpose of education. Dewey's progressivism called for encouraging the initiative of the youngsters by giving them a freer hand to follow up their individual interests while insisting that they do creditable work in the standard subjects. The progressive system subsequently came under severe criticism from other educators—largely because it was introduced haphazardly in many schools and degenerated into mere laxity. But the Lincoln School could command the services of highly expert teachers, classes were small and the instruction was expert and patient. Nelson Rockefeller, at least, could never find fault with it. Years later, after his election as Governor, he would still talk enthusiastically of "wonderful progressive education" and credit his Lincoln School years with instilling in him a zest for new things and ideas that stayed with him. ("I'm never bored," he once said. "Leave me alone for fifteen minutes and I'll find something to do and I'll be able to throw myself into it." It proved a valuable relief from the tensions of a political life.)

The Lincoln School, of course, was a private institution, most of its pupils coming from well-to-do or wealthy New York families, with a sprinkling of children from the families of diplomats assigned to the United States from Europe and the Far East. And, because the school was experimental, there were also a number of scholarship pupils, some of them Negroes, from working-class groups.

So far as Nelson can recall, the question of money simply never came up at the Lincoln School. The atmosphere called for a kind of high-minded democracy, with only achievement and character counting for much. The children, on the whole, went along, being too involved in their own multifarious activities to spend much time on other speculations. The Negro students, rare in private schools of the day, were treated just like everybody else.

Going to school wasn't unalloyed pleasure. It wasn't long after he entered the Lincoln School that it became obvious that Nelson was no scholar. Although he had a quick intelligence, studies came hard to him. He soon raised his grades from the mediocre to poor with which he started out, but he had to turn into a plugger to do so.

His grades troubled his father, who kept telling Nelson that he was scattering his energies in too many directions and insisted that he work harder. Nelson himself was troubled, and, with the self-discipline that was bred into all the Rockefellers, he sweated almost heroically to come up to his father's expectations. But he had a serious handicap in his study. Somewhere along the line some tutor had slipped in teaching the young Rockefeller, and he developed a reading difficulty that has plagued him ever since. For some reason his eye transposes words and, particularly, numerals whenever he reads. The consequence is that reading for him is a slow and tortuous process, and, while he has disciplined himself to read the reports, briefs, studies and other papers that have flowed across his desk in an unending stream for more than thirty years, he doesn't enjoy it. In fact, he reads little outside his working hours, often putting off reading books on subjects that interest, or involve, him for weeks at a time.

He had great difficulty with Spanish, and in his junior year he dropped it as a subject, thereby ending any chance that he would follow his brother John to Princeton. It was, apparently, no great loss to Nelson. He had his eye on Dartmouth where he eventually matriculated. (Some years later, after falling in love with South America, he took a quickie course in Spanish at Berlitz to enable him to operate more easily. His mastery of the grammar remains uncertain.)

But his junior and senior years at Lincoln were far from being totally devoted to the battle of the books. When he could get away from his homework, Nelson led a rather gay social life, going to dances and falling in and out of love. He also indulged a taste for fast driving, picking up a number of traffic tickets while his parents were traveling. These violations he dutifully reported to his father.

All in all it was a happy boyhood. He got through the critical years to his eighteenth birthday without any serious scrapes on his record. He had gradually become aware that he would someday be a very wealthy man and that he would have responsibilities with his wealth, but he was far from being overawed. His school years had been on the whole successful, crammed with activity and the pleasant feeling that he was accepted by, and even popular with, his fellow students. And he was graduated from Lincoln with marks creditable enough to get him into Dartmouth and, more important, acceptable to his father.

5

Dartmouth

BY THE STANDARDS of the 1920's, Nelson Rockefeller was comparatively naïve when he entered Dartmouth in the fall of 1926. He didn't smoke (he never has, having won $2,500 offered by his father for not smoking before his twenty-first birthday) and he didn't drink in an era when needle beer and bathtub gin were the hallmarks of the collegian. Although widely traveled, he'd never hankered after the fleshpots, and the previous summer, he and his brother John, on an unchaperoned bicycle tour of France, celebrated his eighteenth birthday by going to a movie and "sitting up half the night drinking lemonade" as he wrote his mother.

The Dartmouth freshman was a husky, broad-shouldered 18-year-old, sturdily built and looking very much like the man of today, with a shock of brown hair that, then as now, frequently needed cutting. He was also the typical 18-year-old mixture of arrogance and humility, earnest and romantic by turns, and almost grimly determined to get the most out of college. And he was the richest boy at Dartmouth.

Later in life, Nelson was to say that he was never "embarrassed" by his family name or wealth, and certainly there is nothing to indicate that he gave much thought to his money at Dartmouth. He lived on an allowance of $1,500 a year, out of which he was supposed to pay all his expenses (but he frequently needed assists), and he wore the college "uniform" of corduroys and sweaters, easily managing to be as sloppy as collegiate good manners required at the time. He had no car, although there was no campus rule against having one, and he frequently went broke, borrowing, chiefly from his roommate, John French, to tide himself over between checks from home. He had to work hard at his studies to get marks that he could send home without feeling disgraced. And he tackled a bewildering assortment of out-of-class and extracurricular activities, from playing on the soccer team to teaching a Sunday-school class to setting up cultural programs, while putting in as much as six hours a day on his books, exclusive of his classes.

As at the Lincoln School, Rockefeller made friends easily at college, and with his multifarious activities his friendships were widely scattered on the campus. But, as classmates were to recall in after years, he had few intimates. The general belief was that he avoided close personal ties because he wanted to stay away from involvement with those who would impose on his family name or fortune.

There was more to Nelson's aloofness than a natural wish to avoid being made a chump of. For one thing, he was family-oriented to a degree unusual for his age group. He moved, so to speak, from the home to the campus, and as a freshman hadn't had time to develop the vocabulary of intimacy. And since most close college friendships are struck in the first year and ripen through graduation, getting off to a slow start often prevents the development of intimacy. In Rockefeller's case, there was also the matter of his deep respect for privacy, which is almost a fetish.

The recollections of classmates a generation later are hardly prime evidence. Memory accommodates itself more than we know to changing attitudes, with the consequence that the interpretations of a given set of facts are so varied that the facts themselves are called into question. However, the consensus seems to be that Nelson was moderately popular at college without being a campus hero. One classmate reported that "he got along with everybody and just about everybody got along with him." This was only a mild exaggeration.

His acceptance was publicly demonstrated in September of 1959 when Nelson, by then Governor of New York, returned to the Dartmouth campus. His ostensible purpose was to attend the Holy Cross-Dartmouth football game and talk to the students. But, in truth, the visit was the first stop in a series of trips Nelson was making to test what support he could count on if he decided to bid for the Republican presidential nomination in 1960.

Rockefeller was welcomed informally and warmly at a class box luncheon in a grove off the campus even though, as the score or more of reporters traveling with him soon found out, quite a number of his classmates were even then committed to Vice President Richard M. Nixon for the nomination and had no intention of changing their minds, old school tie or no. A complete poll of the class wasn't possible, however, because the luncheon committee, dismayed by the prospect of so many reporters, pointed out to Rockefeller that no arrangements had been made to handle so many extra people. The press obligingly adjourned to the football field to lunch on hot dogs while waiting for the game to start. Holy Cross won.

After the game, Rockefeller was cheered wildly when he addressed a big student rally on the campus. But the undergraduate reaction made no difference to the class of 1930, and Nelson eventually was to stay out of the New Hampshire primary because his soundings indicated that he couldn't rally enough support to beat the state Republican organization, which leaned to

Nixon. Whether this assessment of the situation was correct is
one of the questions that Rockefeller will be asking himself
about 1960 as long as he lives.

Nelson Rockefeller charged into Dartmouth College as he
charged into most situations in his youth. Fired by instant enthusiasm, he set out to prove himself a "regular" fellow, to prepare
for a career, to shine on the campus and to manage half a dozen
side enterprises all at once without giving thought to how he
would find the time. Later along in his college career, he would
be forced to narrow his field of action in order to keep up his
marks.

Nelson's choice of Dartmouth wasn't entirely governed by
the fact that he could get in there. His father was a friend and
great admirer of Dr. Ernest N. Hopkins, president of the college,
and Nelson himself had met Hopkins and been impressed by him.
There was also the consideration that Dartmouth was more or
less isolated from the social attractions of New York and Long
Island, which had taken up a great deal of his time in his last
years in high school. The suggestion also has been made that
Nelson welcomed the chance to strike out on his own without
comparison with his brother John who was already established
at Princeton. On this latter point the evidence is inconclusive.
There was never any undue rivalry among the Rockefeller brothers, and, although John D. III was more like his father than any
of the other boys (Mr. Rockefeller once said that he never gave a
second thought to John's spending at college, but that he had to
keep an eye on the others), he and Nelson never made any great
effort to outshine each other in sibling jousting.

Soon after he arrived in Hanover, Nelson launched himself
as a freshman by calling on President Hopkins. It was an entirely
natural act for young Rockefeller. He'd met Hopkins; he was going to be at the school for four years, and so he called on him.
He'd discussed the prospective visit at home with his father who'd
been mildly taken back by the suggestion, but gave in when Nelson looked disappointed. That newcomers just didn't call on
college presidents simply didn't occur to the new freshman.

Whether Hopkins considered the visit brashness hasn't been recorded. But while Nelson was at Dartmouth, Hopkins wrote to John D. Rockefeller, Jr., to report on his son's progress rather frequently, once sending a letter praising Nelson for his hard work and good grades that moved his mother "almost to tears," as she informed him by letter. And Nelson earned the praise: he was then in the top 3 percent of his class.

Another rather odd circumstance about Nelson's enrollment at Dartmouth was that his mother picked his roommate. Her choice was John French, the son of one of her friends on the Young Women's Christian Association Board. It was a bit of maternal presumption that could easily have been disastrous. But although they met only once—on a visit of the Frenches to Pocantico Hills—before they moved in together at Hanover, the two boys got along so well that they remained roommates for their four years at college. And Nelson later was to credit the arrangement with spurring him to stick at his books, because French, a brilliant, bookish boy, somewhat withdrawn, moved easily to the top of the class and aroused Nelson's always strong competitive spirit. "I was damned if I was going to let him take me," Nelson said later. Throughout the four years, each remained his own man. The two young men studied together, joined the same fraternity after a short-lived revolt against the "rushing" system and managed to avoid bitterness when they occasionally found themselves fed up with each other.

Nelson, diving into college activities in his usual headlong fashion, took even the freshman hazing in stride. He wore his green skullcap, got paddled ferociously and lost his shirt in a roughhouse with sophomores and considered it all great fun. He was shocked however when some sophs got stoned on bootleg liquor and cut loose with profanity the like of which young Rockefeller had never heard. For himself, he never developed the habit of profanity.

In his turn as a sophomore, Nelson participated valiantly in a pitched battle with freshmen on the campus, a battle that raged out of control until Hanover police were brought in to break it up. The row got Nelson headlines in the papers, which distressed him because he worried about how his father would feel about his conduct. It was needless worry. John D., Jr., could take such things in stride.

Mostly, Nelson wasn't newsworthy at college. He had no eccentricities and even his brief attack on the fraternity system was dropped quickly.

Just where Rockefeller picked up his mild hostility to the fraternity system isn't clear. He once said that the only time he was embarrassed as a youth was when he ran into boys from the fashionable prep schools at society affairs and felt shut out from their talk, with its inevitable reference to and grading of fraternities, and that may have been one reason. A more likely reason is that some teacher at the "advanced" Lincoln School spoke out at one time or another against the inherent "snobbism" of fraternities.

Whatever the reason, when Rockefeller found that John French shared his dim view of the fraternities, they wrote a letter to the Dartmouth paper condemning the rushing system. The letter treated of the question only lightly, merely pointing out that rushing was taking up time that could be better spent on study. Nelson noted, in a letter home, that "nobody got sore," when the letter was published. But even before it appeared in print, Rockefeller and French found themselves having a fine time attending open houses at the various fraternities, and before April was out they joined Psi Upsilon. The revolt was completely forgotten.

Soccer was the only organized sport Rockefeller went out for at Dartmouth, and while he made the team and played strenuously, he gave it up without apparent regret after a couple of years when he found it was taking too much time from his other activities. As a player, he was enthusiastic, but not particularly outstanding, and, since soccer was a minor sport, quitting the team didn't affect his campus standing.

He gave considerable time, more than the average undergraduate, to religion. He attended church regularly, sometimes going more than once on Sunday, and besides teaching a Sunday-school class of girls aged eight to ten at White Church, just off the campus, he became a member of the chapel committee in his freshman year and as chairman of the informals committee was charged with lining up speakers and preparing programs for the regular Wednesday night meetings. He welcomed this job because, as he wrote home, it gave him a chance to prove to himself that he could organize meetings and to learn that he could stand up before an audience without nervousness.

Peculiarly enough, young Rockefeller, for all his wholehearted acceptance of college life, took very little part in one of the most cherished undergraduate rites—the bull session. Those who were in Dartmouth with him recall that Nelson rarely sat up for the long gabfests, and that even if he joined a bull session he spoke little except when ethics or religion was under discussion. Part of the reason unquestionably was that Nelson simply couldn't spare the time from his studies, which, as noted, absorbed long hours outside of class. But there was also the fundamental reason that young Rockefeller had little bent for abstractions; he liked to deal with concrete topics, a taste that persists to this day, and the bull session is by its nature given more to imagination than realities.

Complete as was Nelson's assimilation of the Dartmouth pattern, his college years were nevertheless lived under certain pressures. For one thing, he got what amounted to VIP treatment from President Hopkins. From time to time he lunched or dined with Dr. Hopkins and his family, a courtesy that wasn't extended to the vast majority of undergraduates, and Hopkins himself kept John D. Rockefeller, Jr., rather closely informed of Nelson's classes and activities.

Another factor was that Nelson, because of his careless bookkeeping, often spent his allowance within a few days after he got it, leaving himself broke for weeks at a stretch. As a boy, Nelson was used to making up what he spent over his allowance by raising rabbits at Pocantico Hills and selling them to the Rockefeller Institute as laboratory animals. But at Dartmouth there wasn't any easy way to earn money, and though he once toyed with working temporarily as a dining hall waiter at a period when he was particularly broke, a reminder that he might be taking a job away from some student who really needed it was enough to kill the idea. On the other hand, young Rockefeller couldn't borrow as casually as a less wealthy student might.

Then there were family rules. He wasn't allowed a car until his senior year, although cars were not uncommon on the campus in the late 1920's, and in his freshman year, by agreement with his father, he stayed at home when most of the student body traipsed off to Boston, New Haven, New York and various Ivy League points for football weekends. Rockefeller spent most of these weekends walking or studying, and apparently didn't feel at all left out. At any rate, he never became a rabid sports fan, and even as a politician he didn't particularly exploit appearances at sports events, although he did take part in one of the many abortive moves to keep the Brooklyn Dodgers in New York in the 1950's.

Of course there was little social life at Dartmouth. Still comparatively remote even in this day of handy air travel, Hanover was a long haul from the big cities in the 1920's, so most of the students found their contacts with girls during the school year restricted to occasional campus dances. Nelson, who had become a dance fan in high school, invariably attended and, as one classmate was to recall, tried to dance with every girl present. But no lasting attachments came from these dances, nor from the considerably more active social life Nelson led in New York, Seal Harbor, Paris and elsewhere during vacations. Although he had the undergraduate facility for falling in love—he once wrote his mother that he "fell" for about one girl a year—he also fell out of love as easily, with no discernible scars.

His own entertaining at Dartmouth was on the modest side. Unlike his father, who once gave a dance-concert for four hundred while at Brown to reciprocate for the invitations he'd accepted as an undergraduate, Nelson never gave a big party. He did on occasion invite classmates to visit the Rockefellers in New York, but when in his senior year he proposed to take twenty-one of the "fellows"—his favorite college word next to "great"—to Pocantico Hills for a few days, he was advised that they probably would be happier elsewhere, and the group wound up at a resort hotel, with Mr. Rockefeller picking up the tab.

When he looked to the future, at least during his first three years at college, Rockefeller was chiefly concerned with what kind of career would offer him the most scope. His ambition to shine on his own account—"Nelson's crazy ambition," Robert Moses was to call it years later—led him to shift his position almost from day to day. At one point he wrote home that he couldn't see any merit in working his way up in a business "built by somebody else," but at another, he emphasized his hope of working with his father.

At one time Nelson contemplated becoming an architect, but never pursued the idea, although architecture remained a lifelong enthusiasm and he took an active part in designing his various homes. At another period, he and Walter Chrysler, Jr., talked about founding a fine arts magazine. That ended in talk. These ephemeral ambitions usually coincided with some new enthusiasm of young Rockefeller's—and their demise caused no pain. Later in life, Nelson, although still capable of instant enthusiasm, would develop the practice of taking a long hard look at all the angles before throwing himself into a new project.

But while Nelson dramatized his concern about his future, he was never overwhelmed by the problems ahead. And business remained the one constant in all his speculations. As it turned out, he wasn't going to be in any rush to get started after graduation. He was to spend nearly a year in travel with his bride before going into his father's office to start his career.

Of course the elder Rockefellers were familiar with Nelson's mercurial romanticism, and, while his father, a methodical man himself, frequently found his second son something of a puzzle, they didn't take his varied outpourings too seriously.

This was particularly true because Nelson steadied down somewhat after his freshman year, improving his marks and generally displaying an ability to organize his activities better. He even got around to putting his accounts in some kind of order, an accomplishment that his father celebrated by tacking a hundred-dollar bonus on his allowance. Nelson returned the bonus in one of his self-abasing moods, writing that he had been "sailing under false colors" and hadn't really earned it. His father's reaction hasn't been preserved.

Elected to the honorary society, Green Key, in his junior year, Nelson embarked on an expanded and productive work schedule. He was, at the time, beginning his study of Standard Oil as his economic honors project, editing and contributing photographs to *The Pictorial,* the college magazine, and taking a leading role in Psi Upsilon. It was the beginning of the period in which Nelson was to take charge of The Arts group on the campus and reorganize its activities, bringing in as guest lecturers such literary personalities as Vachel Lindsay, Edna St. Vincent Millay and Carl Sandburg as well as the controversial English writer-philosopher Bertrand Russell.

The thesis on Standard Oil was, as noted, a great deal less than objective. Nelson got most of his facts out of an unpublished study of the company written by a former employee. He tried to set up a date with his grandfather to discuss the thesis, but somehow it never came off, and the original John D. never read the finished work. He'd have found little to complain of if he had. Nelson found Standard Oil an efficient and, on the whole, benevolent monopoly, and, while he conceded that it probably boosted prices unnecessarily and raked in profits that "exceeded a fair return" at times, his general conclusion was that the good and bad balanced out. Nelson also advised that John D., Sr., never answered attacks on Standard Oil because "the accusations were false and therefore would fall of their own weight." It was, in brief, a loyal grandson's report, and Dartmouth gave Nelson an *A* for it.

Young Rockefeller was appointed a fellow—a special student allowed to pick his courses—in his senior year by Dr. Hopkins on the special recommendation of an advisory committee. Hopkins wrote John D., Jr., that "unusual importance" should be attached to the recommendation because it shows how successfully Nelson had met the challenges of college. Hopkins reported that the undergraduate reaction to the fellowship was: "Nelson rates it and ought to have it."

The fellowship year was particularly valuable to Nelson. His mother had inculcated him with her own love of art and paintings—her collection of Japanese prints was famous—and he responded with enthusiasm, probably out of empathy, for he had little knowledge and almost no understanding of the pictures he looked at. In his senior year he applied himself seriously to the study of art, and, while he doesn't claim to this day to the expert knowledge of a professional, he has developed a knowing taste that has been and is reflected in the paintings and sculpture he buys and surrounds himself with.

Also in his senior year he gave serious thought to the use of leisure and nearly thirty years later, as Governor of New York, was to break new ground by putting the state in the business of promoting culture in its towns and smaller cities, hitherto cultural wastelands with only an occasional college library or local historical museum to counter the movies and television.

In the spring of 1930, he was graduated *cum laude* as the metropolitan press sedulously noted.

The feeling that he was not living up to what was expected of a Rockefeller is threaded through his letters to his parents while he was at Dartmouth. The correspondence on both sides was rather voluminous. For a youth snowed under by campus activities and inclined to rush into new situations, Nelson wrote to his parents either at home or on their many travels more often perhaps than the average student. And his mother and father, in turn, meticulously kept up their side of the letter-writing.

The letters divide rather neatly, and, considered cumulatively, they offer some revealing insights into the family relationships. To his mother, Nelson wrote exuberantly, gaily and in great detail about his private adventures, including the girls he "loved" from time to time. He also sent her his more self-abasing "confessions," sometimes extravagantly phrased, as when he deplored his "selfishness" in thinking only of fun and swore to turn overnight into a model son. Mrs. Rockefeller, witty and wise enough to overlook the extremes, replied affectionately and promptly, occasionally throwing in a motherly sermon, as when, outraged at an outbreak of lynchings, she wrote that she meant to bring up the subject at prayers "and have it discussed at a family council."

Along with sympathy, motherly advice and frequent warnings to get enough sleep and eat properly, Mrs. Rockefeller spurred her second son to follow up the art interests he had absorbed from her. His own letters revealed how this interest grew.

Nelson's letters to his father were usually more businesslike. Occasionally, he would devote a whole letter to some boyish enthusiasm—for example when thanking him for the Buick roadster—but most of the time he seemed to write with a great earnestness, induced probably by the fact that John D., Jr., although a devoted, loving and frequently indulgent parent, seemed somewhat withdrawn from the everyday concerns of an undergraduate.

The deep affection between father and son shines through the letters. But they also reflected the incompatibility of their temperaments. John D., Jr., who was gay himself in a sedate way when an undergraduate at Brown, seemed to find the rising undergraduate generation, as represented by Nelson, mildly baffling. His letters were always warm and generous to the extreme in crediting Nelson's good intentions, but he found it necessary to fill them with gentle admonitions to his impetuous son. He counseled Nelson to learn patience, to learn to spell, to learn to harvest his time and, above all, to learn the significance of keeping accounts in an orderly and systematic fashion.

Nelson for his part reacted as might be expected from one of his mercurial temperament. He was quick to admit his failings and enthusiastic in promising to change. But he never did learn to spell and his bookkeeping was erratic at best.

The range of the letters was wide, reflecting, at least in part, the occasional difficulties that cropped up when the father and son tried to talk things over. "I cannot forgive myself when my attitude has even seemed to be such as to cause you to hesitate to talk with me freely about anything on your mind," the father wrote once when Nelson informed him by letter about an over-large camera bill instead of discussing it in person. "Forgive me for letting my temporary disappointment so show in my manner as to chill you and hold you aloof."

Yet the elder Rockefeller could grow almost lyrical in praise of his son in letters. On Nelson's nineteenth birthday he saluted him as "a man of whom we are very proud and for whom we have the highest hopes." And when Nelson wrote his father praising a speech on religion the elder Rockefeller had delivered, John D., Jr., fired back a letter, inviting Nelson to sit down with him and go over the speech point by point. "Such a discussion would be very helpful to me," Mr. Rockefeller wrote almost wistfully.

Once in a while Nelson, in thoughtless enthusiasm, would wound his father. Nelson's letter saying that he couldn't see that entering business and working his way up step by step to control at the age of sixty offered much scope for his talents stung the elder Rockefeller to a plaintive rebuttal. Mr. Rockefeller, whose career followed just such a course, didn't rebuke his son, but he pointed out in a long letter that business offered opportunities for a wide kind of service. He also noted that younger executives were taking top command in many key sections of the economy.

The little lecture was probably unnecessary. There is no evidence that Nelson ever seriously wavered in his choice of a business career, and surely he never really contemplated that he would be held back in a subordinate position in any enterprise he undertook. Furthermore at the very time that Nelson, probably in the grip of some new enterprise, questioned the scope of a business career, he was writing to his father for information about the family business, and when at home was often allowed to sit in on his father's conferences.

A measure of the constraint that temperamental differences imposed on father and son is the fact that they continued to write letters and notes to each other even after Nelson left college and entered his father's office to learn something about the family business. There was a practical reason for this of course. Father and son both traveled widely and frequently, and on any given day neither could be sure of finding the other in the Standard Oil office at 26 Broadway. Even when both were present, the elder Rockefeller's heavy schedule often didn't leave time for personal chats, while Nelson usually had enough other pressing activities to keep him on the go. But it was also undeniable that the communication block that sometimes developed between the two in face-to-face talks disappeared when they wrote each other.

None of this is to suggest that a serious schism ever developed between the two. Although he remained sedulously in the background, Mr. Rockefeller until his death in 1960 at age eighty-six warmly supported Nelson in his many endeavors and was quick and generous in his praise. And Nelson, whenever he pushed ahead on one of his projects in disregard of his father's advice, was meticulous in explaining his position and setting out his reasons. One such occasion was when Nelson became a trustee of the Metropolitan Museum of Art at the age of twenty-four although his father counseled him against rushing such things. "In accepting this position," Nelson wrote to John D., Jr., "I realize that I am taking the responsibility upon myself against your better judgment. . . . However, I feel that the advantages which this opportunity offers are of sufficient importance to outweigh the objections."

Nelson added that his "justification" was his feeling that the "aesthetic side of a person's life is almost as important as his spiritual development or physical well-being." And, ever the practical man, he went on to note that "the contacts which such a position offers are not to be disregarded."

It is notable that this disagreement, like most of the disagreements between Nelson and his father, was over a question of timing rather than substance. Mr. Rockefeller had no objection to Nelson becoming a Metropolitan trustee, but he apparently would have preferred having him mature a little more before tackling such an enterprise. And Mr. Rockefeller, who never could arouse such enthusiasm for the far-out art favored by Nelson, may also have hoped that time would give his son a deeper sympathy for more conventional paintings. In any event, no harm was done either to the family relationships or to the Metropolitan. In the long run Nelson found the Metropolitan too confining and shifted his interest to the Museum of Modern Art.

6

Apprenticeship at the Top

WHEN HE WAS running for Governor in 1958, Nelson Rockefeller bore down heavily on the fact that he was a "businessman." The accent was deliberate. His principal promise to the voters was that he would give them an efficient, businesslike administration that would get them more for their tax dollars (he never promised a cut) and would reverse the state's economic drift by accelerating growth. How better to base the pledge than on the indisputable fact that for twenty of his twenty-eight years since leaving college he'd been involved in the management of large affairs in private enterprise? The emphasis also helped him to avoid discussion of national and foreign affairs, which was a basic part of his political strategy.

The term "businessman" has many connotations. But the position of any Rockefeller in business is unique. He starts, as Nelson started, with few worries about financing. Although every new enterprise is scrupulously checked and the hazards evaluated, the money is always available for a worthy project. This, of course, removes one of the initial handicaps faced by most entrepreneurs and makes it extremely difficult to obtain an accurate appraisal of just what Nelson contributed to the success of his various ventures.

The difficulty is compounded because those in the best position to judge are rarely detached enough to make the most impartial witnesses. Associates who have prospered with a wealthy man are bound not only by interest but by their self-esteem to find merit in him. The disappointed too often color their assessments with bitterness. Even the record raises as many questions as it answers. Given a list of accomplishments, how does the outsider determine who should get credit for what? Nevertheless, it is the most reliable guide.

One thing the record clearly proves. Insofar as showing a profit is the mark of a businessman, Nelson Rockefeller is a good businessman. Given his background, he could hardly have been otherwise. Which is not to say that the enterprises he initiated always panned out. He had his failures, but he had a knack for knowing when to cut his losses, and, by any system of bookkeeping, he came out on the right side of the ledger in the long term, which is his way of looking at things.

Rockefeller regards the decade of the 1930's as the period of his apprenticeship. An apprenticeship, of sorts, it unquestionably was. But it was far from the dedicated plugging of the success story. At the outset there was drift, interspersed, as in his school and college years, with flashes of copybook ambition. Moreover, Nelson had the world of adult freedom to discover, as well as business, and other enthusiasms frequently intruded between his nose and the grindstone to which it was never really pressed.

There was also the fact that while Rockefeller assumed that business was his destiny he wasn't in any passionate hurry to bury himself in it. On his honeymoon trip around the world he dined and talked with poets, prime ministers and artists as well as scores of businessmen, and, as he wrote home, he found the businessmen too narrow in their outlook for his wide-ranging tastes. He didn't want to submerge himself in a single interest, and it wasn't until he'd matured a little more that he realized it wasn't necessary.

But if not business, what? The professions had no allure for him; he had the taste but not the talent for art; politics in those days was unthinkable for a Rockefeller; and, while he took his fun where he found it, he was unfitted by character and training to be simply a playboy. Dutifully, he went into the family office in the Standard Oil Building at 26 Broadway to learn something about the far-flung Rockefeller operations and to handle what chores his father deemed him equipped for. It was never exactly Nelson's cup of tea.

It was the beginning of a trying couple of years for Nelson—and for his father. Nelson's brother, John III, already was established in the office and, since it was accepted by everyone, including Nelson, that John would succeed to the mantle of their father, the second son was very definitely the low man. The staff automatically deferred to John III who was taking larger and larger decisions into his hands, while Nelson had no particular province of authority and was left to his own devices. Given his temperament, it made him understandably edgy.

Not, it must be emphasized, that this was an affair of sibling rivalry. Nelson recognized the position of his older brother and fully approved, but he kept up, in occasional bursts of enthusiasm, a certain pressure on his father for more important assignments. John D., Jr., never a man to move hastily, was constantly applying the brakes. A certain strain was inevitable.

At any rate, Nelson was restless. Partly to find an outlet for his energies and partly to prove that he could run a business himself, he joined with two friends in setting up a small company which, for a finder's fee, undertook to bring other businessmen together for mutually profitable deals. John D., Jr., approved the setup at the outset, but later, after Nelson bought out his partners and turned the company into a rental agency for Rockefeller

Center under the name of Special Work, Inc., he objected that it was taking up too much of Nelson's time.

Mr. Rockefeller may also have been influenced by the fact that the aggressive rental policies of Rockefeller Center, including Special Work, Inc., as agent, brought severe criticism from other realty interests, whose tenants were lured away by special concessions in a period when office space was a glut on the Depression market in New York. The late August Heckscher, one of the biggest real-estate operators, was so embittered he sued the Rockefeller interests for $10 million, charging they coerced tenants and used other unfair competition to fill the vast new space they opened up. The suit was never brought to trial. But Nelson has always insisted that the rental practices were both legal and within the framework of real-estate ethics as practiced in New York at the time. Whether those ethics would be condoned in the changed conditions of today is beside the point.

Nelson's interest in Rockefeller Center, which he and his brothers now own, never flagged. A director since right after leaving college, he made management of the huge complex his particular concern in the mid-1930's, and from then until he resigned all his business activities upon being sworn in as Governor on January 1, 1959, he kept in close touch with everything connected with the Center, serving at one time or another as executive vice-president, president and chairman of the board. Of course during his Washington tours of duty, he necessarily turned executive control over to others.

His interest predated his business connections. With the Rockefeller fervor for building, he followed the construction of the Center avidly, and, early in the proceedings, he teamed with his friend Wallace Harrison, who was one of the architects on the job, to speed up lagging work.

"There were about eighty engineers on the job," Rockefeller said a few years ago, "and what with the Depression and all they weren't in any hurry. They kept telling us we couldn't rent the place anyway. Wally and I had to knock a couple of heads together before they got the idea that we'd take our chances on the renting and weren't in a mood for a stretch-out."

He added reminiscently, with an understanding he probably wasn't capable of in his youthful enthusiasm, "You couldn't blame them in a way. There was the Depression, and after that job there was nothing ahead for them. But we were interested in the building."

In the early years Nelson also stood in for his father, who conceived the project and bore the primary responsibility for it, at most of the ceremonial chores connected with Rockefeller Center which needed the presence of a Rockefeller. It was his first experience in public relations, and, in the opinion of those who watched him, he came off rather well.

Less happy was his intervention in the artistic side of the Center. The plans called for a mural in the lobby of the main building at 30 Rockefeller Plaza. The painting, sixty-three by seventeen feet, would be a showpiece for the tourists. Nelson and his mother, the "artistic Rockefellers" to the family, prevailed on the selection of the Mexican Marxist Diego Rivera, a muralist of worldwide reputation, to do the work. Fees and opportunities on that scale were rare in the Depression years, and Rivera, whatever his misgivings about the capitalist system, eagerly grabbed the commission. He submitted a not very imaginative sketch and synopsis for a fresco, in color, portraying American scenes. It was approved by Nelson and his mother as well as the directors.

Once the contract was signed, however, Rivera's Marxist artistic "integrity" reasserted itself. He threw away the sketch and went to work on a painting glorifying Lenin and the Russian Revolution, with such "typical" American scenes as police riding down demonstrators on Wall Street. The shock to the Rockefeller Center directors can be imagined.

Nelson was appalled. But Rivera, so charming and cooperative while negotiating the contract, wouldn't even acknowledge suggestions for a change. Nor would he stop working. On May 10, 1933, he was paid off in full—$21,500—and fired. The painting was chipped from the wall to the amusement of the general public and to the glee of the Communists who had a fine time picketing against this capitalist destruction of proletarian art.

Eventually, José María Sert did the mural, portraying various American scenes, that still decorates the lobby.

Nelson's determined respect for artistic integrity was shaken.

Before settling down to concentrate on Rockefeller Center, Nelson had what might be called an indoctrination fling in another enterprise largely dominated by his family: the Chase National Bank, now the Chase Manhattan and now headed by his brother David. In the 1930's, the president was Nelson's uncle, Winthrop Aldrich, and Nelson traveled the country with him, a valuable experience for a young man whose business world was bounded by New York. He also served in the London and Paris branches of Chase. His European chores, which were chiefly in public relations, also involved a considerable amount of entertaining for Standard Oil. He found the work pleasant enough, but there was nothing in it to tempt him to stay.

Back in New York, Nelson began assuming more and more responsibility in Rockefeller Center. He sparked an executive reorganization that shook out a lot of fat cats, and took over the presidency himself. As president, he showed a true Rockefeller flair for cutting costs while maintaining standards, but he couldn't turn the $125-million complex into a money-maker. Office space remained in oversupply in New York all through the thirties, and it wasn't until the war put an end to construction that Rockefeller Center began showing profits. They've been piling up ever since.

One of the things Nelson is proudest of is that even while Rockefeller Center was losing money he instituted a labor policy that has been hailed by many in the building trades unions as one of the most enlightened in the industry. The success of the policy is beyond question: Rockefeller Center has never had a major strike or work stoppage.

The installation of the policy was the more remarkable because it came about without a crisis. When Rockefeller Center opened for business, most of the employees were members of a company union which was functioning more or less smoothly. But under the impetus of New Deal legislation, the militant building service unions were beginning to look with disfavor on employer-dominated associations. Whether Rockefeller foresaw an inevitable clash and moved prudently to head it off, or whether he accepted the growing opinion that company unions couldn't fairly represent the workers, doesn't matter. He presided at the voluntary dissolution of a company union at a time when other employers were fighting savage battles to preserve them, and he extended recognition to nine American Federation of Labor unions as bargaining agents. Labor didn't forget. He got a surprising amount of covert support in the labor movement in his first run for Governor in 1958, and, when he sought reelection in 1962, he was openly endorsed by nearly half the labor unions in the state, an unheard-of thing for a Republican.

The labor relations program, it should be added, later was broadened to provide the first pension plan in the building management industry and, eventually, a scholarship program was set up for the children of Rockefeller Center employees.

Deep though his involvement in Rockefeller Center affairs in the late thirties, it was in this period, also, that he began developing Latin-American interests, interests that would lead him first into government and then into some of his most imaginative and successful business undertakings after the war. It came about almost by happenstance.

Rockefeller made his first trip south of the border in 1933 when he spent a month vacationing in Mexico. He found himself drawn to the people, although, having failed to master Spanish in school, his contacts were limited almost entirely to the educated classes. But even after his investment in Creole Petroleum in 1935 won him a place on the board as a minority stockholder representative, he showed little interest in Latin America until 1937 when he abruptly decided to make a three-month tour of seven South American republics. The stated reason was that he wanted to look over Creole's properties.

As usual Nelson organized all the way. He prepped for the trip by taking a cram course in Spanish at the Berlitz School (a few courses later and after much practice, his Spanish would become somewhat better than passable), and he got himself briefed by experts on the political and social conditions in the countries he would visit. He also persuaded South American experts from Chase Bank and Standard Oil of New Jersey to go along. The party was rounded out by his wife, her cousin, Eleanor Clark, and his brother Winthrop. Standard Oil and Chase executives in the field were alerted to arrange meetings with government officials and others along the route. There would be time for sight-seeing and meeting poets and artists, but the accent was on business, which, undoubtedly, was rather dull at times for the ladies in the party.

It was a voyage of discovery and shock. Nelson was entranced by the beauty of the southern continent from the austerity of the Andes to the lushness of the jungles. He found the people individually friendly. He saw and was told of great natural resources ready for fantastic development once the capital and know-how could be found. He felt, as he said later, that here was a land rife with opportunity. At the time he had no ideas how to grasp it.

On the unpleasant side, he was distressed to find a virulent anti-Americanism nearly everywhere in these Europe-oriented nations where the North American concept of democracy occasionally got some lip service, but in practical cases was suppressed by the ruling classes. The endemic illiteracy and poverty appalled him.

He was distressed to find American business firms, including his own Creole Petroleum, callously exploiting the people and the countries where they operated. Creole at that time ringed its properties in Venezuela (which would become a second homeland to Nelson for many years) with barbed wire and paid no attention to the shantytowns on the perimeters where the casual laborer scrounged out their lives without sanitation, without schools and without rudimentary health services. And worse, as he saw it, without anybody caring.

Everywhere he found the Indians oppressed and disenfranchised to greater or less degree. In Peru he was shocked to learn that the government refused to provide money to preserve priceless Indian mummies because the Spanish-descended rulers looked down on the Indians. (This so offended his respect for art that he arranged for U. S. sources to supply the money, one of those nice little gestures open to a Rockefeller.)

As he traveled around South America, mostly by plane but sometimes by Standard Oil yacht, he encountered the Communist movement feeding on the misery of the discontented and displaced in country after country. The Reds paid him the compliment of attacking him savagely as an exploiter and robber wherever they had a paper. He would get more of the same, and even more savagely, a few years later when he would actively fight the Latin Communists as a government officer.

Rockefeller returned to New York without any new plans and not realizing, perhaps, that somewhere along the line he'd made a subconscious commitment that would absorb his interest and a great deal of his time over the next two decades. But he brought back two profound convictions: that the callous behavior of U. S. companies in South America would endanger their assets over the long run; and that the private enterprise system itself in Latin America faced the challenge of meeting the humanitarian needs of the people or going under.

Later that year, Nelson summed up his findings for three hundred Standard of New Jersey executives brought together from all over the world for a stockholders' meeting. His theme was "the social responsibility of corporations." Ownership, he said, must recognize that it has a responsibility to the community that goes beyond simply making profits, or take the dire risk that it will be driven out. The speech was received politely—it could hardly have been otherwise considering the speaker and the setting—and the executives quickly changed the subject.

But the following year, the Mexican government of President Lázaro Cárdenas made Nelson's point for him by seizing U. S. owned oil fields. The expropriation hit Standard Oil particularly hard, and sometime later Nelson undertook an informal approach to President Cárdenas in an effort to work out a settlement. Nothing came of the talk, but Cárdenas and Rockefeller hit it off well and became good friends.

The Standard Oil speech, however, did encourage some of the

rising men in Creole Petroleum who shared Nelson's assessment of the situation. With an important stockholder in their corner, they were emboldened to begin a series of reforms that began with a requirement that all field executives learn Spanish and take part in community life. In time, the barbed wire around the Creole camp would come down, medical help would be provided for the shantytowns and local authorities would be prevailed upon to provide sanitation. Eventually there would be schools and even scholarships to train Venezuelans for technical and professional posts with the company.

In 1939, the year of Rockefeller's second trip to South America, Creole, on his urging, commissioned an engineering survey of Venezuela to develop plans for improving conditions. The principal finding was that the great immediate need was to develop local food production, which had fallen below sustenance levels when the economy shifted to oil, in order to cut the cost of living by eliminating or at least reducing food imports.

The recommendation pointed out an area in which free enterprise could operate to serve humanitarian needs. Rockefeller and his friends, after examining the situation carefully, hit on the device of a development company, financed in part by local capital in order to involve the interests of the local government, as the best approach. This would provide funds for necessary studies, to pay technicians and experts and to obtain needed machinery and equipment.

The first of the many development companies Rockefeller would help set up in South America was organized in Venezuela to help increase food production. Unfortunately by the time its preliminary work was finished, the war in Europe intervened and the project ground to a standstill. However, another Venezuelan development company, founded about the same time, built the highly successful Avila Hotel in Caracas, which was a paying proposition from the day it opened and richly rewarded the investors. Rockefeller also had interests in Brazilian development companies that helped build a paper mill and a steel plant during the war years.

And in the summer of 1940 when Nelson went to Washington

to become Coordinator of Inter-American Affairs, he put his private Latin-American plans on ice for the duration.

The Washington assignment developed directly out of Nelson's early involvement with South America, and in the five years on the job he lived South American problems day and night. He was able, as related elsewhere, to get programs started toward some humanitarian reforms, by use of U. S. money when it was available and by obtaining the interest and cooperation of the home governments in many cases. But he knew it was only a start.

When Nelson returned to his desk in Rockefeller Center in the late summer of 1945, this time donning the hat of chairman of the board, he was more determined than ever to follow through on his personal Latin-American program. War spending in the United States already had been cut back sharply, and with the nation's own economic future uncertain and the problem of the reconstruction of Europe engaging the foreign-policy makers, he foresaw that this country would again lose interest in its neighbors to the south. His fears were prophetic.

"I felt," Rockefeller said later, "that if private enterprise didn't step in and get things started nobody would do anything."

But Nelson's thinking on what could be done in South America had sharpened under the impact of his Washington experiences. On the one hand were the broad social problems such as health, sanitation, education which usually are dealt with in the public sector of the economy in the United States. On the other were projects designed to improve economic conditions directly, to provide jobs and to modernize business; projects, in brief, that, within the free enterprise system, are generally left to private capital.

Never one to enlarge the public sector of the economy unnecessarily at the expense of the private, Rockefeller conceived the plan of setting up two distinct organizations which would supplement but not impinge on each other. To handle the general welfare problems, he founded the American International Association for Economic and Social Development (AIA). The International Basic Economy Corporation (IBEC) was organized to stimulate economic growth under accepted business practices.

Both were highly successful and both are still in operation today.

The AIA was set up as a nonprofit, philanthropic organization with the Rockefellers putting up the money and contributing to it regularly. It also got $3 million in outright grants from the oil companies in Venezuela, which were worried about their future in the postwar years. Latin-American governments and local governments contributed on a matching basis on specific projects.

No dollar value can ever be put on what the AIA operations have meant to the people of South America. But a measure of its success is that it is constantly expanding, with a backlog of appeals always at hand. It can expand because it follows the practice of turning its projects over to local authorities once they are running smoothly, thus freeing its funds for new undertakings.

As for IBEC, the Rockefellers put about $16 million into it, all in all, and the oil companies about $15 million. Its start was ragged, but after four years the corporation began breaking even. By the late 1950's when Nelson withdrew from active management, it was netting more than $2 million a year on a turnover of about $80 million. That's sound business by any cash register.

Operating on different levels, AIA and IBEC had, nevertheless, a common goal: to use the tools of private enterprise to encourage a rising standard of living that would create the demand necessary to attract the huge capital investment needed to lift South America out of its semifeudal state.

"We had to run two operations," Rockefeller once commented. "I don't believe you help people by just handing them money. You've got to get them involved. AIA started a lot of things the local governments took over. But IBEC proved that you could make money on a straight business basis. We had to make it pay. There's nothing convinces a businessman like a profit."

Venezuela and Brazil were the starting countries for both operations but both expanded as their experience grew. AIA now offers information services to all of South America and is a partner in a cooperative farm project in far-off India. IBEC spread around the world. It now has enterprises in nine Latin-American countries and Puerto Rico; it introduced the supermarket to Italy; and it has interests in the Middle East, Pakistan and Thailand. It is also heavily engaged in an international finance company set up to provide capital for underdeveloped nations.

Rockefeller was far more than the Maecenas who found the money to launch the two projects—the original contributions to the AIA came from the Rockefeller Brothers Fund, a corporation set up in 1940 to handle joint philanthropic enterprises of the third-generation Rockefellers, and the IBEC capital was put up by the Rockefeller Brothers, Inc., a holding company for joint ventures, although Nelson poured additional millions of his own into the IBEC operation to get it on its feet. He took on the active management of both efforts.

As president of both AIA and IBEC, he commuted to South America, consulting with government officials and local investors, reviewing plans and programs on the spot, troubleshooting and not infrequently using the prestige of the family name and his own recognized ability to get along with people to straighten out public relations rows that cropped up from time to time. For the Rockefeller programs weren't by any means accepted on his say-so. The political left, both in Brazil and Venezuela, saw in them a dark plot by the "Standard Oil magnate" to get his hands on oil lands for future exploitation; certain businessmen and landowners frankly feared that Rockefeller would "rock the boat" and endanger the system under which they thrived personally. The propertied people also echoed the Communist line that Nelson would aim for monopoly in any field he entered. In time, Frank Jamieson would devise an efficient public relations network to deal with these attacks (never wholly successfully, of course), but at the start Rockefeller felt he had to be on the firing line when the going was rough and key projects were endangered.

In these efforts he often barged in on his critics—editors, politicians, landowners and businessmen, alike—to sit down and argue out their objections with them. "I don't know that I convinced very many of them," Rockefeller has said, "but usually they'd listen and once in a while as we talked I'd spot something that we were doing wrong and was causing the trouble, something we could do something about."

AIA, by its nature, attracted few attacks. It was, and remains, a grass-roots operation. It was modest in its approach. It always had the blessing of local authorities, it acquired no land, and it, quite patently, didn't make any money. Superstition and ignorance were its principal foes, although occasionally it would become a matter of contention between the outs and the ins in a local political squabble. Rockefeller, when he ran into one of these situations on his field trips, would call community meetings and challenge the critics to state their case. As often as not he found that the attacks were based on misinformation, and when the projects were explained they would get full support.

Of necessity the emphasis of the AIA was on education and vocational training. The people of the back country of Venezuela and Brazil were mostly of Indian descent, overwhelmingly illiterate. They lived on the ragged edge of malnutrition and their farming was primitive. The infant mortality rate was high; life expectancy was low; and they had no access to medical care nor even primitive concepts of sanitation. They needed just about everything.

Nelson Rockefeller was never under any illusions about what the AIA could accomplish. In a note to his father at the start of operations, he conceded it might seem a "preposterous" project for private undertaking, but expressed hope that even the most modest beginnings might set an example that could be expanded by popular support. It was a hope destined to be disappointed in the main. Venezuela and Brazil followed up and broadened the programs within the limits of their resources, but their chronic economic difficulties restricted the program to only a small fraction of their people. Years afterward, Rockefeller acknowledged that the job was beyond private efforts. "There is just too much to be done," he said. "It's too big, too vast. It will take a massive effort they can't afford right now."

Yet the gains of the AIA were not inconsequential. Spending

at a rate that averaged out to about a million a year overall, it made definite contributions to the postwar increase in agricultural productivity—as much as 50 percent—in Venezuela and Brazil, and to a dramatic drop in the infant mortality rates.

Its methods were unobtrusive. Its medical teams, consisting of a doctor and nurse, traveled the back country by jeep and truck, sometimes carrying along a portable movie projector to lure in the "patients," and vaccinated thousands (once, at least, forestalling the threat of a smallpox epidemic). In the villages, clinics were held to instruct the women in how to care for their infants and to teach basic first aid. Medicines were distributed as needed, and disease-breeding swamps were drained and sprayed in cooperation with the local authorities. The local government also was aided in setting up schools to attack illiteracy.

Agricultural experts of the AIA ran what might be likened to county farm bureaus to help the villagers improve their crops, and, of course, their diets. Simple tools were provided for farmers; improved seed was made available.

But it was never in any sense a giveaway program. As local governments were required to share in any project undertaken in their localities, so the people were expected to show good faith by putting forth their best efforts when help was extended to them. This was particularly true for the farmers with whom the AIA experts worked closely to see that they followed up on what they were taught.

On occasion, the farmers got help beyond this. In the Brazilian state of Minas Gerais, for example, farmers cooperating with the agricultural program were stymied by lack of credit. The governor, who had been worried about the problem, invited AIA and Rockefeller, personally, to see what could be done.

It was a problem that had long engaged Rockefeller's attention. But AIA was not and could not become a financing agency. Nelson and his experts, however, came up with a plan to minimize the risk on farm loans, and, with the cooperation of the Minas Gerais government and a state bank, it was put in operation.

The plan was simple. Teams of experts were formed to select suitable applicants for loans and put them through a super-screening. The teams consisted of a man and a woman, the man charged with planning the improvement of the prospective bor-rower's property down to deciding what crops were to be sown, how much livestock was needed, where and how to irrigate. He also taught the use of fertilizers and supervised the spending of the money step by step down to the last penny. The woman's primary function was to help the farmer's family improve its health and sanitation programs, stimulate a desire for education and get them started toward a higher standard of living, which, in itself, made them better loan risks. Loans were made at 8 percent, dramatically lower than the prevailing rate for high-risk farm credit, by a state bank with government encouragement. Defaults were so rare the loans became a profitable enterprise for the moneymen.

Originally there were only a few teams in Minas Gerais state, but the scheme worked so well it was expanded swiftly into other states. Eventually, the federal government of Brazil undertook its sponsorship on a national basis.

The overall AIA operation, although it was philanthropic in concept and humanitarian in practice, merits discussion in con-nection with Rockefeller's business career, however, because (1) it provided an outlet through which business (chiefly the oil companies) could discharge some of the "social responsibilities" that Nelson believed devolved upon corporations, and (2) it was an opening wedge toward raising standards of living which he considered the *sine qua non* for creating the demand needed to expand the economy.

For Rockefeller, who always put his faith in accelerated growth, making it the keystone of the fiscal policy of New York State when he became Governor, believed South America was on the verge of tremendous expansion, and the parallel opera-tion of the International Basic Economy Corporation was con-ceived to encourage that expansion under free enterprise, and profit by it. Whatever abetted demand, therefore, contributed to the climate for expansion. After all, families with cash incomes as low as seventy dollars a year can't buy a lot of anything.

It was the opinion of Rockefeller and his advisers in IBEC that the South American venture could best be launched with a big splash. The theory was that large-scale investment, distributed broadly in a number of spectacular enterprises, would jolt the economy into forward movement and, by stimulating competition, encourage local capital to look for opportunity at home. This view was encouraged by the government of President Rómulo Betancourt, a onetime critic of Rockefeller, who wound up as his great friend. Betancourt's government, already involved in a vast program to free Venezuela from its almost total dependence on oil, put $4.5 million into nonvoting stock in Venezuela Basic Economy Corporation, which was set up as an IBEC subsidiary. VBEC was absorbed by the parent company several years later with the government withdrawing.

IBEC and VBEC had their splash, but it came very close to washing them out. Spawning subsidiaries at a rate that outsped their planning and administrative capabilities, the two corporations were soon overextended and forced to shrink their operations drastically. Only the fact that Rockefeller and the other sponsors were in a position to pour in more capital saved them. Later Rockefeller acknowledged that he should have listened to his father, who had counseled him to take things one at a time. But in the beginning Nelson wanted a dramatic achievement, and his wish, supported by what appeared to be sound economic thinking, was enough reason to overrule John D., Jr.

It is not within the purview of this book to trace the intricate financial manipulations required to keep IBEC and VBEC afloat. Among the subsidiaries there were more than a score of reorganizations, mergers, consolidations and liquidations. Cherished programs had to be drastically revised; some were liquidated outright. The scope of nearly all of the projects had to be cut back. It was a trying and galling period for Rockefeller. However, after the shake-out was well along and things began to look up again, he got a wry kind of comfort out of the changed attitude of the Caracas business community. Initial hostility from those fearing competition was softened by the spectacle of IBEC's floundering, Rockefeller noted, and gradually Nelson became a "member of the club" in the Venezuela business world.

Yet IBEC made lasting contributions to the economy of Venezuela and Brazil. If it failed to create a modern Venezuelan fishing industry because the fishermen preferred to use their modernized boats for smuggling when the market was slow and because there was no wide taste for fish, it nevertheless instituted a system of supermarkets that revolutionized retail trade in Venezuela and evoked so much local competition that food prices declined 15 percent. If its first vegetable crop at Monte Sacro in Venezuela's Chirgua Valley rotted on the ground because nobody had made arrangements to get it to market, it also took an insignificant milk-pasteurizing operation, serving only a handful of the wealthy, and developed it into a major industry, with more than a dozen local companies competing, that made pasteurized milk available for the first time to most city dwellers.

It introduced a hybrid corn strain in Brazil that could survive the hazards of jungle agriculture, and founded a seed industry. It imported heavy farm equipment that cleared more than a hundred thousand acres. It built coffee processing plants in Guatemala and El Salvador. It built grain elevators in Brazil. And, everywhere, it conducted basic research, the benefits of which remained even after specific projects were canceled out.

In a related activity, IBEC also entered the low-cost housing field in the United States and built successful developments in Florida and Puerto Rico.

But the focus always was on South America. There Rockefeller proved himself as a businessman—as the balance sheet shows—who met the tests of competition on a stern level and survived financially against the odds. He would be entitled when he turned to politics to cite his business background as he might not have been entitled had he chosen the safer course of sticking strictly to Rockefeller family affairs and safely established interests.

Not that he accomplished all, or even most, of what he hoped for in South America. He was particularly disappointed that other risk capital, on the whole, stayed out of hemispheric development. Perhaps his early difficulties deterred some. More potent inhibiting factors, however, were, and are, the political instability and inflation that bring recurring threats of expropriation.

"There's a great deal that can and must be done in South America," Rockefeller said sometime ago, "but we can only help. It's up to the people and their governments to give us the kind of climate business can work in."

7

Marriage

THE WEDDING OF Mary Todhunter Clark and Nelson Rockefeller on June 23, 1930, immediately after Nelson's graduation
from Dartmouth, drew a fashionable crowd of fifteen hundred
to Bala-Cynwyd, a Philadelphia suburb, and was dutifully and
respectfully reported in the society columns. Their divorce,
nearly thirty-two years later, was a worldwide sensation on page
one of nearly every important newspaper.

The special importance of the divorce—which, standing
alone, was big human-interest news because it involved a Rockefeller and the breakup of a marriage that lasted three decades—
stemmed, of course, from the unique position Nelson occupied

after the 1960 election as the Republican most likely to be nominated for President in 1964. For this reason, it will be discussed
in a later chapter.

The marriage of Nelson and Mary Clark occasioned no surprise. They were summer neighbors, so to speak, at Mount Desert
Island in Maine where the Clark place in the Bar Harbor Society community was only a short drive from the Rockefeller estate
at Seal Harbor, and, from their early high-school days, the
Rockefeller boys and the six Clark brothers sailed and played
away their vacations together. The future Mrs. Rockefeller was
sometimes included in the fun. More often, she was not.

There was no teen-age pairing off. Nelson discovered girls
about the time his father gave him a sporty little Ford roadster
to drive around Seal Harbor, and he plunged into the study of
this delightful subject gaily and enthusiastically. By his own
recollection he fell in love at least once a year—and fell out just
as facilely. His letters home carried frequent references to the
"peaches" he met on his travels in Europe and in his first years
at Dartmouth. Always, however, he seemed to go out of his way
to emphasize that he realized the various attachments were temporary.

Though Nelson "played the field" in his first two years at
college, his most frequent girl at the big dances was Miss Clark,
and in his junior year, while far from forsaking all others, his
focus in her direction sharpened. By January, 1929, when Mary
Clark made a trip to Europe and Egypt with Mr. and Mrs. John
D. Rockefeller, Jr., and Nelson's brother David, he began making sounds like a jealous suitor. Still no pledges were exchanged.

That didn't come until the end of the summer of 1929 which
Nelson spent with his brother Laurance, his particular buddy
at this period, sailing in the Arctic with an expedition headed
by Sir Wilfred T. Grenfell, noted missionary and explorer. It
may have been that a girl-less summer gave him time to think.

At any rate, Nelson no sooner returned to Dartmouth for his
senior year than he and Mary Clark became engaged, without
the formality of obtaining the consent of the elder Rockefellers.
John D., Jr., highly approved of Nelson's fiancée, but he took a

dim view of college boys making major decisions without consulting their parents. It took Nelson a few weeks to get back in his father's good graces.

Mr. Rockefeller, however, never held Nelson's impetuousness against his daughter-in-law-to-be. And once he got over his peeve at Nelson, he went out of his way to show approval of the marriage, spending weeks picking out a fabulously expensive and beautiful pearl necklace as a wedding gift, and sending the young couple around the world on their honeymoon.

The other Rockefellers welcomed Miss Clark to the family as enthusiastically as their parents. Even after she and Nelson were divorced in 1962, she continued to occupy their home at Pocantico Hills, while Nelson moved into his grandfather's house about three-quarters of a mile up the hill on the estate. Frequently both were in residence at the same time.

In 1930, however, Mary Todhunter Clark, generally known as "Tod" by her intimates, was making a drastic change in her life in moving into the Rockefeller clan. She was accustomed to intense family life, but as a Clark of Philadelphia, daughter of Percy Hamilton Clark, an investment banker, and granddaughter of George B. Roberts, onetime president of the Pennsylvania Railroad, her family connections were as extensive as Philadelphia's Main Line Society itself. She was brought up among people who went to the right schools, joined the right clubs, vacationed at the right resorts and, in short, played the Society game. It was a measure of her personal independence, however, that after attending the very proper Foxcroft School in Virginia, where she rode to the hounds in Virginia tradition, she spurned the traditional French finishing school, spending her year in Paris taking French literature at the Sorbonne.

The Rockefellers, on the other hand, paid no attention to formal Society. The original John D. and John D., Jr., were too wrapped up in their own undertakings, and, while the third generation played in Society's playgrounds, they never seemed to take its pretensions seriously. And, although they had cousins in abundance, they were inclined to regard "family" as meaning the Pocantico Hills Rockefellers, whose tight little circle represented the direct line. Within this grouping there was intense social activity in the early 1930's, but nothing like what Tod was accustomed to.

There was never any question that the bride would fit in. Slender, brown-haired, with aristocratic features, she demonstrated her tact and deep thoughtfulness on her wedding day by wearing flat ballet slippers to avoid seeming to tower above the bridegroom—the two are exactly the same height, standing 5 feet 10. It was a typical gesture.

After a few weeks at Seal Harbor, the Nelson Rockefellers left on their ten-month wedding trip around the world, a trip which turned out to be a combination of a honeymoon and the kind of ceremonial visit that royalty makes. Alerted to the young couple's coming, representatives of the Rockefeller interests and the various connections of the Clark family competed to outdo each other in setting up welcomes and programs, programs such as a visit to Hawaii's leper colony, which the young Rockefellers found interesting but depressing, and which seemed a little incongruous for honeymooners. Additionally, the Rockefellers carried letters of introduction guaranteed to open almost any doors they wished to enter. The scheduling involved so much protocol that Nelson and his bride at frequent intervals had to contrive to sneak away for a little time to themselves.

It was nevertheless a memorable journey. Besides the leper colony, the young Rockefellers visited a native feast in Hawaii, and dined with the governor. In India, they hunted with the Viceroy and walked and talked with the holy man, Mahatma Gandhi. They rode elephants in the jungle and were shocked at the bound feet of women in Manchuria. Korea, Burma, Siam and Peking all were visited, with Christmas in Bangkok, before the young couple moved on to Europe for the windup of their trip.

The America the young couple returned to late in April, 1931, was deep in the most savage depression in history, but they had neither the experience nor the need to realize it. Their primary concern was to set up housekeeping and begin making a life for themselves. They plunged at once into outfitting their first apartment in East 67th Street, New York, and picking up where they had left off nearly a year earlier. The East 67th Street apartment proved to be temporary, and they later moved into a triplex atop 810 Fifth Avenue. Mrs. Rockefeller still has an apartment there as her town residence.

While Nelson was still very much a young man in search of a career, Mrs. Rockefeller, whose own tradition, while not so strict as the Baptist upbringing of the Rockefellers, nevertheless abhorred idleness, interested herself in a number of activities from garden clubs to church societies. But she found her most enduring interest, aside from her family, in her work as a member of the Board of Managers of the Bellevue School of Nursing, which she began in 1932. She continued this work until Nelson's election as Governor when she reluctantly resigned.

Rodman, the first of the Nelson Rockefellers' five children, was born in 1932 and as the others came along at two-year intervals—Ann, now Mrs. Robert Pierson, wife of an Episcopal minister who was to be arrested as a Freedom Rider in 1961; Steven, whose marriage to Anne Marie Rasmussen, a onetime maid in the Rockefeller home, was the Cinderella story of 1959, and the twins, Mary, now Mrs. William Strawbridge, and Michael, who lost his life in a tragic, senseless accident in far-off Dutch New Guinea in 1961—the focus of their home life shifted to Pocantico Hills and Seal Harbor where the children would grow up much as their father had.

As a parent, Nelson followed the methods of his father. The children were impressed with the importance of thrift and were given limited allowances to teach them the use of money, as Nelson himself once got a small allowance. But he also encouraged self-reliance and independence, giving the youngsters increasing latitude to encourage them in making their own decisions as they grew older. Always, however, the family was close-knit. When Nelson moved to Washington in 1940 to take over the Office of the Coordinator of Inter-American Affairs, Mrs. Rockefeller and the children followed a short time later. And although the burden of raising the youngsters rested mostly with Tod, Nelson managed to see them every morning at breakfasttime in the house on Foxhall Road where they lived during the war years. When time allowed, he started off their day with prayer or a brief reading from the Bible at breakfast. More often than not, however, his intensive work schedule required him to rush off before the family assembled. On those mornings the youngsters would drop in on him in his dressing room if they had anything they wanted to talk about.

As the children grew older, the public image of the Nelson Rockefellers as a nearly "ideal" family gradually evolved. The young Rockefellers were not angels, of course, but none of them ever got into a serious scrape. And they managed to stay out of the papers.

When the family finally was subjected to unrelenting publicity after Nelson became a candidate for Governor of New York, this public image was a definite political asset.

But it was precisely because this image was so firmly established that the divorce of the Nelson Rockefellers shocked so many people who couldn't have cared less about Nelson's politics or his political career.

8

Washington Assignment

NELSON ROCKEFELLER SERVED in Washington under three Presidents and liked and admired them all, each for separate reasons. In a nostalgic summing-up of his Washington duty tours about a year ago, Rockefeller said of his commanders in chief:

"I've been pretty lucky I guess. They weren't at all alike, but I could like and respect each one of them even though I couldn't always agree with them."

Not that Rockefeller ever had a serious disagreement with any President he served, not even with Harry S Truman, "who kicked me out. I've always believed in teamwork," Rockefeller explained. "I'll fight like the devil for programs I believe in, but if somebody else's program is adopted I'll fight just as hard for that. That's the only way you can run an administration.

"Of course," he added, "I was never asked to go along with anything I couldn't honestly support. Nothing like that ever came up. If it had, I suppose I would have quit. You can't be only a part-time member of the team."

Rockefeller admired Franklin D. Roosevelt, who recruited him into Federal service, for his breadth of vision, the scope and grandeur of his ideals and his tremendous personal magnetism. He liked President Truman for his saltiness, his political courage and his last-ditch loyalty to the people around him even when the loyalty seemed misplaced. And he found in Dwight D. Eisenhower a "warmth and humanness that seem to reach out to everybody."

The assessments tell a great deal about Rockefeller himself, for he embodies to a greater or lesser degree all the qualities he found in the three Presidents.

Like Roosevelt, Rockefeller thinks big. Accustomed all his life to the Rockefeller world view, Nelson brought this habit of thought into government with him, but the scope of his interests is so broad that he can turn from world-planning and talking to give utmost seriousness to the selection of a painting, much as Roosevelt turned from his desk to his stamp collection. The Rockefeller personal magnetism is so widely known that after his election as Governor in 1958 some political writers compared him to FDR as a campaigner. The comparison was superficial. As a campaigner, Rockefeller is a "natural," with a great deal of innate talent; Roosevelt not only had as much or more natural talent, he was an incomparable master of the techniques of campaigning. And, of course, as an orator FDR would leave Rockefeller tongue-tied. This, however, does not invalidate the proposition that Nelson found in Roosevelt qualities he himself possessed to some degree and sought to develop.

Rockefeller, of course, has none of the saltiness of Harry Truman nor has his political courage been tested on the grand scale—as in Truman's decision to fight for Korea or the firing of General Douglas MacArthur. But on his own political level, Rockefeller has shown he is willing to stand up for unpopular programs and make hard decisions in the face of political risk. And at least twice he has put his prestige as Governor on the line to back up a political ally under fire.

As for warmth, Rockefeller will never be an Eisenhower. Nelson has a deep feeling for the problems of his fellowmen and takes real pleasure in meeting and talking with them. But he has no experience of those problems. His was a hothouse youth, despite the elaborate charades to dress it up as "a normal American boyhood," and, while he earnestly wants to like and be liked, the trailing glamor of his name and uncountable wealth set him apart as one who has never sweated out everyday living worries. People respond to his outgoingness, but they can't identify with him, and this imposes a barrier that never intrudes in the case of an Eisenhower.

With all three Presidents, Rockefeller enjoyed a special relationship. Only in his last year in Washington when he was Special Assistant to the President did his official rank entitle him to easy access to the White House. But doors open to Rockefellers where others can't penetrate. Presidents Roosevelt, Truman and Eisenhower all found time to listen to Nelson in person when he pressed for decisions on matters within his special competence. And he exploited the open door when the chips were down. It was a circumstance that outraged and embittered many bureaucrats and rising career men, who could get their ideas up to the top only through the chain of command, and in his last year in Washington it would from time to time put a strain on Nelson's relations with Eisenhower's Secretary of State, John Foster Dulles. But Rockefeller was never one to see the second-in-command when the head man was available.

Rockefeller was thirty-two years old when he first went to Washington. For ten years since leaving Dartmouth, he'd been making frantic, short-lived rushes in search of a career, dabbling in various business enterprises (most of them more or less successful), without finding any absorbing interest that he felt offered sufficient outlet for his talents; talents, it may be said, which were more apparent to Nelson than to outsiders. A role in the management of the worldwide Rockefeller interests might have provided something of the scope he wanted, but his father and his older brother, John D. III, had that situation well in hand, and, anyway, Nelson was never one to start at the bottom of somebody else's operations; he preferred to start his own. So far as the public knew, he was just an extremely wealthy young man, a dilettante of art—he'd been elected president of the Museum of Modern Art in 1939—and some sort of an executive at Rockefeller Center. "Playboy" was the tag Washington correspondents hung on him even before he got his first Washington job.

"I got the job the way I get all my jobs," Rockefeller said later. "I thought up something that had to be done and somebody said, 'O.K., it's your idea. Now let see you make it work.' "

The go-ahead in this came from President Roosevelt. It was, in many ways, a curious order. Rockefeller's "idea" was rather revolutionary. With most South American countries being put through the economic wringer by the war in Europe which was cutting off their foreign trade, he proposed that the United States undertake a massive effort to replace the lost trade, not only by huge purchases of materials needed for the military effort, but also by helping develop the internal economies of the threatened nations. This, he contended, was necessary to bulwark the democratic forces south of the border at a time when the democratic ideal was under unrelenting attack. It was a program in keeping with the general aims of Roosevelt's Good Neighbor Policy. But Nelson was an untried young man, recommended chiefly by his money and his name. High advisers within the Administration were against turning over to him the disposition of perhaps hundreds of millions to be spent abroad; some frankly didn't want a Rockefeller butting in. Had the anti-Rockefeller group anticipated the full expansion of the program, they might have fought even harder. But Roosevelt rode down all objections and to the end gave the fullest support to Nelson. He never explained, however, just why he picked Nelson for such an important role.

The Rockefeller "idea" was really a group idea as most of

Nelson's projects are. "I'm sort of a catalyst," he once explained. "When I see a problem I get people together to talk about it and we make studies. When we've got all the facts, I usually can put my finger on what's to be done and how to do it. That's what an administrator's for."

The outbreak of World War II in September, 1939, made the South American situation acute. Businessmen whom Rockefeller had been trying to interest in South American investment as a long-term proposition lost what little interest they had. The British blockade cut off one-third of Latin America's foreign trade and Nazi U-boats crippled shipments to the Western Allies. On the whole, American industry, gearing up its plant for the cash-on-the-barrelhead profits of war production, couldn't have cared less about the situation to the south, although there were a few notable exceptions.

Through the months of the "phoney war," before Hitler turned his armies west to devastate the Low Countries and topple France, the economic condition of South America steadily worsened. Rockefeller and an informal brain trust he'd assembled to discuss world affairs watched with deep foreboding the expansion of Fascist and Communist propaganda in countries facing economic destruction.

Rockefeller and his friends—they would later constitute a more or less recognized advisory panel on South American affairs known as The Group—were unable to enlist any important support for their view that the United States was risking great danger by neglecting its hemispheric problems. It was a first-things-first time, and the first thing in the minds of most planners and policy-makers, in and out of government, was Europe and what would follow the "phoney war."

The answer came when Hitler's armies smashed Norway to protect Germany's flank and then turned westward. For the first time, the specter arose of Hitlerism triumphant with a war potential that could be turned toward the United States. The danger was too naked to be ignored.

A great many people beside Rockefeller and The Group had been contemplating just such a situation during this period, but

the Rockefeller pipelines to high places gave The Group a running head start. In May, 1940, as the Nazi campaign in Norway
was drawing to a close, Nelson began a series of confidential
talks with the late Harry Hopkins, who was possibly the most
powerful man in the United States after the President although
there was no statutory base for his power. A onetime New York
social worker, who served Roosevelt as troubleshooter, plenipo-
tentiary extraordinary and in dozens of other capacities, Hopkins was a global thinker after FDR's heart. And since he
thought of the war in world terms, Hopkins saw U. S. defense
in the same frame of reference. The weakness of our position
vis-à-vis the Fascist-Communist world (the weird Nazi-Red alliance of 1939 was still in effect, not to be breached for a year)
in the event of a Hitlerite victory was all too apparent. To leave
our southern flank exposed to Hitler-Stalin hegemony was clearly
suicidal.

Hopkins was the needed key. Interested from the first, he
asked Rockefeller early in June to prepare a program for action
on the ideas they had been talking about. The resulting paper
was a distillation of the thinking of The Group, but it was
drawn chiefly by Rockefeller and Beardsley Ruml, the New York
business economist who fathered the withholding tax. Their
joint production was a thousand-word memorandum, entitled
"Hemispheric Economic Policy," which they placed before Hopkins in the White House on June 14th, just eight days before
the fall of France.

The memorandum was a typical Rockefeller presentation:
broad in the statement of the goals; emphatic about their necessity; optimistic about the prospects; and on the skimpy side on
details. For the overworked Hopkins, even then deeply involved
in FDR's third-term bid, it had the merit of tying up the problem in a package that could be acted on. It is probable, also,
that his social worker's interest was enlisted by the Rockefeller-
Ruml proposal to link up the economic rescue act with cultural
and educational programs that, though vaguely stated, were
patently basic in the plan.

At any rate, Hopkins, although obviously very tired, gave up

several hours that night to finding out just how much Rockefeller knew about the situation in Latin America. He questioned
Nelson closely about how he would handle specific aspects of
the program, and he let the always-enthusiastic Rockefeller
throw out ideas. In the end, Hopkins appeared satisfied. He kept
the memorandum and promised to take it up with "the boss."

There was a legend in Washington at the time that the
Roosevelt New Deal government was an administrative laby-
rinth in which even the most surefooted could wander hope-
lessly and forever. But when Harry Hopkins spoke to "the boss,"
all difficulties disappeared. And Hopkins was a direct actionist
once he'd decided on a course.

Within a day after getting the Rockefeller-Ruml memorandum, Hopkins had it on Roosevelt's desk. And the President,
long interested in Latin America himself, was as vigorous as
Hopkins. After reading the paper, he circulated it to the State,
Commerce, Treasury and Agriculture Departments for comment. Curiously enough, the military departments, whose strategic interest could be presumed to be paramount, weren't can-
vassed on the first go-around.

The replies were in by the June 20th deadline set by
Roosevelt, but he didn't like them. The departments, jealous of
their prerogatives, wanted to keep their respective jurisdictions
over South American affairs. Roosevelt promptly brought the
matter up at a Cabinet meeting, reading the memo aloud. Under
Secretary of State Sumner Welles, himself an expert on Latin
America, who was sitting in for Secretary Cordell Hull, again
interposed objections. He felt that any policy-making program
should be kept in State, which, of course, would keep it in his
hands.

The Cabinet meeting ended on that note. But on June 28th,
the President abruptly activated the new economic program, and
the State Department lost the project. Following a suggestion
advanced by Rockefeller, FDR turned the program over to a
Presidential assistant. The man he picked for the job was the
fast-rising James V. Forrestal, lately a New York investment
banker.

The selection was fortuitous for Rockefeller. Had the project gone to the State Department, Rockefeller might never have gotten to handle it. For, as Nelson was to remark later, Welles never welcomed private persons in foreign policy. "He never tried to block our work or to interfere," Nelson said, "but he never warmed up to us. He helped us when we asked; he didn't volunteer anything. And he was always formal: he called me Mr. Rockefeller and I called him Mr. Welles. I can't remember him ever talking about anything but the business in front of us." Nelson, who thrives on informality and has been a first-name user all his life, seemed bemused.

It is doubtful that Roosevelt ever intended Forrestal would actively run the inter-American program. Clearly marked for cabinet rank—he was to be named Under Secretary of the Navy within a month on his way to becoming the nation's first Secretary of Defense—Forrestal, in that summer when Hitler bestrode Europe and only Britain stood at arms against the Nazi menace, was the all-around man among the White House Special Assistants to the President. Roosevelt had developed a habit of shunting all new problems to him. His function at this period, which he performed with great skill, was to screen out the flaws, set up the guidelines and kick off the new programs, turning them over to others to administer.

In working up the inter-American policy, Forrestal went to the source and summoned Rockefeller to Washington. The two dined on the night of July 9th in one of Forrestal's clubs, and for hours Rockefeller did a totally unnecessary selling job on the White House aide. Forrestal listened with great patience, possibly because he was still making up his mind. Then he neatly capped the Rockefeller selling job. Would Nelson, in view of all he'd said, be willing to come down to Washington and work full time on the project? Forrestal asked. He added, "The President is ready for action."

In later years Rockefeller would say the job offer surprised him, but all the evidence is against the claim. After all, in 1940 Rockefeller was a young man in search of a career who hadn't yet found a project big enough to offer him what he considered a satisfactory challenge. For months he'd been working on the hemisphere economic scheme, consulting with Hopkins and others. He couldn't possibly have thought the astute Forrestal had invited him to Washington just to hear him talk.

But a Rockefeller, even one as impulsive as Nelson, just doesn't rush his fences. From the time of the original John D., the Rockefellers avoided personal entanglement in government. The leap from the sidelines into a policy-making role in the New Deal Administration was a grave one, no matter how you looked at it. And the Rockefellers, including Nelson, were about to support Wendell Willkie for President against FDR.

Nelson went home to consult the family.

There was no problem. His father gave the project his blessing and who was there among the Rockefellers to disagree with a decision of John D., Jr.? Nelson had all the go-ahead he needed. But he still wanted to talk about the new job. He flew out to Salt Lake City to lay the matter before Wendell Willkie.

Rockefeller later said he made the trip as a courtesy to Willkie and because he really wanted advice. What Willkie thought about the visit hasn't been recorded. But the 1940 Republican nominee gave Nelson the answer he wanted.

"He told me," Rockefeller said, "to go ahead and do the best job I could. He said if he were President he wouldn't think much of anyone who would turn down an assignment in a time of national crisis.

"After that there was nothing to stop me."

Back in Washington on July 25th to accept his appointment, Rockefeller found that events had outstripped him. Forrestal was ready to make his move from the White House to the Navy Department, and Rockefeller, instead of working with Forrestal, was ticketed for top command of the new program.

A more politically sophisticated man of thirty-two might have boggled on taking full charge of a new foreign-policy project from a standing start; Rockefeller was serenely undismayed. In fact, he told the President across his cluttered desk in the White House, he had a few questions he wanted answered. His first two questions were: Was FDR at all concerned that the Rockefellers were not only substantial contributors to the Republican Party but heavily involved in Standard Oil and its Latin-American operations? And, two, would Rockefeller have a free hand in picking his staff? The answers were "no" on the first and "of course" on the second.

There was a third question: Who was going to draw up the guidelines for the new program?

"See Jim Forrestal on that," Mr. Roosevelt said.

That was the end of the business at hand. For about twenty minutes Nelson and the President chatted about their respective South American enthusiasms and Rockefeller got the full charm treatment. He left the White House deeply convinced that Mr. Roosevelt shared his own passionate interest in spreading culture along with economic aid in hemispheric undertakings.

Long after FDR's death, Rockefeller, who remains proud that he never contributed to a Democratic campaign, would pay high tribute to the President's vision and understanding. Of his own relations with FDR, he would say: "He gave me all the backing I could have asked for, but I had to settle my own fights. You could always count on him for a fair hearing."

When Rockefeller followed the President's advice to "see Forrestal," he found out just how much he was going to be in charge. Forrestal congratulated Rockefeller on his appointment and listened politely when Nelson asked him for the political ground rules. "That," remarked Forrestal dryly, "is your first assignment."

From there on in, Rockefeller was on his own.

On August 16th the White House issued an executive order creating the Office for Coordination of Commercial and Cultural Relations between the American Republics—a name that, happily, was soon to be shortened to the Office of the Coordinator of Inter-American Affairs or CIAA in the New Deal alphabetese. Nelson Rockefeller was named director at no salary. To get things started he was given a "guess" budget of $3.5 million drawn from the President's emergency fund. When more money was needed, Rockefeller would have to fight his own battles with the Budget Division, the State Department and the Congress. Rockefeller would learn a lot from that.

Nelson Rockefeller ran the Office of the Coordinator of Inter-American Affairs for a little more than four years. In that period, the CIAA spent $140 million, built up a staff of 1,100 in this country, with 300 specialists in the field. Its operations ranged from undisguised press agentry to solid educational programs, from rudimentary planning to arranging for massive economic credits and benefits, from persuading business to go along, to threats to take reprisals against companies that insisted on retaining Nazi business agents. Its staff included experts in everything from economics, finance, agricultural and industrial planning to editors, photographers and folk dancers. Its scope was as wide as the spectrum of Pan-American hopes, and it functioned, as one staffer put it, "by God and by guess, but somehow we got things done—some of them our own and a great many chores handed us by other departments."

Evaluation of the role of the CIAA in helping South America avoid the war-threatened bankruptcy that might have opened the way for a postwar Communist take-over awaits the verdict of history. The office was small by wartime standards, and many of its programs were carried out through the regular government departments—State, Commerce, Agriculture and Treasury—and by various agencies such as the Export-Import Bank, although the projects were conceived in what became known in its early years as the "Rockefeller shop."

Certainly the CIAA was a great deal more than the "propaganda mill" that one embittered early aide called it after being pressured into resigning because he didn't fit "on the team." Not that propaganda ever was neglected. The growth of Nazi propaganda in South America in the late 1930's was one of the things that first alarmed Nelson and The Group and led to the original memorandum to Hopkins on the inter-American program. As Coordinator, Rockefeller rushed his press division into action because he believed that only "an informed public opinion" in the Latin countries could provide the support needed to get cooperation for the overall program, and because it was, as a simple, practical matter, the easiest to set up. The challenge and the targets were known from the outset, and the indicated course was clear. Other undertakings of the CIAA required months of study and investigation before even preliminary steps could be essayed.

But while Nelson fought for his propaganda arm as fiercely as any lioness ever defended a cub, he never considered propaganda to be the paramount objective of the CIAA. "It was very, very important," he said later. "It was a big part of a big job that had to be done and we were the only ones who knew how to do it. But it was still only part of the job. We had to really help those countries, not just talk about it. All the clippings in the world wouldn't have meant a thing if we'd let it go at that. . . . Propaganda alone doesn't solve problems," he added reflectively, "though it may help you get them out in the open where something can be done about them."

When the Rockefeller shop started operations, the problems were known only in the most general terms. It was obvious that the South American economy was hurting badly and the situation would get a lot worse before it got better. But the specific plans were still to be hammered out. And Rockefeller had for his guidance only a broad directive to set up the office and do something. The undertaking was a brand-new one, and the ground rules had to be made up as the program itself came into being.

President Roosevelt in setting up the CIAA directed its head to clear his programs with the State Department to avoid conflicts on policy. But for the first few months the old government hands at State showed little interest in the new agency. State, of course, was busy on other matters, but at least part of what appeared to be its calculated indifference unquestionably reflected the bureaucratic principle that any new agency, given enough rope, will hang itself by its excesses without the guiding hand of the bureaucrats. And in State, it must be remembered, Rockefeller admirers weren't exactly legion.

For a time it looked as though the bureaucrats might be

right. The Rockefeller shop was set up in the Commerce Department Building, and, even while the staff was being recruited, the word went out in Washington that Roosevelt's latest "tame millionaire" was masterminding a kind of cultural boondoggle for South America. It was an angle that reporters covering the lighter side of the Capital could get mileage out of, and they played it for all the white space they could get. One consequence was that a large part of the public and some Congressmen got the impression, never completely eradicated, that the CIAA was an expensive sideshow.

FDR never shared this opinion. In the last letter he wrote Nelson, dated March 31, 1945, the President expressed his "high appreciation" of Rockefeller's CIAA activities.

"You have made a magnificent contribution to the unity of this hemisphere and its ability to emerge with renewed strength from a grave period in its history," the President said. "The people of this country and, indeed, of the other American republics are well aware of the significant progress attained under your leadership."

At the start, however, Rockefeller's almost frenetic activity seemed to lend credence to the frivolous early assessment of the CIAA. He had a lot to learn, and he was here, there and everywhere trying to learn it all at once. As director of the CIAA, he was also chairman of an interdepartmental committee on inter-American affairs, a member of the advisory committee of the National Defense Council and chairman of the Inter-American Development Commission, which functioned as a research and planning development section of the Pan American Union. Merely attending the meetings necessary to keep all these balls in the air at once crowded his schedule. And there was much more to learn. Rockefeller soon became aware of the overlapping jurisdictions common to Washington in 1940 when Hitler seemed on the verge of crushing free Europe, and he found himself dashing from department to department to keep the channels clear. And, of course, since all government activities require money, he came up against the hard fact that the executive proposes but Congress disposes, and he had to spend long hours on Cap-

itol Hill, soothing the feathers of the self-important, lobbying
for appropriations and recruiting allies. In consequence at any
given moment in those first few months he was the "man in
motion," spending only a fraction of his long day—he habitually
worked from about 8:30 to 6:30 and then held extra conferences
at home after dinner—at his desk.

To those unfamiliar with Rockefeller's work methods, all this
running around indicated disorganization. Quite the opposite
was true. Rockefeller has always prided himself on his organizing ability (he not infrequently overorganizes with occasionally
bizarre consequences), and he was putting together a staff that
would develop into a smooth-functioning machine before the
program really got rolling.

Partly by choice and partly by necessity, Rockefeller went
outside government to get his key people. The choice was his
because he knew few people in government; the necessity was
forced on him because at the start it seemed the Rockefeller shop
had too uncertain a future to attract talented people from established departments. The consequence was that the hard core of
the CIAA advisers came from business backgrounds, and all
shared Nelson's enthusiasm for South America.

As his top aide, who would succeed him as Coordinator when
Rockefeller switched to the State Department, he brought in his
architect friend, Wally Harrison, and the post of general counsel
went to John E. Lockwood, the lawyer who now is the key
man in the intricate Rockefeller legal setup. Others included
Joseph Rovensky of the Chase Bank (usually referred to as the
Rockefeller bank); Jay Crane, an oil executive with wide-ranging
interests; Percy Douglas, later chairman of Otis Elevator Co.;
and three associates in a short-lived Venezuelan development
company Rockefeller had started in the thirties—Carl B. Spaeth,
Edward H. Robbins and Kelso Peck. Louise Boyer, still a key
figure on the Rockefeller staff, was principal liaison for the
group.

Soon to join the inner circle was Frank Jamieson, known to
Rockefeller at that time only as an aide who'd worked with his
brother Winthrop on the Greater New York Fund campaign in

1938. Jamie was an invaluable find. He was politically more sophisticated than Rockefeller, knew his way around Washington and enjoyed wide respect in the Washington press corps, all of which helped smooth rough spots. He took over the press division of the CIAA and ran it with quiet efficiency, but he also became one of Nelson's closest friends, and with Harrison and Lockwood made up the trio that Rockefeller turned to most often in good times and bad. In the next twenty years, until Jamie's death in 1960, Rockefeller would rarely make a major decision without talking it over with Jamieson.

Others brought in from the outside included John S. Dickey, who would later become president of Rockefeller's alma mater, Dartmouth; Karl A. Bickel, retired president of the United Press; John Hay Whitney, who would become President Eisenhower's Ambassador to the Court of St. James's, and Will Clayton, a Texas businessman who was destined to rise high in government. Victor G. Borella was drafted from the Rockefeller Center staff to run day-to-day operations as assistant coordinator.

Rockefeller was the boss. Accustomed to being top dog in all his undertakings (years later, when Governor of New York, he remarked: "I never wanted to be vice-president of anything."), he called the shots for the CIAA, subject to conformity (sometimes reluctant) with the overall policy of the State Department, and stamped the decisions as his own. He relied on the experts for the facts, and he would take an idea from any source if it fitted his general scheme, but when the chips were down he put his faith in his own intuition. When now and then his intuition, plus his enthusiasm, led him into errors that others had foreseen, he took the rap for the goofs.

He also did most of the fighting for the CIAA when raids were made upon its authority and its budget or prestige were imperiled.

9

Fights for Survival

ROCKEFELLER WAS RATHER luckier than he had any right to
expect in the savage bureaucratic warfare that goes on eternally
in Washington. Because the CIAA operated largely outside normal diplomatic channels, its projects, no matter their merit,
were subject to constant sniping by ambassadors who resented
infringement on their presumed prerogatives and sought to veto
or take over various operations. These skirmishes had to be
fought, sometimes ambassador by ambassador, over every new
program undertaken by the agency, but they were more an annoyance than serious threats, and Nelson usually managed to
get his way with only minor arm-twisting.

Not that he was in the slightest hesitant about using his muscle when muscle was called for. On one occasion, when Ambassador George Messersmith, a tough and experienced protector of ambassadorial privilege, moved to take over the Mexican office of the CIAA information service, which was making a splash by rehabilitating the film industry, Rockefeller flew to Mexico City to face him down.

Rockefeller told Messersmith bluntly that unless he kept hands off the CIAA would pull out of Mexico and turn all its projects over to Messersmith to be financed out of embassy funds. And, Rockefeller added, CIAA would make sure everybody was told, in detail, just why it pulled out.

The U. S. involvements in the economy of Mexico were heavy. At this point besides helping the film industry get back on its feet, we were giving massive assistance to rehabilitating the Mexican trunk line railroads to guarantee an uninterrupted flow of strategic materials despite the shipping shortage, and efforts were being made to stimulate stockpiling and development of new industry. Later in the war $24 million of CIAA money would be poured into twenty short-term projects to spur war production.

It was a challenge Messersmith couldn't accept. There was no money in his budget to run the CIAA operations, and he couldn't kill off the various projects because they were patently successful.

Like a good diplomat, he capitulated.

When word of the encounter got around, as it did very soon, other ambassadors quickly got the message. And the CIAA's path was probably a little smoother thereafter.

But the really big battles, the ones in which the life of the CIAA was at stake, were fought out against skilled bureaucrats in Washington. The major battles were three in number and the prize in each case was the same issue that had brought Rockefeller's showdown in Mexico: control of the CIAA's propaganda which, in governmentese, was called "the information service" on the principle that only the bad guys spread propaganda; good guys spread facts.

Rockefeller liked to say that CIAA survived in the bureaucratic jungle because "we really believed in what we were doing." The evidence, however, indicates that the survival factor was compounded of intrigue, upmanship and savage undercutting of those on the other side. And, although the ground rules were more or less observed, the losers didn't easily forget or forgive their scars.

Rockefeller lost his first major battle before he knew the fight was on, falling victim to an adroit State Department ploy that was a *fait accompli* by the time he heard of it. He saved the situation only by backpedaling furiously and "joining" State, so to speak, because there was no way to fight back.

What happened was simple enough. Anxious to get started with a bang, the CIAA whipped up a $600,000 campaign to offset Nazi propaganda in South American papers. The Nazis were getting their stuff in print by outright subsidies and by paying off editors. The CIAA disdained these undercover methods (which were, in any event, repugnant politically and morally to U. S. concepts) and proposed instead to tell our story in paid advertisements recounting the adventures of a Latin-American couple traveling in this country. The text of the ads bore down heavily on the morality of democracy, the glories of Western Hemisphere unity and like themes, all with the aim of winning us friends.

Friends we certainly didn't win. When the ads were published early in 1941, there was literally no shipping available to carry South Americans on vacation trips to the Colossus of the North, and the "advertising gimmick" was exposed as a fraud to howls of sardonic Latin laughter. Even worse, the advertising mind had looked at the circulation figures rather than editorial policies of the papers it placed the ads in with the consequence that the biggest pro-Nazi organ in Brazil and smaller ones elsewhere got big, fat chunks of CIAA money for printing ads that made the United States a laughingstock.

Ambassadors south of the border reported the fiasco almost gleefully. They hadn't been consulted in the first place, and they'd have been less than human if they hadn't grabbed the opportunity to beef. The complaints, of course, went to the State Department, not the CIAA. And State went to the President.

Roosevelt, who had troubles of his own with the State Department, wasn't about to add to them. In a letter dated April 22, 1941, FDR sharply recalled to Rockefeller that he'd been instructed to clear policy with State. The President said he "observed impairment of our total effort . . . in the other American republics" and demanded assurances that "in all instances projects initiated by your Office shall be fully discussed with and approved by the Department of State, and a full meeting of minds obtained before action is undertaken or commitments made."

It was a cold rebuke and Nelson took it big. It was true the advertising campaign had been okayed routinely with an assistant secretary of state, but the monstrousness of the failure was so great that raising this technicality might have raised more embarrassing questions about the CIAA's cavalier habit of assuming State Department clearance was only a formality. The idea, in hindsight, had been no good in the first place; trying to pass the buck wouldn't change that.

The ebullient Rockefeller was down in the dumps. The CIAA had been on the move under a light State Department rein, proceeding buoyantly on the assumption that it enjoyed special status at the White House. As Rockefeller saw the altered situation, tight State Department control would stultify the program for Latin America as well as end his usefulness.

Convincing himself that the letter of rebuke was written for the President in the office of Under Secretary of State Welles, Rockefeller decided to take up the rebuke with the top man. General Edwin M. (Pa) Watson, the Presidential appointments secretary, set up the date.

Rockefeller never got to state his case, whatever it may have been. FDR, with his uncanny instinct for handling men, forestalled any chance of a showdown at the top even before he got through greeting Nelson.

The President told Rockefeller that he was aware of his troubles with the State Department, but that it was up to him to fight his own battles. Running to the White House, FDR suggested, couldn't change what had happened and might compel Mr. Roosevelt, if backed into a corner, to rule for State in any foreign-policy dispute. The President then chatted amiably of other things.

Rockefeller took the hint. To protect himself in future clinches, he went to Welles and promised the fullest possible consultation and cooperation on all projects—a promise that was meticulously kept. And Welles, having got what he wanted all along, a veto over new projects, cooperated on his side by giving the CIAA a free hand in most of its program. The Under Secretary also used his considerable powers to keep ambassadors in line.

Although Rockefeller had suffered a defeat because the President's reprimand still stood, he hadn't fared too badly: the CIAA was preserved intact; it continued to initiate most of its programs, and, in the long run, the State Department supervision probably helped more than it obstructed CIAA operations.

And Rockefeller had learned a valuable lesson: never put the top man on the spot unless you're ready to be wiped out.

In the CIAA's two subsequent fights for life, both of which wound up on the President's desk, Nelson sedulously avoided pushing himself to the forefront, although he made adroit use of high-placed allies to sway the Presidential decision. The first of these tests came when the office of the Coordinator of Information, set up in July, 1941, after the uneasy Russian-Hitler peace exploded into war, made a determined grab for the CIAA's information service.

The COI was headed by a skilled Republican politician-soldier, William J. (Wild Bill) Donovan, a World War I hero who would wind up running the secret Office of Strategic Services as a major general, and Donovan nearly pulled off his coup. An order for the President's signature was already at the White House when Rockefeller enlisted the intervention of Mrs. Anna Rosenberg, a member of Mr. Roosevelt's inner circle since his Albany days and an adviser to CIAA. The order was amended.

In the second threat in March, 1942, after the attack on Pearl Harbor had brought the war to the United States, the Budget Bureau came within an ace of blanketing the CIAA information service into the Office of War Information. Intervention with the President by Vice President Wallace and Under Secretary Welles got a special dispensation reserving the right to handle South American propaganda for the CIAA.

This was a tremendously important point. The OWI was geared to a worldwide effort without the specialized interest that Rockefeller and Roosevelt felt was essential to putting our case before the people of South America in terms affecting their own direct interests. Loss of the information service might well have crippled the CIAA over the next several years.

While fighting its battles, the CIAA had developed into a going organization. Although cultural activities—trading visitors with South American countries, attempting to stimulate the theater and films—got the most attention, solid work was being done to displace Nazi agents and sympathizers from their key positions in the economic and propaganda fields. Health and sanitary services came into being in several countries and a flow of economic aid, in various guises, was started.

10

::

The War Years

JUST HOW MUCH economic aid was channeled to South America as a result of CIAA operations, it is impossible to say. As noted, the agency itself directly spent only $140 million on all operations from the day it was founded until it faded out after peace was restored. But its reason for being, to Rockefeller's thinking, was basically economic, and from first to last the agency inspired, fought for and developed programs that were aimed at maintaining a flow of hundreds of millions of dollars south of the border to ease the dislocations of war.

The bulk of this economic aid was made available through the regular departments of government, the war procurement agencies and the various bank and credit facilities, which would have proceeded with their own limited programs in South America if CIAA never existed. The special role of the CIAA, as Rockefeller saw it, was to expand the existing programs and to obtain the maximum political effect of this vast spending and credit by tying it into the economic needs of the countries on the receiving end. The agency also handled chores—notably its health and sanitation programs—that were outside the scope of the usual departmental operations and which might have been neglected without the CIAA. Furthermore, it acted as liaison between South American countries and American industry and finance, and one of Rockefeller's first efforts in this area was to persuade the Export-Import Bank to set up credit lines for Latin-American purchasers to allow them to pay for goods after receipt through U. S. banks, a move that greatly aided importers.

The CIAA also undertook to get the Export-Import Bank, which got a boost in lending authority from $200 million to $700 million in September, 1940—a move that was in the works before the CIAA was conceived—to soften its terms on surplus commodity loans to aid particularly hard-pressed sections of the Latin-American economy. After the war the bank got tough in collecting its loans, undoing some of the goodwill it originally created, but Rockefeller was out of government and his protests were ignored.

Rockefeller also persuaded the President to write a letter on September 27, 1940, to department heads and the Advisory Committee on National Defense, directing them to give priority to Latin America in overseas buying for this country's swiftly growing defense buildup. The aim was twofold: to firm up the South American economy with our defense millions and to deprive the Nazis of strategic materials which they were buying up wherever they could be found and shipping across the Pacific to Vladivostock to evade the British blockade in the Atlantic.

The American buying certainly raised prices for the Nazi purchasers in South America, but, given the Axis leanings of a great many industrialists, it still left them plenty of scope to grab up the materials they needed to fuel their war machine.

To correct this, and maintain the U. S. position of neutrality—in 1940 isolationist pressure was at its peak in the United States—the Council of National Defense assigned the CIAA to negotiate contracts, country by country, with Latin-American nations to take the total output of certain products for fixed terms of one to five years. A number of the contracts outlived their usefulness because after Hitler turned his armies eastward against Russia in June, 1941, the Nazis had no way to ship their purchases to the homeland, but in the short-term run the "preclusive buying" shut off some vital supplies.

A corollary assignment of the CIAA was to root out Axis agents who held key economic positions all over South America as representatives of U. S. corporations. This was a particularly sensitive area: sensitive in the political zone because FDR in the 1940 election campaign "again and again" promised the American people their sons wouldn't be sent into "any foreign war"; sensitive under international law because the United States as a "neutral" would be proceeding against German and Japanese nationals; and sensitive in our relations with South America because the operation would disrupt, at least temporarily, normal trade channels and might be regarded as unwarranted interference.

Yet Harry Hopkins was insistent. Anticipating what he undoubtedly saw as the inevitable war between the United States and the Axis, he wanted to avoid repetition of the chaos that wrecked hemispheric trade in World War I when a blacklist of German nationals and firms was issued the day war was declared. Valuable months were lost in 1917, he noted, before new trade lines could be set up. But in 1940 the "blitz" was an established fact of war; the risk of lost time would be immeasurably greater.

A "top-secret" tag was hung on the project and an immediate survey was begun to determine the full extent of Axis influence in U. S. firms with large interests in South America. Most of the fieldwork fell on the CIAA, which, as a new and only partly understood agency, would arouse the least suspicion by its inquiries into business setups. But both the State Department and the

Federal Bureau of Investigation took part in the investigation, which proceeded over a period of months.

The findings were more shocking than anybody anticipated. With few exceptions, German and Japanese nationals who represented U. S. firms as distributors, franchised dealers and agents were shown to be pushing anti-American propaganda by every means at their command. A few of the more brazen used funds allotted to them for advertising to pay for this propaganda; others financed it out of their profits. United States trade secrets were being readily betrayed to the Axis powers, and Axis officials were being put on payrolls, which amounted to setting up an intelligence network for the Axis that was paid for out of U. S. funds.

On the basis of the survey, it was decided to bring the facts out in the open. Many American firms refused to believe their agents in South America were pro-Nazi and resisted suggestions that they change them. The resistance was easy to understand. Most agents had long-term contracts; they were successfully established in thir various communities; and they were able businessmen, returning a steady flow of profits to their principals. To cut such ties, with the inconvenience and expense such dislocations would cause, was repugnant to many executives, particularly as it would rock the boat at a time when American industry was concentrating on the cash profits to be made out of supplying Europe and was disinclined to make a massive effort to reorganize a dwindling South American trade.

In January, 1941, Rockefeller announced some of the findings of the survey to the press. The reaction was good. The country was still strongly antiwar (most Americans remained antiwar until the bombs fell on Pearl Harbor), but there was little sympathy for the Nazis. The idea of Nazi infiltration of South America at a time when Hitler seemed sure to triumph in Europe was alarming.

The CIAA was assigned to get voluntary agreements from American firms to get rid of their Axis agents. Naturally, the task devolved on Rockefeller. He knew a great many of the top executives involved personally and he could talk their language. Further, when he made the point that failure to go along would be bad for private enterprise both in the United States and in South America, his hearers would listen.

Most of them did go along. He tackled the twelve largest American corporations with extensive Latin-American interests first, and with eleven of them he had no trouble. The twelfth balked, although it employed nineteen agents shown by the survey to be pro-Nazi. Its chief negotiator told Rockefeller the company was international in its operations and that it could not get involved in "political matters." Rockefeller was aghast, but he had no intention of taking a "no" for an answer. Coldly he told the recalcitrant executive that he knew he had no power to enforce compliance, but that if the company persisted he would simply call in the press and lay out the whole story for the reporters. That settled that.

With the big boys in line, other American firms readily joined in firing their Nazis. Within six months, more than a thousand accounts had been taken away from suspected Axis agents, and by the time of the sneak attack on Pearl Harbor 85 percent of the business that once passed through Nazi or Japanese hands had been diverted to more reliable managers. When the United States went to war, the State Department took over blacklisting and made it mandatory.

While cooperating with other agencies in the blacklisting operation, the CIAA, on its own, set out to break the grip the Nazis held on a large section of the South American press. The Nazi dominance was no happenstance. A great many Germans moved to South America to escape the post-World War I misery in the Fatherland, and after Hitler came to power he set out to exploit their loyalty with the hope of binding their adopted countries to his cause. Propaganda was a vital weapon.

The principal instrument of Nazi propaganda in South America by 1940 was the German Transocean news service, which served up the National Socialist line disguised as news stories and numbered among its clients hundreds of papers, small and large. Heavily subsidized, Transocean undersold the regular

U. S. wire services by so much they couldn't compete. The Nazis also obtained influence by their payoffs to favored papers and to editors and writers on papers that did not or would not subscribe to their "news service." All in all, it was a formidable setup.

One of the prices exacted by democracy is that you can't always fight fire with fire. Challenging the Nazi propaganda machine on moral grounds, the CIAA couldn't adopt totalitarian tactics. It couldn't subsidize papers, buy up editors or set up a fake news agency. It could and did use legitimate advertising to tell its story in friendly papers, and it persuaded the Treasury Department to allow institutional advertising as a tax deductible business expense by U. S. corporations temporarily deprived of their South American markets to channel private funds to helpful papers.

The CIAA also persuaded the President to use some of his emergency funds to help pay the cost of shipping newsprint, which was in short supply all over the world, to the South American markets to guarantee democratically oriented papers that they could continue to publish. In this connection, Rockefeller arranged through a development company set up privately before he joined the CIAA to establish a paper mill in Brazil. Eventually, the mill produced about thirty thousand tons of newsprint a year.

The frontal attack was made, however, by the CIAA press division under Frank Jamieson. The initial problem was to place before democratically inclined editors, who were in the majority, an alternative to Nazi propaganda they were often forced to print because their papers were too poor to buy a legitimate news service and had to take German Transocean or do without. One approach was to help the legitimate news agencies improve their report, thus setting up standards that the Nazi propagandists could not meet and compelling editors to look beyond the Transocean for their news. This, it must be emphasized, was no mere press agentry. The CIAA furnished the news agencies with hard news and objective background material, but carefully refrained from trying to turn the wire services into U. S. counterparts of Transocean. There was no effort to "sell" the CIAA program through the wire services, and, in fact, most of the material the Rockefeller shop developed dealt strictly with Latin-American affairs, mentioning the United States and American plans only when they were basic to the story.

Working directly with South American editors, the CIAA arranged intensive briefings on world and hemispheric problems to lay the facts before them and give them a perspective from which to view the slanted Nazi "news" stories. The agency also set up a feature service that supplied papers with articles, cartoons and pictures without charge. Authoritative writers were recruited in the various countries to prepare the local material, and Jamieson's staff in Washington supplied the world and U. S. news.

The critical period in the propaganda confrontation with the Nazis was from the fall of 1940 until Pearl Harbor. In that time, the press division built up a list of 1,200 subscriber papers to which it furnished 2,000 features a month. (After the United States got into the war and the Nazis were forced to pull back in South America, the CIAA output skyrocketed to 33,000 pieces a month.)

But long before Pearl Harbor, the Nazi propagandists were badly mauled. Only a few of their papers were starved out of existence by the newsprint shortage, but nearly all of them were forced to dilute the Axis line in order to meet the competition of the democratically inclined press. During and after the war, many South American politicians credited the CIAA with a major role in the fight for public opinion. And Rockefeller felt, with good reason, that his strenuous battles to keep his information service as a specialized, autonomous agency were well worth the effort.

The press division also put out a glossy Spanish-language, news picture magazine, *En Guardia,* which achieved a circulation of nearly 550,000 by mid-1944. Aimed at the professional classes and focused primarily on hemispheric solidarity, it achieved considerable status by providing source material for the editors, professors and broadcasters who shaped public opinion. Before the war ended, a Portuguese edition was being circulated in Brazil and a French edition in Haiti.

On other propaganda fronts, radio broadcasts to South America were doubled by the CIAA and its motion-picture division, organized by John Hay Whitney, producer of *Gone With the Wind,* hit the Nazis where it hurt by getting U. S. moviemakers to withhold their pictures from theaters showing German propaganda films. Since U. S. features were box office, this was spectacularly successful. The division also stepped up newsreel coverage of South America, again displacing Hitlerite products. At one period, the CIAA had two hundred trucks, mounted with portable projectors, touring the hinterlands and showing film shorts in remote villages.

Fortunately for Rockefeller all these operations were running smoothly when the Japanese attack on Pearl Harbor plunged us into war. For with Pearl Harbor, all programs became "emergency." The economic plans being developed and painstakingly negotiated abruptly were put on a crash basis. The jump from an uneasy peace to a full war footing stepped up the tempo of all government activities. South American projects, previously regarded as desirable, now became mandatory because the Japanese fleet stood between us and the raw material sources of the Far East.

Pearl Harbor also posed a personal decision for Rockefeller. He was thirty-three, fit and, although he was the father of five, distinctly eligible for military service. Was he justified in remaining a civilian at a time when men were desperately needed in the armed forces?

"I went to the President," Rockefeller recalled years later, "and told him I was ready for anything he wanted me to do. He told me to stay put. He told me I was doing a job nobody else could step in and take over without long delays and that he'd let me know when he wanted me elsewhere."

Six months later at a White House luncheon, Rockefeller brought up the question with FDR again and got the same orders. "The President told me," Rockefeller was to relate, "that he'd gone through the same sort of thing when he was Assistant Secretary of the Navy and President Wilson ordered him to stay a civilian in World War I. I had to accept that."

It was about the time of Pearl Harbor that the CIAA made its first direct contribution to the war strategy. Some months before, a survey had shown that a German-owned airline, staffed by veterans of World War I, controlled airfields within striking distance of the Panama Canal, some of them in Bolivia. Rockefeller had taken the finding to General George C. Marshall, Army Chief of Staff, who expressed deep concern.

With Marshall's strong backing, Rockefeller got the Reconstruction Finance Corporation, headed by his friend and frequent adviser, Jesse Jones, to set up a subsidiary corporation to take over the airline and bases from the German interests. The German pilots were fired just before Hitler declared war on the United States.

The operation cost $8 million and the RFC, which was hard-nosed in its negotiations at all times, eventually got its money back. But even if it hadn't, the price would have been small considering the havoc that could have been wreaked on the Panama Canal by a few well-placed bombs.

The state of the war found Rockefeller deeply involved in trying to get off the ground with the CIAA's most ambitious project and one very close to Nelson's heart because it was strictly humanitarian in purpose: a massive assault on the malnutrition, disease and illiteracy that were endemic in large sections of South America. The idea was conceived in the CIAA earlier in 1941 when the United States, expanding lend-lease after Russia had entered the war against the Nazis, allocated $150 million in lend-lease to South America.

Widespread fear was expressed at the time that the dictators running many of the South American countries would use lend-lease to arm themselves against their people rather than to arm their nations against foreign invaders. To counterbalance this, CIAA proposed that the United States spend as much again on humanitarian projects that would directly benefit the people rather than their governments.

It was big thinking—too big for the actualities as it turned out—but it was the type of project that struck a responsive chord in President Roosevelt. Rockefeller sent the plan to FDR

through Harry Hopkins, after equipping Hopkins with charts
and a book of statistics giving the details, and, without ever seeing Mr. Roosevelt, got a $25 million allocation from the Presi-
dential emergency fund to get things rolling.

It was one thing to have the President cut red tape and make
the money available; it was quite another to comply with all the
legal requirements before the spending could begin. Furthermore there was the question of getting cooperation from the
South American governments. It was the CIAA thinking that
the beneficiary countries should match U. S. contributions dollar
for dollar on all projects—a rule later changed to give the bene-
ficiaries credit for materials and labor in lieu of cash because of
their dollar shortage—and this meant they would have to be
consulted.

The legalities were taken in charge by Senator Kenneth D.
McKellar, chairman of the Appropriations Committee, who
started out as a severe critic of the CIAA but later turned into
a firm friend and a warm admirer of Rockefeller. McKellar was
at first dubious, but agreed to set up the Institute of Inter-
American Affairs as the corporate subsidiary to handle the program on being prodded by Jesse Jones, who sympathized with the
plan although he refused to put RFC funds into it. The IIAA
was chartered in March, 1942, by Congress.

Under Secretary of State Welles undertook to line up South
American support. Rockefeller had gone to him for advice while
Welles was preparing for the conference of the Pan American
Union to be held in January, 1942, in Rio de Janeiro. The prime
purpose of the conference was to commit the American republics to a U. S. resolution requiring them to break off relations
with the Axis countries. In that Welles failed, a failure that outraged the always testy Secretary of State Hull and was to be used
in his successful campaign to drive Welles out of the State Department. The Argentine government, strongly pro-Nazi as it
would remain throughout the war despite some *pro forma* back-
tracking after the West's victory was assured, objected to the
mandatory feature of the resolution and raised the old cry that
the United States was dictating to Latin America. Since this is a

taunt that scares Latin-American politicians, the resolution was watered down to a mere recommendation. (In practical effect, of course, this was only a paper defeat: all South American countries except Chile and Argentina severed relations with the Axis less than a month after the conference, and Chile joined the club within a year, leaving Argentina isolated.)

But Welles had no difficulty getting unanimous South American approval for Rockefeller's program for mutual efforts to attack the pressing problems of health, sanitation, food production and illiteracy.

The IIAA made a unique contribution to the war effort and inter-American affairs in a time of crisis. It was credited with saving the emergency rubber program in the Amazon Valley by sanitary programs that held back endemic malaria. Its agricultural program helped provide food for American troops stationed in South America as well as for the local populations when there weren't enough ships in the Western world to maintain adequate supply lines. And it provided Latin-American countries with some twelve thousand agricultural and sanitation technicians to carry on their own program, giving them training on the job they never could have gotten otherwise.

Yet it was in no sense a giveaway. From 1942 through 1945, the IIAA spent $40 million on projects in eighteen countries with the recipient nations putting up perhaps half as much again in materials, labor and cash. Initial grants were for up to 80 percent of the financing, but the programs were phased out by reducing the IIAA outlays by 20 percent a year until the local governments could carry on unaided.

It was an undertaking that epitomized, in many ways, Nelson Rockefeller's approach to large problems. It was bold in concept, massive in scope, practical in operation. It was humanitarian. It created conditions in which free enterprise could operate more efficiently, but it never intruded on the private sector of the economy—a cardinal principle with Rockefeller who believes government should intervene only in those situations manifestly beyond the capacities of private capital.

No wonder, then, that Rockefeller would later look back on

the health and food programs as major successes of the CIAA. They worked, they were inexpensive in the framework of war spending, and the fact that they were carried on after the United States pulled out was an emphatic testament to their worth to South America.

One reason for the success of course was that the IIAA's programs permitted direct action. Most of the other economic jobs falling to the CIAA were more complex. All involved priority of goals, and, where a clear and present military gain couldn't be established, it was extremely difficult to get the cooperation of other government departments, no matter how worthy the project in terms of the overall war effort. A case in point was shipping for South America.

Almost from the day war broke out in Europe, South American shipping was hard hit. The British Navy blockaded the North Sea, which cut off the German vessels that normally carried a substantial part of the tonnage between South America and Europe. And the increasing European demand for war materials that could be produced in the United States but not south of the border led to removal of most of the merchant marine fleet normally engaged on hemispheric runs.

By the time the CIAA was set up, the situation was acute and Rockefeller knew it. His fear was that the economic losses which were threatening to strangle the one-crop countries would lead inevitably to political upheavals that could end in formation of a pro-Nazi bloc of South American dictators. His fears multiplied when the Nazi U-boat campaign in the Atlantic began taking its toll.

Early in 1941, Rockefeller turned to the Navy for help, noting that the shipping shortage was obstructing the flow of materials to the big base the United States was building at Natal in Brazil and other bases elsewhere in the strategic defense screen around the Panama Canal. Secretary Frank Knox and Under Secretary Forrestal were sympathetic, but they couldn't spare any ships. What bottoms they had couldn't fully satisfy the needs of the military.

Nelson took his case to the White House. But the American

shipbuilding industry, which would turn out a fantastic eight million tons of shipping in its peak war production year, was then only just gathering for the big push. The President did, however, create a committee on inter-American shipping, consisting of Admiral Emory S. Land, chairman of the War Shipping Administration, Forrestal and Rockefeller, with authority to set minimum requirements.

The committee did its earnest best, but its task was impossible. For as the war effort increased and the Nazi submarine wolf packs sharpened their techniques, more and more of the world tonnage was absorbed for direct military uses. At one point the situation got so desperate that Rockefeller assembled a wooden sailing fleet to carry nonstrategic cargoes in the Carribbean trade. The subsidiary corporation set up to handle this phase of the shipping problem actually got fifteen small ships into service before the wolf packs were driven from the western Atlantic as the tide of war changed late in 1943. After that more bottoms became available and the crisis in South America eased, although shipping remained in short supply.

The experience was a frustrating one for Rockefeller. Unquestionably the U. S. program in South America would have been more efficient had adequate shipping been available. But, in retrospect, Rockefeller conceded that, given the circumstances of the war years, nothing much could have been done about it.

Mexico got one big break out of the shipping crisis. Its nationalized railroad system, run by the labor syndicates, had been falling apart for several years because of divided authority and lack of planning. Suddenly, with coastal shipping cut off, it became the principal carrier under war supply contracts negotiated by the Mexican government. The increase in carloadings nearly finished off the roads. Neither the equipment nor the personnel was adequate for capacity operation. Wrecks rose to an alarming rate, endangering train crews and sometimes destroying freight.

A CIAA survey, ordered by Rockefeller on urgent pleas from his staff in Mexico, found the rail system basically sound but backward in management and maintenance techniques. However, a crash program was needed to repair and strengthen bridges, modernize freight yards and institute a more efficient dispatching and control system.

On Rockefeller's recommendation, the U. S. Government put up $7.5 million for a crash program to put roadbeds back in shape, improve signal systems and generally get the trains running safely and on schedule. A CIAA mission of experts was lent to Mexico to teach American railroading know-how to the Mexican managers of the lines. This aid, plus the recovery of millions of dollars worth of equipment which had been stockpiled by Mexico for development programs but never used because the plants were delayed, resulted, in the long run, in the complete rehabilitation of the rail system, an important factor in Mexico's postwar economy.

The success of the rails program probably influenced the thinking of Presidents Roosevelt and Ávila Camacho, of Mexico, when, at their meeting in Monterrey in April, 1943, they set up the Mexican-American Development Commission for Economic Cooperation with Rockefeller as the ranking U. S. member. By 1944, the commission launched twenty projects, involving U. S. investment of $24 million, to aid war production, and a backlog of programs was developed that contributed importantly to the Mexican economy in the postwar period.

Rockefeller tried to set up similar bilateral commissions in other countries after the success of the Mexican experiment was demonstrated, but was thwarted by the State Department. Had the scheme been adopted, it seems probable a great deal of the Latin-American bitterness that developed when the United States began its lavish aid to European reconstruction might have been avoided, and the Communists, who became the South American menace of the Cold War, at least would have been deprived of their claim that we were neglecting this hemisphere.

Part of the Mexican success was due to the fact that Rockefeller insisted on consulting labor. Although there was no official labor representation on the Mexican-American Commission, Rockefeller personally called on the most important union leaders to enlist their support.

Labor never did officially endorse the program. At the outset the union leaders were openly suspicious of the "Yanqui" capital-ist, Rockefeller, and received him coldly. Nelson wasn't abashed. Accustomed from the 1930's to meeting initial (and occasionally lasting) hostility in his contacts with Latin-American laborites, he resorted to the shock treatment that he can use so well to dis-arm those who base their attitudes toward him on preconceived notions. He was aware, Rockefeller said, that the labor federations couldn't come out and support a program they hadn't been officially consulted on, particularly a program that would cause the certain loss of some jobs in its early stages. But, he empha-sized, if labor used its political power to set up roadblocks, the development projects would fail. In the longer view, he said, this would retard industrialization of Mexico and prevent the creation of new jobs. He added that, so far as he was concerned, if Mexi-can labor wanted to fight the plan he'd be glad to forget the whole thing. It's your country, he said.

The union leaders weren't precisely entranced. But after satis-fying themselves that development would really provide the new jobs, they agreed to keep hands off the projects. The pledge was scrupulously observed. And, later, after the program succeeded, the labor men let it be known that they'd had more than a little to do with its success. In claiming the credit, they, of course, had to acknowledge that the United States had acted handsomely, thus getting the message out to the people.

The Mexican situation was a special case, but on most of the CIAA's undertakings Rockefeller strove for and got the support of labor. Even Communist-oriented unions, hostile until Russia entered the war, swung into action on our side after the Moscow line shifted. Labor difficulties did crop up, but, given the scope of the project and the antagonistic attitudes that some Latin-American unionists feel it necessary to take toward capital, this was inevitable. But there were no major troubles.

Hemispheric unity, of course, was always relative. Neither economic aid, nor propaganda, nor cultural exchanges, nor the combination of all could put down traditional rivalries and con-flicting ambitions. The competition of the various countries to get aid matching or exceeding that going to their neighbors, both for political reasons at home and because of honest differences of opinion, kept the CIAA and Rockefeller hopping to head off open quarrels. And, from start to finish, Argentina was divisive and obstructionist, a bully to her smaller neighbors, a naysayer to all inter-American cooperative efforts, and, only at the very last when it no longer mattered in the war effort, a reluctant declared enemy of the Axis.

Rockefeller ran head on into the Argentine obstructionism almost as soon as the CIAA came into being. The antidemocratic government bet on Hitler when the war broke out in Europe and never wavered in its loyalty to the Nazis. But it quickly and greedily demanded U. S. aid when cattle and wheat piled up on its docks because shipping was driven from the seas. The CIAA moved in to ease the crisis by helping to move the surpluses, only to find that the Argentine ruling clique would accept help only on its own terms. Those terms, it was soon made apparent, included official suppression of news about American aid.

The situation distressed Rockefeller through 1941. Try as he might—by negotiation, through his press division and through other aspects of the information service—he was unable to reach the Argentine people, who he always maintained were prodemocratic and would exert pressure on their government if they knew the facts. With the U. S. entry into the war and the Argentine government's refusal to break relations with the Axis powers, the blackout became critical.

For the bulk of the press, already gleefully pro-Nazi, took its guidance from the government and became more and more anti-American. Even democratically oriented newspapers, including *La Prensa,* of Buenos Aires, were at best noncommittal in the shadow of totalitarian controls.

Rockefeller was determined that the American story would reach the Argentine people. He knew *La Prensa,* one of the truly great newspapers in the Western Hemisphere, was followed by a large segment of Argentina's press. He knew, also, that *La Prensa*'s editor and owner, Alberto Gainza Paz, who later would win world acclaim for courageously fighting the dictatorship of Juan Peron until *La Prensa* was suppressed and he himself jailed, abhorred

the totalitarianism abroad in his country. The problem, as Rockefeller saw it, was to persuade Gainza Paz that this was the time
to make the fight for his principles.

It was a decision, Rockefeller realized, involving great risks
for *La Prensa* and its editor. But Nelson regarded the question as
so important that he went to extraordinary lengths to make sure
Gainza Paz got the U. S. point of view from the highest possible
sources. He invited the editor to Washington for a private
dinner.

It was a dinner that any editor would have given his right
arm to attend. The other guests were President Roosevelt's two
closest military advisers—General George C. Marshall, the architect of our victory, and Admiral William D. Leahy. Another
guest was Rockefeller's friend and CIAA associate, Wally Harrison.

It was a quiet dinner, deadly serious. Gainza Paz needed the
answer to many questions. The Allied cause did not look hopeful
in early 1942, with the U. S. Pacific fleet destroyed at Pearl Harbor, daily Japanese invasion scares panicking our West Coast
states, and the strong voices of the isolationists still echoing loud
in the land. Hitler's armies were on the march in Europe and
Africa; Russia was still in the war only because of massive U. S.
lend-lease, and Japan was scourging Asia and the western Pacific
almost without opposition. Millions around the world doubted
that the United States had the will or the capacity to win the war.

Patiently, point by point, Marshall and Leahy spelled out the
U. S. position for Gainza Paz. They made it clear this country
accepted the war as a global conflict that must be pressed to
total victory. They reassured him there would be no separate
peace that would expose our friends to Axis take-overs. They
sketched in for him the vast industrial resources that were being
organized, and sometimes conscripted, to build the greatest war
machine the world had ever seen. In the end, they convinced him.

Gainza Paz returned to Buenos Aires to lead one of the great
fights for freedom in the history of the press. *La Nacion*, the second most important daily in Buenos Aires, followed *La Prensa's*
lead, and a number of provincial papers soon began daring to

print prodemocratic news and opinions. Not that the press, or even most of it, became overwhelmingly pro-Allied. Nazi influence was too strong, Nazi money was too plentiful, and many editors were too slavish or fearful in the face of totalitarianism.

In the later light of Gainza Paz's lonely and gallant fight against Peronism, it must be regarded as certain that he would have followed his principles if there had never been a dinner with the military chiefs in Washington. Yet the dinner remains important. For on the basis of it Gainza Paz made his declaration for democracy earlier perhaps than he would have if he'd waited on the logic of events. Therefore, there was a democratic press in being when the Colonel's Revolt, led by Peron, seized power in the name of a military junta in June, 1943.

The nascent free press would be short-lived. Peron would crush it after he consolidated his power. But in the war years, before Peron perfected his mastery of the dictators' technique of rule-by-mob, it would give the Argentines unbiased glimpses of the Free World and occasional exposures of the brutalities of Fascism.

The affair of *La Prensa* was, for Rockefeller, only the first of many confrontations he would have with Argentine totalitarianism. It was also an exercise in the kind of extracurricular diplomacy that would become almost his trademark when he moved over to the State Department and that would irritate and enrage the professional diplomats. That there was no criticism of the Gainza Paz dinner must be attributed to the fact that it was hush-hush. Until after the war only a handful of people ever knew there had been a dinner.

Before going to State, however, Rockefeller would get some thorough, although strictly unofficial, on-the-job training in diplomacy. For as the war wore on and the military tide turned in our favor, the economic and other sections of the CIAA smoothed out their operations and began rolling on inertia. Nelson continued his overseeing of the program, but, increasingly, he was called upon to unsnarl the problems of allies in South America, problems frequently complicated by Argentine interference.

It was a peculiar position for Rockefeller. The CIAA had

been chartered to work out and execute a program for economic cooperation in the Americas within the framework of policy laid down by the State Department—and Rockefeller had been rebuked for overstepping an early directive—but in late 1943 this carefully nurtured unity was in definite danger because policy was betraying our goals.

By January, 1944, Rockefeller was ready to act. After consulting with his CIAA advisers, he went to Secretary of State Hull with a plan for a boycott of Argentina. The old Secretary quite probably was personally sympathetic. His rage at what he called Under Secretary Welles's "appeasement" of Argentina in the 1942 Rio Conference had cost Welles his job, and Hull would have liked to show muscle.

There was also the logic of Rockefeller's position. He told Hull that so long as this country and Britain helped make Argentina rich by buying huge quantities of her cattle and other foodstuffs, the United States was going to look pretty silly trying to fight the South American dictatorship on other levels.

Regardless of his sympathy, however, Hull didn't have the final say. That belonged to Winston Churchill, and the British Prime Minister cabled President Roosevelt that Britain could not survive without Argentine imports. That was that.

A couple of weeks later, Hull did get a chance to vent his wrath. Argentine interests got caught fomenting a revolution in Bolivia, and, to take the heat off, the Peronist military junta abruptly broke off diplomatic relations with the Axis. It was a rupture more symbolic than meaningful, but the junta had the gall to follow up the break with a demand for military aid from the United States. Hull blasted back with a reply that barely came within the limits of diplomatic language and imposed limited sanctions on Argentina. But Britain, mindful of its food needs, and Argentina's immediate neighbors, mindful that the Argentines had meddled in one revolution, refused to go along. The net effect was to stir dissension in South America without materially gaining anything.

This might have ended the boycott proposal except that the State Department went on to ruffle further the always sensitive

South American feelings. First it turned down a proposal by Foreign Minister Ezequiel Padilla, of Mexico, for another inter-American conference, and, second, it opened the Dumbarton Oaks talks with Russia, Britain and China in late May without so much as informing the Latin-American countries. Since the Dumbarton Oaks meetings were preliminary to drafting a charter for the proposed world organization, the Latins claimed they were being taken for granted.

In an attempt to rebuild morale, on August 19th Rockefeller made his last pitch for a boycott. The CIAA experts, increasingly worried by deteriorating relations in South America, came up with the suggestion that since Britain absolutely couldn't cut her meat imports, it was up to the United States to tighten its own meat rationing and send the savings to Britain, thus permitting her to stop trade with Argentina. In retrospect, it seems incredible that such a proposal could have been seriously advanced; 1944 was an election year, with President Roosevelt bidding for a fourth term, and, with victory in sight, Americans everywhere were cursing rationing and buying meat where they could find it in the black market. Hull, an old pro politician for a generation before he became Secretary of State, wearily told Rockefeller the boycott was dead.

At the same time, Hull killed off Rockefeller's plea for support of Padilla's suggestion that the United States call a new conference of Inter-American foreign ministers to develop joint action against Argentina.

In his concern that the drift in U. S. policy might nullify all the work and care that went into the South American program, Rockefeller felt impelled to state his position in writing for the record. It was a risky move. Hull was notoriously jealous of his prerogatives and sensitive to anything remotely like criticism. It seemed to Rockefeller's advisers that there was an even chance that the only result of such letter-writing would be to get Nelson fired. Sit back and wait for a break, he was told.

But sitting back was just one of the things Rockefeller couldn't do. At age thirty-six, in 1944, he was still rushing headlong into new situations. In the immediate instance he regarded the impasse over Argentina as an overriding emergency. That his view might have been exaggerated in the context of the larger war problems in the State Department probably never occurred to him.

The six-page letter and accompanying memorandum to Secretary Hull were drafted after much careful thought. Every effort was made to make the language diplomatic. But it is simply impossible to tell a Cabinet officer, especially a wise old bird like Hull, that his department has fouled up and make him like it. Neither Rockefeller nor his advisers had any illusions on that score.

What Rockefeller's criticism boiled down to was that authority was so fragmented in the State Department because of its system of assigning operations by function that no one had an adequate understanding of regional problems or needs. The consequence, Rockefeller said, was that policy could be made only by the overburdened Secretary himself, and he, frequently, was compelled to improvise *ad hoc* programs because he couldn't take the time for full-dress studies.

The correspondence was sent off, and all concerned sat back to wait for the explosion.

Nothing happened. Whether Hull knew that Rockefeller had taken out insurance of a sort by checking with Harry Hopkins and getting the word that the White House had no objections to criticism of State's handling of Argentina is not known. The Secretary never so much as acknowledged the letter.

Sometime later, President Roosevelt put out a statement echoing the standard CIAA line contrasting the "democracy" of the Argentine people with the dictatorship of their government, and some within the agency saw in this a reflection of the views Rockefeller sent to Hull. At best, it would appear, this estimate was overenthusiastic; no evidence ever was turned up to support it.

The riposte to FDR's statement came in October. Argentina, proceeding probably on the strategic cliché that the best defense is a good offense, abruptly called for a Pan-American Conference so she could answer the U. S. charges against her. To Rockefeller, it was the break of breaks.

By letter and in person, with all the eloquence he could command, he urged Edward R. Stettinius, Jr., who'd succeeded Welles as Under Secretary of State, to grab the opportunity. Since Argentina had brought up the question of her sins, Rockefeller argued, a conference would give the United States a chance to present a complete, detailed indictment to the world in an international forum. To Rockefeller's mind, the indictment would be unanswerable, and, by following it up with a reaffirmation of the Good Neighbor Policy, the United States could smash Argentine obstructionism.

The handsome Stettinius, who'd been working closely and sympathetically with Rockefeller for some months past, was interested. But Hull was affronted. He would have no part of a conference suggested by the upstart Peron, and twice the Secretary intervened to prevent action on the Argentine proposal by the board of the Pan American Union. Nor would he consider an alternative proposal to call a conference in Mexico City, the scheme Padilla and Rockefeller had been pushing at every opportunity.

There the matter rested on November 27, 1944, when Hull resigned as Secretary of State. On November 29, Stettinius became Secretary and promptly called Rockefeller home from Haiti where he was on a CIAA inspection tour and informed him that he was to be Assistant Secretary of State for Latin-American Affairs, a brand-new post.

The appointment, Stettinius added, came from President Roosevelt.

11

Mr. Assistant Secretary

THE APPOINTMENT OF NELSON ROCKEFELLER as Assistant Secretary of State was confirmed by the Senate on December 20, 1944. Counting the three weeks he put in on the job before the Senate acted, he served just short of nine months as head of the State Department's division of Latin-American Affairs. In that period he was never in any danger of winning a popularity contest; he was damned as anti-Russian and pro-Fascist; he put together and helped guide an international conference that produced one of the great documents in the history of the Western Hemisphere; he fought his colleagues and public opinion to bring on one of the first diplomatic confrontations with Communism as it hardened into its old mold with the approach of victory in World War II; and he tasted the intoxication of being among the movers and shakers of the world, albeit in a subsidiary role.

He enjoyed himself immensely.

Later Rockefeller was to say that he had to take the job in the State Department because he'd been, in his words, "knocking the ears off" the professional diplomats from his post in the CIAA and couldn't very well run when he was called on to do the job himself. The remark was rather too ingenuous. All Rockefeller's criticism of State had emphasized the need for creating the very job he got, and there can be little doubt that he would have been bitterly disappointed if it had gone to someone else.

This is not to say that Rockefeller was responsible for creating the new post. There is evidence that President Roosevelt set up the CIAA as an independent agency in the first place because he was dissatisfied with the way State was handling South American affairs, but couldn't risk offending Hull. With the reorganization of the department after Hull's retirement, an opportunity arose to incorporate the continuing functions of the CIAA, soon to be phased out because its work was done, in the regular departmental structure.

With his new job, Rockefeller got a shock. The economic program for South America, which he'd been handling in CIAA, was transferred in the State Department reorganization to another assistant secretary, Will Clayton. But Clayton was a friend and associate of Rockefeller in the early CIAA days and there was no reason to fear a feud. As it turned out, Rockefeller's duties so absorbed him on the diplomatic level that he had almost no time to think of anything else.

For at last he was about to come to grips with what he regarded as the worst menace to hemispheric unity: Argentina.

The timing of Rockefeller's move into the State Department couldn't have been better from his point of view. President Roosevelt was taking direct control of policy-making in a way that was politically impossible to him while the strong-minded Hull commanded State, and the new Secretary, Stettinius, an able administrator but inexperienced in making policy, went along willingly. Furthermore, Stettinius and Rockefeller had been working closely together for several months, and the Secretary was inclined to defer to the Latin-American "expert" who was "handed him," so to speak, by the President. A mutual liking also helped.

Almost as soon as he took office, Rockefeller revived Mexican Foreign Minister Padilla's proposal for a new inter-American conference—and ran head on into a collision with his colleagues. There were still a lot of "Hull men" around, and they opposed the meeting out of loyalty to their old chief. Potentially more serious opposition developed among the group planning for the San Francisco Charter Conference of the UN—then known popularly as the United Nations Organization (Organization was dropped from the title in 1945). Their objection was that the conference Rockefeller wanted might in some way detract from the formation of the world organization.

But the Rockefeller of December, 1944, had a far shrewder understanding of the State Department than the young Coordinator of Inter-American Affairs in the opening years of the decade. Exploiting to the full the prestige attached to his selection for State by the President, Nelson moved swiftly to protect his flanks before the snipers could get into position. He modified the Padilla proposal to call for a conference excluding Argentina, thus isolating her in the Western Hemisphere, and set about winning over Stettinius. As Under Secretary, Stettinius had been sympathetic to the idea of the conference. As Secretary, he was still sympathetic, but he was now running a department, and, with his wider responsibilities, he had a natural reluctance to begin his new job by reversing his predecessor's policy in a field in which he could claim no special competence. He insisted on getting White House clearance, which turned out to be a big break for Rockefeller. For the President not only gave prompt approval, but made it clear that he would give personal attention to the project. Time and again in the next three months, Mr. Roosevelt, despite failing health and the complex problems arising out of the Yalta Conference and the war, would intervene actively, with suggestions, with support for Rockefeller when he needed it, and with assurances to Latin-American delegates when they ran into rough going.

As soon as he got the go-ahead from Stettinius, Rockefeller went to work. He and his old and valued friend, Padilla, spent long hours reviewing all aspects of inter-American problems and going over the mechanics of getting out invitations to the conference, which Mexico would sponsor. Late in December, after his confirmation by the Senate, Rockefeller gave one of his private luncheons for the ambassadors from Chile, Colombia, Costa Rica and Peru. Out of the after-lunch conference came the rough draft of an agenda.

On January 3, 1945, Stettinius and Rockefeller discussed the Mexico City conference with President Roosevelt at the White House. The President initialed a memorandum approving the tentative agenda, already subscribed to by the Latin-American envoys stationed in Washington, and he gave Rockefeller a go-ahead to send a special representative to Buenos Aires to test Juan Peron by offering him an invitation to the Mexico City meeting if he would declare war on the Axis and restore constitutional government to the Argentine.

The special representative was Rafael Oreamuno, a Costa Rican diplomat, who was attached to the Inter-American Development Commission. After keeping Oreamuno dangling for several weeks, Peron, as expected, rudely refused to meet the conditions on the eve of the conference. Peron reiterated the refusal two weeks later when another last-chance invitation was sent him from the conference itself.

The tentative agenda okayed by FDR had four main points: the joint war effort, inter-American relations, joint economic activities and support of the burgeoning world organization. But what turned out to be the heart of the conference came out of a talk Mr. Roosevelt had with Eduardo Santos, former President of Colombia, on January 9th. Rockefeller, who helped set up the meeting, sat in.

Santos told the President that the dictators of South America had used lend-lease and U. S. military aid to build war machines far beyond any foreseeable needs. He argued that the peace of the hemisphere was in serious danger and that the danger would grow unless a means was devised to curb military adventuring. His idea was that Mr. Roosevelt should bring the problem before the Mexico City conference (Santos didn't know, of course, that FDR was getting ready for Yalta) and suggest a mutual guarantee of borders against attack. Mr. Roosevelt approved at once, but said the proposal probably would look better coming from Colombia. Santos undertook to sponsor a resolution, with Venezuela as cosponsor. Rockefeller was authorized to follow through. As a guideline Mr. Roosevelt defined an attack as one armed man crossing a border.

Out of the Roosevelt-Santos talk there evolved what became known as the Act of Chapultepec, which was the single most important achievement of the Mexico City conference and turned out to have international significance far beyond anything its sponsors anticipated. The Act called for an inter-American treaty (finally signed in 1947) declaring that an attack on one country in the Western Hemisphere was an attack on all, requiring joint action against the aggressor. This principle of mutual defense among friendly nations, written into the United Nations Charter at San Francisco by the American nations, later was invoked as a legal precedent for the North Atlantic Treaty Organization and other alliances developed by the democratic nations for the containment of international Communism in the Cold War.

But the State Department planners found the principle of regional groupings repugnant when Rockefeller broached the Roosevelt-Santos proposal at a staff meeting. State was then heavily engaged in planning for the charter conference and wanted to leave all matters of national security to the world organization. Spearheading the opposition were Leo Pasvolsky, special assistant for international organization, and Alger Hiss, executive secretary at Dumbarton Oaks, who would be secretary-general at San Francisco. Their stated reason was that world and, especially, Russian opinion might resent "ganging up" by the Americas. Rockefeller at last rode down the opposition, with undiplomatic bluntness, by telling the critics the proposal already had the written approval of the President.

Pasvolsky never did give up though. He was so passionately opposed to the pact that he tried to split the U. S. delegation in Mexico City right up to the last minute before the vote was taken. His attitude so angered Rockefeller, who was in charge of the delegation, that he threatened at one time to send Pasvolsky back to Washington. That silenced him, but left him an implacable foe as Rockefeller would find out in San Francisco.

Whether Hiss had ulterior motives would become a matter of national debate a few years later when his conviction and imprisonment for falsely swearing that he never delivered U. S. secrets to the Communist spy courier, Whittaker Chambers, ended his brilliant career. In 1945 Rockefeller had been shown an FBI report critical of Hiss and was wary of him. Later Nelson would say of Hiss: "We never got along; I didn't like him and he didn't like me, but I could have said that about a lot of people in State."

Certainly Rockefeller's conduct of the Mexico City conference wasn't calculated to make him friends in the Foreign Service. He outraged traditionalists at the start by chartering a plane to fly to the meeting with a group of Latin-American ambassadors. As ranking State Department officer, he clashed with Stettinius, who flew into the conference from Yalta and found himself called on to go along with things he'd never been briefed on; he "leaked" decisions approved by the President to the press before one of the key U. S. delegates was consulted, and he talked far too freely and informally with other delegations to suit the strict adherents of protocol.

Nevertheless, the conference proceeded rather more harmoniously than expected. All major items on the agenda, including the Act of Chapultepec, were enacted, and as its final act the conference set the terms for readmission of Argentina to the Western Hemisphere Community. These conditions included: declaring war, joining the war effort, democratization of the Argentine government, and full adherence to the pledges made at Mexico City.

Rockefeller flew home well-satisfied with the outcome.

He reported to the President on his mission at lunch in the

White House on March 16th. Mr. Roosevelt, who would die within a month, had returned from Yalta drawn and so weary that he had left off wearing his leg braces even in public appearances, but he followed the details keenly. He also initialed a memo approving a pledge to support Argentina for membership in the United Nations if that country declared war and fulfilled the conditions laid down at Mexico City. It was a directive Nelson would need.

Argentina stalled along until March 27th and then declared war on the Axis, agreed to the conditions laid down at Mexico City and announced it would adhere to the Act of Chapultepec. To Rockefeller it spelled victory. To others it was only a further proof of the cynicism of Juan Peron, then ruling from the office of vice-president. Germany's defeat was only weeks away, and Japan was never more than a side issue to Argentina. And it was noted that Peron rewarded himself for declaring war by seizing Axis assets.

Whatever the merits of the arguments, the facade of hemispheric unity was restored on April 9th when the American republics, led by the United States, resumed diplomatic relations with the Argentine, and France and Britain followed suit. Ambassador Spruille Braden was shifted from Cuba to Buenos Aires on the theory that his reputation as a hard-nosed, militant democrat would show that this country wasn't knuckling under. Braden, perhaps, overplayed his hand. He talked so tough, before and after he was recalled to Washington to replace Rockefeller a few months later, that Peron made him an issue in the election he finally allowed his people in February, 1946, and whipped up "anti-Yanqui" sentiment anew.

Within the State Department, recognition brought on a new fight after Mr. Roosevelt's death. Under the Mexico City agreement, the United States was now bound to support Argentina's application for membership in the United Nations. But the so-called liberal bloc that organized around Assistant Secretary Dean Acheson and the old "Hull men," who looked to Assistant Secretary James C. Dunn for leadership, were united against "appeasing" any pro-Nazi nation, which Argentina certainly was, and public opinion and most of the press supported them. When Rockefeller, hoping against reason that Argentina would really mend her ways under the pressure of moral force, tried to force the issue on the ground that our word was pledged and that the late President had approved, he was curtly reminded that there was no timetable on our commitment.

The death of President Roosevelt at Warm Springs, Georgia, on April 12 brought on a world crisis that made all questions temporarily academic. Briefly there was doubt whether there would be a San Francisco Conference. The new President, Harry S Truman, was known chiefly for his able work as chairman of the Senate War Investigating Committee. However, he ordered the conference to proceed on the lines laid down by FDR.

Incredible as it seems in view of all that has happened since, it wasn't until after FDR's death that U. S. planners woke up to the fact that Russia was ruthlessly lining up supporters for a power play at the San Francisco conference. Belated though the realization, however, it came in time to allow the West to rethink its tactics before the opening gavel banged down.

The State Department began counting noses to see how many friends it could call on in a showdown. But the career men of the international division, still sore about the Mexico City conference, were inclined to overlook Latin America. On April 20th Stettinius called in Rockefeller, the one State officer who had been in close touch with the South American situation, and told him he would have to stay in Washington. This was one the "pros" wanted to handle themselves, Stettinius said. Rockefeller knew just what was going on, but he was helpless.

Before the day was out, the signals were changed. The United States had been arming and feeding the Free World, but the nose count showed that our Allies intended to put first things first, meaning themselves, on meaningful issues. Latin-American support suddenly loomed as very important, and Rockefeller was asked to go to San Francisco for "a few days" to talk up the U. S. viewpoint.

The next day Rockefeller and a group of his friends among the Latin-American delegates flew to San Francisco in a char-

tered plane, a touch of swank that tweaked the noses of his disappointed foes. Rockefeller, who charters a plane as casually as
the next fellow hails a cab, saw the special plane as a goodwill
gesture. But he certainly relished the fact that he remained at
the conference to the end and sat in on high-level huddles from
which the career men were barred.

What lingering hopes there may have been that Russia would
act with sweet reasonableness in the light of the worldwide aspirations for peace were quickly dispelled at San Francisco.
Soviet Foreign Minister V. M. Molotov started out bullying the
conference, apparently expecting disorganization among the
Western Powers because of the death of President Roosevelt.
He disappointed U. S. hopes that Secretary Stettinius would be
named chairman by insisting on a system of rotating chairmen;
he insulted the Latin-American nations, when Mexican Foreign
Minister Padilla seconded the nomination of Stettinius, by calling them stooges of the United States and treating them as satellites, an attitude he maintained to the end of the meeting, and
he brazenly attempted to railroad the Communist-puppet, Lublin Polish cabinet into the United Nations despite a Yalta agreement to defer seating Poland until a new government could be
chosen.

The bullying apparently was intended to split the United
States and the rest of the Americas. The consequence was directly opposite. The offended Latin-Americans, far from being
intimidated, solidified in their determination to pressure the
United States to honor its Mexico City commitment to support
the admission of Argentina. And the State Department and the
U. S. delegation were forced to the conclusion that the time was
here and now to make a stand in support of Argentina, distaste-
ful as it might be.

Molotov kept the pressure on. At Yalta it had been agreed
that two Soviet satellites, the Ukraine and White Russia, would
be admitted as full members of the United Nations as a sort of
counterbalance to the votes given the Dominions of the British
Commonwealth as independent nations. If the satellites could be

rushed through, the question of admitting Argentina, which was widely unpopular, could be isolated and probably defeated.

A Rockefeller suggestion for a three-week delay in seating new members so the stalled conference could get on with the work of organizing was spurned by the Russians. On April 27th Molotov rammed a resolution to seat the Ukraine and White Russia through the steering committee and was on the point of getting preliminary approval from the conference when Foreign Minister Lleras Camargo, of Colombia, interposed an objection that shunted the question to the executive committee for study.

Stettinius, who shared widespread Western fears that the tough-talking Russians were looking for a pretext to wreck the conference, made one last effort to head off the confrontation, setting up a meeting of the Big Four with Latin-American spokesmen in his suite at the Fairmont Hotel. All it produced was a cynical offer by Molotov to trade Soviet approval of the admission of Argentina for Latin-American votes to seat the Lublin puppets. This would directly violate the Yalta agreement. The deal was spurned as totally unacceptable.

The U. S. delegation, after a bitter debate, called President Truman and got permission to vote for admission of all three applicants. On April 30, White Russia and the Ukraine were approved unanimously and without debate. Molotov made a savage attack on Argentina which was voted in by 32 to 4, with the Soviet bloc casting all the nays. The Russians remained at San Francisco.

Nobody was pleased. We were still in a deadly serious war with the Axis, although total victory over Germany was only days away, and neither the American people nor the press was in a mood to applaud any gesture that could give comfort to a pro-Nazi. This feeling was exacerbated by indisputable evidence that the Argentine government, having enriched itself by its paper declaration of war on Germany and Japan, was going its old Hitlerite way toward an ever-tighter dictatorship—controlling the press, stamping on individual liberties and preaching an ever-more-virulent hatred of the United States.

Stettinius, Rockefeller and the Latin-American foreign ministers were the whipping boys. The Secretary and Rockefeller were damned editorially across the country for their "cynicism" in pandering to the Latin-American bloc, while the foreign ministers were, with impartial fervor, accused of blackjacking the United States in time of need. Russia's obstructionism was largely overlooked.

Rockefeller felt that the State Department erred by not putting the full story of Molotov's role in the Argentine maneuvers on the record. But Stettinius preferred taking the criticism to risking anything that might give the difficult Russians an excuse to stir up more trouble. Nelson had to go along.

Returning to Washington to testify at a Congressional appropriations hearing, Rockefeller found the criticism following him, and new critics honing their adjectives. He was required to deny that he was anti-Russian and pro-Fascist and to explain the U. S. delegation's vote in San Francisco although he was not a member of the delegation.

Rockefeller got back to San Francisco on the first Saturday in May to find the U. S. delegation had agreed with the Soviet, British and French to support what he considered one of the most dangerous articles proposed for the United Nations Charter. He was the more shocked because he'd discussed the question at some length with Secretary Stettinius a few weeks earlier and thought they had an understanding to examine the matter more fully before any course would be recommended. At issue, as Rockefeller saw it, was the future of mutual security pacts, including specifically the defense treaty envisaged in the Act of Chapultepec.

The proposed article, endorsed by the Soviet, would have permitted military alliances among the United Nations against former "enemy states." This, in effect, would have allowed Russia to erect alliances in Europe and Asia against Germany and Japan, leaving other regional agreements subject to a Big Power veto in the Security Council. The international division of the State Department had obtained a consensus in the U. S. delegation for the proposal on the ground that the world body could handle any disputes that arose. But this made no specific provision for a Western Hemisphere alliance.

Mistrustful always of the veto—a couple of weeks later he filed a prophetic memorandum, still in the archives of the State Department, predicting it would be misused against the West— Rockefeller wanted firm protection for mutual security pacts written into the Charter. The Latin-American nations wanted even more: a specific approval of the treaty promised in the Mexico City agreement.

When Rockefeller tried to get hold of the Secretary to discuss the matter he was told that Stettinius wasn't available. He was advised to take his problem up with Assistant Secretary Dunn or Leo Pasvolsky. It was unacceptable advice. Dunn and Pasvolsky had fought him in the past, and, anyway, both could be counted on to support the line taken by State's international division. Even if one of them had been open to Rockefeller's ideas, it wouldn't have mattered particularly as neither was influential enough. For what Nelson was about to undertake was to reverse a policy that was all but official. Mentally canvassing the delegation for a possible ally with an open mind and enough stature to make his opinion count, Rockefeller decided his best hope was Senator Arthur Vandenberg, of Michigan, ranking Republican member of the Foreign Relations Committee.

Vandenberg at that time occupied a unique position in the Senate. Starting out as a far-out isolationist, he had under the pressure of the war years moved steadily toward international-ism. He enjoyed tremendous esteem in his own party and close relations with the White House. He'd been picked for the U. S. delegation by President Roosevelt, before his death, because Mr. Roosevelt, always mindful of the Senate uprising that killed the League of Nations, was determined to assure Republican sup-port for the Charter. Vandenberg also worked in close harmony with Senator Tom Connally of Texas, the chairman of Foreign Relations, who was the Democratic Senatorial delegate.

Rockefeller called Vandenberg at once and invited him to dinner that night, explaining that he was worried about the tentative agreement to vote the U. S. delegates in favor of the

military alliance proposal. Vandenberg, who had misgivings of
his own, readily agreed to talk the matter over. The two dined
privately in Rockefeller's suite in the St. Francis Hotel.

The talk was a long one. Vandenberg was concerned, as he
noted in his diary, that failure to write a specific sanction for mutual security into the Charter would gut the Monroe Doctrine.
He sympathized with Nelson's fear that hemispheric unity would
be a dead letter unless Latin America was assured that the Act
of Chapultepec would be honored. The difficulty was to find a
formula to cover all angles of the situation. Neither the Senator
nor Rockefeller could devise one on the spot.

Vandenberg regarded the matter as so urgent, however, that
he decided to put his objections in writing in a letter to Secretary Stettinius. With Nelson offering occasional suggestions,
Vandenberg dictated the letter that night. He pointed out that
Senate approval of the Charter would be impossible to obtain if
the Monroe Doctrine were in any way endangered. Vandenberg
said that, for his part, he'd oppose ratification unless the agreement was amended.

Rockefeller counted it a successful night. He would go into
this fight with a powerful ally—two, really, because Senator Connally would back Vandenberg all the way.

The predictable hell broke out right on schedule at 9:30
Sunday morning when Stettinius read the letter, which Vandenberg had dropped off before going to bed. The Secretary, aware
that he didn't enjoy the full confidence of his President, was
under tremendous pressure. And here was a matter he'd thought
all buttoned down threatening to cause another crisis. He felt
he had cause for anger.

Others were just as bitter. John Foster Dulles, a powerful
Republican lay spokesman in the delegation, later to become
President Eisenhower's Secretary of State, said bitterly that the
letter could "wreck" the conference. Although the letter was
signed by Vandenberg, most of the bitterness was aimed at Rockefeller. He didn't let it bother him. "I was the one everybody
was sore at," he remarked later, "but I'd do it all over again.
It had to be done."

Senator Vandenberg was shocked, but not dismayed, when the fury broke at the regular meeting of the U. S. delegation on Monday. Dulles, an international lawyer of vast experience in world conferences, called the Vandenberg proposal frivolous and unnecessary. The other ranking Republican candidate, Harold E. Stassen, onetime governor of Minnesota, at first sided with the State Department line.

Vandenberg was not to be moved. Confident that Connally would stand with him to the showdown, the Michigan Senator demanded specific guarantees for the security of the Americas. Unless such guarantees were written into the Charter, he said, he would be forced to support a move to oppose it in the Senate. Since Vandenberg and Connally held the power between them to nullify everything done at San Francisco on the Senate floor, this was an ultimatum. The acrimonious session broke up with the matter being placed in the hands of a technical committee. But the dreary wrangling dragged on and on. It would be necessary to take a six-day recess from the charter conference to allow time to settle the affair.

Within the delegation, Rockefeller was the villain. He was charged with trying to run the conference and he was blamed for "stirring up" Vandenberg despite the Senator's statement that he'd had serious reservations about what would happen to the Monroe Doctrine even before he talked to Nelson. Feeling ran so high against Rockefeller that Dulles refused to speak to him for several days.

It became, now, a question of finding a formula. The technical committee had got nowhere. The delay was grating on everyone's nerves. After a great deal of hesitation, Stassen accepted an invitation to have dinner with Rockefeller and for long hours they worked over the problem. It was Stassen, an old hand at legislative drafting, who came up with an acceptable proposal. He suggested linking the Act of Chapultepec's basic premise of mutual defense with the inalienable right of any nation, anytime or anywhere, to defend itself as the legal foundation of the formula. Working from this concept, Vandenberg drew up a two-part section of Article 51 of the Charter, writing in the specific guarantee of self-defense and recognizing the "principles" of the Monroe Doctrine and the Act of Chapultepec. By long-distance telephone, Stassen, with Rockefeller at his side, explained the proposal to President Truman and got his personal approval.

Now the British got into the act. They were willing to go along with the guarantees sought by Vandenberg and the Latins, but they objected to the specific naming of the Monroe Doctrine and the Act of Chapultepec, fearing it might make the difficult Russians still more difficult. As finally amended, the key section of Article 51 provided "nothing in this Charter shall impair the inherent right of individual or collective self-defense if an armed attack occurs against a member of the United Nations."

The South American foreign ministers were then called in and the situation was explained to them. It wasn't a happy meeting. Most of the United States delegation seemed aggrieved at spending so much time on the question, and even Senator Connally, although he stood with Vandenberg on the Monroe Doctrine issue, upbraided the Latin-Americans for what he called their ingratitude. The Latins weren't to be budged. Beset by political problems at home, which few in the American delegation fully comprehended, they were fearful that the Act of Chapultepec might never be implemented unless it was pledged in the Charter. But they finally agreed to accept the formula after getting word that President Truman would call a meeting in October to draft the hemispheric defense treaty.

On June 9th, Article 51 became part of the United Nations Charter by unanimous vote.

The full significance of Article 51 wouldn't be realized for several years. Only after a series of arbitrary Soviet vetoes in the Security Council bedeviled the United States and a number of Russian Cold War offensives threatened peace would Dulles, a man who could cherish a grudge, offer his hand to Rockefeller and apologize, with an acknowledgment that only Article 51 had made the North Atlantic Treaty Organization possible in a time of crisis for the West.

As for the Latins, they would have to sweat out their treaty for two years. For reasons beyond the control of those at San Francisco, the pledged October conference ran into a series of delays. There would be wide rejoicing when the hemisphere treaty was finally approved in 1947, but by that time only a few would remember the role Rockefeller played and give him credit.

On the day Article 51 was adopted, however, Rockefeller, vindicated in a fight far more important than even he anticipated, still had a major job ahead at San Francisco.

With the conference now pointing toward a hopeful conclusion, the two Senators had to get the Big Power veto in the Security Council approved. The veto had been agreed to at Yalta, and the Senators felt that the UN treaty would fail in the Senate without it. The complication was that the smaller nations, including a number from South America, were organizing to fight the veto at any costs. Rockefeller was asked to line up his friends from Latin America. From then on he held daily meetings with them.

It was an unwelcome assignment. Rockefeller had set forth his personal misgivings about the veto in his memo to Stettinius some weeks earlier, and nothing had happened to change his mind. He was aware, also, that opposition to the veto was a matter of principle with some of the Latin-Americans. But he agreed to do what he could. "I don't see, even now, what else I could have done," Nelson said years later. "Van stood by me when I needed him, and, anyway, all I had against the veto was that I was suspicious. I had no alternative to offer."

Rockefeller balked, however, at twisting arms to get a unanimous Latin-American vote for the veto. He explained his position to the foreign ministers and asked them to go along if they could do so without embarrassing themselves politically at home. Most of them voted with us or abstained on the roll call.

The United Nations Charter Conference closed on June 26th to world rejoicing. Europe had been at peace for nearly six weeks; Japan's defeat was now only a question of time, although there was fear that the cost would be frightful. But the world was crying for peace and the Charter seemed to offer a hope there would be no more wars.

In the U. S. delegation and staff nearly everybody was happy, except, perhaps, Secretary Stettinius, who landed at Washington Airport to find that his resignation had been accepted. He was promptly named United States Ambassador to the United Nations.

Nelson Rockefeller returned to Washington to see what time and the new Secretary of State had in mind for him.

The new Secretary, James F. Byrnes, a South Carolina politician of unbounded ambition, apparently had very little in mind for his Assistant Secretary for Latin-American Affairs, even if his name was Rockefeller. Byrnes was too busy accepting resignations, reorganizing his department, and preparing for the Potsdam Conference to sit down and discuss South American affairs.

That left Rockefeller to pick up where he'd left off before going to San Francisco. And that, of course, brought him back inexorably to his old problem and worry: Argentina.

The situation was far worse than he had anticipated. Rockefeller never believed that the Argentine government would reform itself except under pressure from the people and from the other American republics. But there was no pressure. In the months following Argentina's readmission into the American community of states on April 9th all eyes had been turned on San Francisco and Fascism had a rank growth in the Argentine. The militant democracy preached and practiced by Ambassador Braden, which Rockefeller found entirely praiseworthy and which he would publicly applaud, had been the single, lonely voice crying out against dictatorship, and Peron had exploited its loneliness to build up a bogey of Yanqui domination. Anti-American feeling was strongly on the rise.

Rockefeller felt, with considerable prescience, that hemispheric unity would soon become meaningless unless the crisis of leadership was resolved. He set about finding ways to mass the moral and economic policies of the Western world to bring down Peron.

Then the bomb dropped on Hiroshima and man's way of life was forever changed.

Secretary Byrnes returned from Potsdam to confront a world

without a recognizable power structure. The precarious balance achieved at San Francisco was drastically altered, and the new balance of terror that would sustain an uneasy peace into the 1960's was still in the future. All postulates of our foreign policy had to be reexamined. With the whole world cowering under the mushroom clouds of the atomic bomb, it was no wonder the Secretary had little time for Latin America, which had no atomic potential and which, to oldline diplomats at least, existed only on the fringes of power.

All through the early weeks of August as he watched the Argentine situation deteriorate further, Rockefeller was unable to get to the Secretary. "I was pretty sure," he said later, "Jimmy Byrnes was going to get a man of his own, but I just couldn't let everything go." He finally won an audience by sending Byrnes a text of a speech he was slated to deliver in Boston. The Secretary didn't even want to talk about it; he told Nelson that he'd informed the President that Rockefeller wanted to resign. There was no need to make the speech, Byrnes said.

Rockefeller's temper flared. He told Byrnes he didn't want to resign and that Byrnes knew it. Rockefeller said he'd make the speech as an Assistant Secretary of State or he'd make another speech as a private citizen and tell the whole story of what was happening in the State Department under the new Secretary. Byrnes was furious, but had no alternative except to approve the speech.

On August 24th in his last official act as Assistant Secretary of State for Latin-American Affairs, Rockefeller arraigned Argentina before a Pan American Society audience in Boston. The Peron government, he said, carefully distinguishing the Argentines from their rulers, was embarked on a reckless and brutal drive to impose totalitarianism on a basically democratic people. He called for strong leadership by the other American republics, particularly the United States, to check the rising Fascism before it became an enduring blot. The cry went largely unheeded. Peron endured for a dozen years, and Argentina is still bedeviled by Peronism.

The morning after the Boston speech, Rockefeller's resignation was announced and Braden was recalled from Argentina to take his place. A few newspapers gave favorable, if passing, mention to Rockefeller for his service in government, but most editorial comment was reserved for Braden, the current hero because of his tough speeches.

"I went over to see the President," Rockefeller reminisced a couple of years ago, "and told him I didn't want to resign. I said South America was too important. I said I'd like to finish the job if he wanted me to. Harry was very decent about it. He told me I'd done a good job. But he fired me."

"He fired me," Nelson repeated, wonderingly.

There was no rancor in the firing. Later Rockefeller would observe, "Truman couldn't have done much else. It was the way he was. He wanted to back up his Secretary, and Byrnes wanted no part of me." As for Mr. Truman, he called Nelson back to Washington in November, 1950, to head the International Development Advisory Board to study U. S. aid programs. The commission submitted a comprehensive report, "Partners in Progress," but its recommendations were passed over by the Truman Administration, although some were later incorporated in our foreign aid program. The second parting, a year later, was "entirely cordial," to use Rockefeller's description.

12

....

A Semi-Private Citizen

His FIVE YEARS in Washington gave Rockefeller a lasting taste for government. He returned to private life in the latter part of 1945 and was soon deeply involved in his big socioeconomic experiment in South America to test, as related elsewhere, whether private enterprise could contribute significantly to the advancement of the underdeveloped countries and still show a profit, but he kept one eye on the nation's capital.

The years immediately ahead, however, were barren of opportunity. As the war emergency and Mr. Roosevelt's New Deal, with its heavy latter-day "national" government overtones, gave way to the frank partisanship of Mr. Truman's Fair Deal, the political credentials of the Administration's appointees were examined with increasing care, and to Harry S Truman, Democrat, Nelson Rockefeller, who would, in any event, contribute to Thomas E. Dewey's campaign in 1948 and who never gave a dime to the Democrats, had no credentials. It looked as though Nelson would be an outsider for some years to come.

In 1946, however, he accepted appointment to Mayor William O'Dwyer's committee to find a permanent site in New York City for the United Nations, then housed temporarily in quarters at Lake Success on Long Island. The prospects weren't bright. Philadelphia, San Francisco and a number of other cities, here and abroad, were competing for the headquarters, and no one in New York seemed able to come up with an acceptable site.

Matters drifted. Rockefeller was only one member of a rather large committee, he was heavily engaged in major business undertakings, and at the United Nations the talk droned on and on, with no sense of urgency on a decision. But as the Christmas recess neared, the tempo changed. Abruptly the UN decided to vote on December 11th whether to keep trying in New York (which many delegates wanted, at least in part, because the United States was ration-free and luxuries were abundant) or to look elsewhere.

Rockefeller was in Mexico on business when he got word of the scheduled vote and flew back immediately. He landed in New York on the afternoon of December 10th, with only about twenty hours to spare before the roll call would start at Lake Success.

It was the kind of go-for-broke situation, as in San Francisco, that Rockefeller nearly always accepts as a challenge. The Mayor's Committee, bankrupt of ideas, wasn't even meeting. Anything that was to be done, he'd have to do on his own. That wasn't too displeasing. True, he would get no advice. But then nobody would be looking over his shoulder telling him what he couldn't do. The difficulty was that he had no more ideas than the Mayor's Committee, and time and the United Nations seemed to be slipping away.

As usual at such times, Rockefeller, Frank Jamieson, John

Lockwood and Wally Harrison got together in Nelson's office in Rockefeller Center to kick the problem around. It was quite a problem. Nelson's first thought was to give the United Nations a 200-acre plot known as Rockwood Hall on the family estate at Tarrytown. His brothers agreed, but his father took a dim view of the plan. The United Nations, moreover, was insisting on Manhattan. But to assemble such a property might be the work of months or years, even if the power of condemnation could be invoked, and no one was sure it could be.

Harrison, who as an architect kept track of major real-estate happenings, knew of just one likely parcel—a seventeen-acre plot lying along First Avenue, north of 42nd Street, on Manhattan's East Side. It wasn't the best spot; just below, Consolidated Edison's East River plant belched forth smoke night and day, and from below that the slaughterhouses smelled out the neighborhood when the wind was wrong. The subways were some blocks distant. But it was a large plot and it was in the hands of William Zeckendorf, a real-estate promoter, with whom Harrison had been associated in the past. Harrison "guessed" it could be had for about $8.5 million.

This information was about as useful as a map to Fort Knox when you need money. Nelson telephoned his father, interrupting him at dinner, for advice. He got a great deal more than advice. After listening a few minutes, John D., Jr., who knew as much about Manhattan real-estate values as any man alive, agreed that $8.5 million seemed a fair price. He added that if Nelson could get the property he'd give it to the United Nations. Nelson has always claimed that the offer surprised him as much as it did everyone else when it was made public the next day.

The rest of the night was spent getting an option, state, Federal and city clearances, with the city promising to do something about the smoke and slaughterhouse nuisances, and the next day the $8.5-million gift proposition was offered to the United Nations in a neat package. It was accepted immediately.

Nelson gave his father all the credit for the operation, but Mr. Rockefeller insisted on calling it a "joint accomplishment." At any event they exchanged mutual congratulations.

Although the brief adventure stimulated Nelson, it was to be his last "official" action for several years. For most of the period he was too deeply involved in his own affairs to do more than keep a close watch on world developments, but in January, 1949, he was moved to put himself on record in favor of the Point Four program to give technical assistance to underdeveloped countries that President Truman presented to the world in his inaugural address. Point Four was new only in name. A sort of "pilot" program had been tested by the Institute of Inter-American Affairs and, in fact, a former assistant of Frank Jamieson had suggested using the idea in the inaugural speech.

Rockefeller, on the basis of his Washington experience and because he'd been dealing in private business with some of the problems of exporting know-how and capital in a private enterprise system, quickly fired off a letter to Mr. Truman, praising his boldness in applying the plan to the world. He offered to lend a hand in getting it started. Nothing happened.

The letter went unanswered, but it quite apparently was not forgotten. For with the Point Four bogging down in the fall of 1950, Mr. Truman invited Rockefeller to take charge of the International Development Advisory Board to devise a policy for aid to underdeveloped countries. Rockefeller asked and got authority to approach the question on the broadest possible base, and then went to work.

The "Partners in Progress" report was completed in five months, and that should have been the end of the chore for Rockefeller. Instead, he spent most of 1951 commuting to Washington, seeking support for his board's recommendations from such outstanding nonspenders as Virginia's Senator Harry Byrd and "Mr. Republican" himself, Senator Robert A. Taft, who already was campaigning for the GOP Presidential nomination in 1952—the nomination that would go to General Dwight D. Eisenhower. The reception given the report was cool.

But Nelson's intense activity generated a suspicion—which Rockefeller claims was completely unwarranted—that he wanted to become head of a new agency proposed by the board to distribute all aid to the underdeveloped countries. One who shared the suspicion was W. Averell Harriman, later his opponent in the 1958 state election. Harriman, originally receptive to Rockefeller's ideas, apparently saw in the broad recommendations a threat to his control of foreign aid as head of the European Cooperation Administration and interposed his objections when Rockefeller wanted to go to Key West, Florida, to present his report in person to Mr. Truman. An official coolness developed between Rockefeller and Harriman over this point, and they never quite warmed up to each other again.

Rockefeller always claimed that President Truman was enthusiastic about the Point Four program and would have supported major points in the "Partners in Progress" report if they'd been presented to him properly. This view overlooks the political realities. The nation was deep in the Korean War in 1951, a Presidential election was only a year away, and Congress was in no mood for experimental spending ventures, even though they were aimed at promoting the use of private capital in developing private enterprise abroad.

The fact that many of the proposals were enacted into law piecemeal in the politically more stable climate after the end of the Korean War would appear to indicate that timing had as much to do with the sidetracking of the advisory board efforts as any opposition. But Rockefeller, being human, couldn't see it that way at the time, and he was rather bitter about the matter for a while, although his bitterness never extended to Mr. Truman.

Less than a year after quitting the International Development Advisory Board, Rockefeller would be back in Washington, pitching in on the preliminary planning for the incoming Administration of President Eisenhower. He would serve three years under Mr. Eisenhower, part of it in the White House, and he would come very close to Cabinet rank before his next return to private life.

In the 1952 election, Rockefeller was an enthusiastic and generous, but strictly behind-the-scenes, supporter of General Eisenhower. Nelson's cash contributions were graciously accepted, but the men running the campaign—Thomas E. Dewey, then in his last term as Governor of New York, and Herbert Brownell, who would become Attorney General—"wanted no part of me," as Rockefeller commented some years later. He went along with their wishes.

But while leaving politics—a field in which he claimed no special competence—to the professionals, Nelson felt impelled to be more than just a contributor and went to work in the area that intrigued him most: ideas. With the tremendous research facilities of the various Rockefeller organizations at his disposal, he collected a group of economists to survey the nation's problems and come up with suggested speeches for the General.

"I got him some of the best writers in the country," Rockefeller has said, "and he used a lot of our material in the campaign."

From this activity it was but a natural step for Rockefeller to accept eagerly when President-elect Eisenhower invited him late in November to become head of a tight little group of planners to advise the new Administration. The other members of the group were Dr. Milton Eisenhower and Arthur S. Flemming, who would later become Secretary of Health, Education, and Welfare. After President Eisenhower took office, the group was constituted by executive order as the President's Advisory Committee on Government Organization, with a charter of responsibility so broad as to encompass nearly every phase of administration.

It was an assignment that Rockefeller suggested. Here, at the start of a new Administration, with a popular new Republican President and a Republican Congress that might be expected to follow his wishes, Nelson was handed a chance to help streamline executive departments at the policy level. It was heady wine. Big planning was called for, and big thinking. He was superbly confident he could supply them.

The climate was conducive to optimism. President Eisenhower named big businessmen to key offices in his Cabinet, and Rockefeller could talk their language. In his six years in reorganization planning, which he quit only to run for Governor of New York, he always had the cooperation of the department heads.

The first chore Rockefeller was handed as a planner was to work with Oveta Culp Hobby, pulling together the widely scattered government activities that would go into the new Department of Health, Education, and Welfare. It was an extraordinarily complex job. Bits and fragments of various programs, in health, in general and specialized welfare, and in different phases of education, were embedded in the structures of existing departments, sometimes with several departments involved, and the bureaucrats were, as always, reluctant to give them up.

For all its complexity, the work proceeded smoothly. Congressmen, jealous of the prerogatives of departments in which they had special interests for one reason or another, were persuaded that the new department would continue the activities in the various states without any interruption in services. By April, the legislation was ready for action, and before the end of the month the Congress approved it under Senator Robert Taft's guidance.

Side by side with putting the HEW together, Rockefeller was drawn into military planning for the first time. Defense Secretary Charles E. Wilson, who was always one of Nelson's strongest boosters, named him chairman of a special committee on the reorganization of the Defense Department on February 19, 1953. This was a vitally important area. General Eisenhower had been critical of the conduct of the Korean War in the 1952 campaign, and he wanted fast action on defense reorganization.

The special committee included Flemming and Dr. Eisenhower, Nelson's colleagues on the President's planning board, and former Defense Secretary Robert A. Lovett, General Omar Bradley, a longtime friend of the President, and Dr. Vannevar Bush, the scientist. Recruiting the nation's top retired military commanders, including General George C. Marshall, former Secretary of Defense and World War II commander in chief, as experts, the special committee went on a crash schedule, holding executive hearings three days a week during March. It came up on April 11th with a plan that got enthusiastic backing from Secretary Wilson.

The major recommendations for strengthening the powers of the Defense Secretary and the service secretaries to tighten civilian control over the military and for relieving the Joint Chiefs of Staff of paperwork were incorporated in President Eisenhower's message to Congress on April 30th, proclaiming the reorganization. (Other suggested reforms were put through by Secretary Wilson by administrative order.)

The reorganization provoked the expected outcry from the armed services, and Rockefeller was called before Congress on June 19th to defend it against charges that it would lead to an all-powerful general staff on the Prussian order.

He apparently was persuasive. A motion to reject the reorganization plan in the House of Representatives was beaten down by 235 to 108 on June 29th and the recommendations became law the next day by Executive Order.

While the Pentagon reorganization was being fought over, President Eisenhower named Mrs. Hobby, a Texas newspaper owner and World War II commander of the Women's Army Auxiliary Corps, as the first Secretary of Health, Education, and Welfare. Named as Under Secretary was Nelson Rockefeller— another instance, he remarked, of finding himself told to make his own plans work.

It was the start of a year and a half of hard, frequently tedious and mostly anonymous work. HEW came into being with a staff of 35,000, a budget of $2 billion and responsibility for distributing $4 billion in Social Security payments. It had a blueprint of organization, but no tradition of loyalty to sustain morale, and many of the employees, transferred from other departments, were something less than ecstatic about moving into a new organizational setup.

Rockefeller threw himself into the work as into a game. He and Mrs. Hobby worked closely together on major policies, and she gave him his head as the executive officer of the department. He found plenty to do. It was one thing to draw a blueprint; it was another to set up a going department. He found that many of the programs now falling in the HEW portfolio had atrophied from neglect or lack of funds in other departments. He set about to revitalize vocational rehabilitation of relief clients, to make an imaginative attack on juvenile delinquency, to reform and update some parts of the Social Security program. He worked on Administration programs for education aid, getting an insight into the school problem that would stand him in good stead some years later as Governor of New York.

His activities were not always expansionist, however. One of his first acts in HEW was to cut off the Office of International Cooperation, which handled overseas health programs, and transfer its functions to the Foreign Operations Administration on the ground that HEW was primarily concerned with domestic affairs. This, like other key plans, was fully approved by Mrs. Hobby who kept a close check on all developments.

As Under Secretary, Rockefeller had a hand in making policy, and he drafted or helped draft all the legislative proposals HEW sent to Congress in its first two years to flesh out the skeleton of the fledgling department. He also found himself spending many hours on Capitol Hill testifying before committees and lining up support for the programs.

This was to Rockefeller a great opportunity. For the first time in his government experience, he was a part of the Administration, and for the first time he was seeking partisan advantage. He believed the Republican Party needed to broaden its popular support, and he felt that a soundly based social program under the aegis of HEW would best prove to the people that the Republicans weren't about to cut back the advances made after the Depression. It was a view shared by many in the Administration, but the Congress was (and remains) divided on just what the Federal Government could and should do.

In 1953, however, Nelson was optimistic. The legislation he helped draft and fought for was congenial to his humanitarian thinking. He enjoyed the confidence of the President, and the bills that came out of HEW were carefully fitted into the overall goals of the Administration, often bearing the President's personal imprimatur. But, as was the case with the "Partners in Progress" report he prepared back in the days of the Truman Administration, the timing was off.

A decade later the questions of Federal aid to education and health insurance, which Rockefeller worked on assiduously at

HEW, were still deeply enmeshed in Congressional controversy, but Rockefeller continued to feel both would eventually be enacted. His thinking on health insurance changed over the years, however, and from a proposal for an experimental program in 1953 to handle the problem through private insurance companies, he gradually shifted by 1960 to a belief that "medicare"—then hotly contested—should be keyed to Social Security, with certain safeguards against it becoming compulsory. This changed attitude brought him into a direct clash with President Eisenhower and Vice President Nixon as the presidential campaign opened that year.

Over the years, a number of the legislative proposals that came out of HEW while Rockefeller was Under Secretary became law, notably proposals to increase Federal responsibility for basic research in various health fields, and several national conferences he proposed—on health, education and the like—were held. He continued to follow these developments long after leaving the department.

By the late fall of 1954, HEW was a going concern and Rockefeller considered his job done. He'd accepted the assignment to get the department on its feet, and, although he'd continued to wear his hat as chairman of the President's Advisory Committee on Government Organization, the daily routine demands on his time kept him to some extent out of the mainstream of the Administration. Besides he was anxious, in those troublous Cold War days, to have a greater share in foreign affairs.

He was also aware that when C. D. Jackson resigned as Special Assistant to the President for Cold War planning a few months earlier, he'd recommended Rockefeller as a likely successor.

When Rockefeller mentioned to the President that he thought it was time to change jobs, he found Jackson's White House spot had been held open for him, but with a significant increase in the area of operations. In a letter of appointment, dated December 16, 1954, Mr. Eisenhower told Nelson:

> I shall look to you for advice and assistance in the development of increased understanding and cooperation among all

peoples. I shall also look to you for assistance in reviewing
and developing methods and programs by which the various
departments and agencies of the government may effectively
contribute to such cooperation and understanding.

You are requested to attend the meetings of the Cabinet,
the National Security Council, the Council on Foreign Economic Policy and the Operations Coordinating Board.

This directive put Rockefeller about as high as one could go
on the policy-making level of the Administration without Cabinet
rank. It also exploded him to the center of the stage where the
strong men of the Administration, notably Secretary of State John
Foster Dulles and Treasury Secretary George Humphrey, were
accustomed to brook no dissent. Inevitably, Nelson would step
on some toes. Inevitably, also, although his innate optimism probably obscured the fact at the start, he was in for a certain amount
of frustration. For the lot of a Special Assistant to the President
is rarely a happy one. He has no fixed place in the chain of
command, and the departments are likely to resent his "interference" even when the logic of the situation compels them to
approve his ideas.

Nelson wasn't so naïve as to expect easy sailing. He still remembered his fights with the State Department at San Francisco
ten years before, and, although his personal quarrel with the
strong-minded Dulles had long since been patched up, Rockefeller
knew that State's career men weren't going to put out any welcome mats for him. On the other hand, he had no intention of
taking his job at any less than its total responsibility. To this
end, he always refused to be categorized as a Special Assistant in
a specific field, preferring the wider scope of a general assignment.

Most of his difficulties were with the State Department, but
Rockefeller encountered resistance also from Treasury Secretary
Humphrey and Rowland Hughes, the Budget Director, who had
him tabbed as a "spender" and consistently opposed his programs
on the ground they would cost too much. In the end, Humphrey
would put the crusher to Rockefeller's chances of entering the
Cabinet on these grounds.

The occasion arose late in 1955, after Nelson already had decided to resign the White House post, when Defense Secretary Wilson asked him to become Under Secretary of Defense. Since Wilson was straightening out his affairs to get ready to retire, this would have paved the way for Nelson to advance to Secretary within a relatively short time.

"I talked it over with the President and it was agreeable to him," Nelson said afterward, "but when Humphrey got wind of it and George told the President I'd wreck the budget with my spending. That settled that. George had a lot of influence in those days."

A lot of Rockefeller's difficulties with the State Department traced to his strained relations with Under Secretary Herbert Hoover, Jr. A traditionalist, Hoover didn't want any "outsider" mixing around in State Department affairs and said so. Furthermore, Hoover seemed to take it as a personal affront when Rockefeller was named to head an inner planning group in the Operations Coordinating Board, of which Hoover was chairman. The inner group, recommended by Budget Director Hughes and approved by the President and the National Security Council, lasted only a few frustrating months, and Rockefeller himself recommended its dissolution when it became apparent that it was getting nowhere. Nelson always maintained that State's obstructionism sank the project.

Nelson's dealings with State also were complicated unwittingly by President Eisenhower himself. "The President would pick up a phone," Rockefeller has said, "and say 'Foster, Nelson has an idea,' and that would be enough to get Dulles's back up."

Dulles's testiness over presumed invasion of his preserves did not affect the personal relations between the two men, however, although they disagreed over many of Nelson's ideas.

At the peak of his operations in the White House, Rockefeller had a staff of twelve specialists on loan from other departments and about fifteen administrative and secretarial employees, all under Major General Theodore W. Parker, who was assigned as his chief of staff by the Defense Department. Parker hadn't been eager to give up his command in the Chicago area to take the

Washington job, but he and Rockefeller got along well and functioned smoothly.

The staff worked hard, Rockefeller himself put in his usual
long hours and a good part of his nights on various aspects of
his job. The multiplicity of his interests was staggering. Broadly
interpreting the directive of his appointment, he became an
advocate of economic aid as an indispensable prop to our national security. In the contest for the loyalty of the emerging
nations, he argued, the United States needed to involve their
self-interest or leave a void that Communism would occupy in
default, by subversion or token economic penetration. This, he
said, based on his experience in South America in the CIAA and
in private business, required taking the long-term view of our
outlays.

This was a thesis bound to bring him into conflict with others
in the Administration. The complex question of foreign economic
aid involved political, budgetary and emotional factors that af-
fected the whole of the Administration. Although Rockefeller
always checked with President Eisenhower before undertaking a
project, he often found the go-ahead meant merely that Mr. Eisenhower wanted another point of view on the subject. When the time
for decision came, the President was inclined to let Secretary Dulles
have the final say on foreign policy, and to defer to Secretary
Humphrey on spending. This did not deter Rockefeller. He conceived it his duty to lay before the President the facts as he saw
them: he was under no illusion that his proposals would be controlling. But he had the satisfaction of initiating new lines of
thought, and sometimes of directly influencing policy. However,
most of his successes were incorporated in others' policies and
shrouded in the anonymity of the Special Assistant.

He was not without allies, of course. Nelson recalled recently
that Vice-President Nixon, with whom he'd worked on HEW
legislation, was "always very helpful" and on occasion the two
teamed to put over projects of mutual interest, notably a speedup
in the construction of the Pan American highway in Central
America and in getting more money for the United States Information Agency. Nelson also had a close working relationship

with Sherman Adams, then second only to the President in the Administration.

Throughout his service in the White House, Rockefeller proceeded on the assumption that the Cold War was here to stay and that short-term policies were inadequate to our need. He believed, as he still does, that negotiation with the Communists in the give-and-take of normal diplomacy is impossible. His position was, and is, that the Soviets will honor their commitments only when confronted by overwhelming strength that leaves them no alternative, or when their own interest is so heavily involved that any other course would be unprofitable, militarily, economically or both. From this conviction, he argued for aid to Indonesia and for Nasser's government in Egypt to tie them to the West at a time when the State Department was putting on the brakes. Whether Indonesia's drift to Communism or Egypt's seizure of the Suez Canal could have been averted by timely aid must remain a matter of speculation.

His concern over the danger of negotiations deepened as the Soviets launched their so-called "peace offensive" in the spring of 1955, highlighted by the Moscow call on May 10th for general disarmament. As the President prepared for the Summit Conference to be held at Geneva in July, Rockefeller got his authorization to convene a panel of experts to make a top-secret assessment of the U. S. position in the psychological aspects of the Cold War. The meeting was held at the Marine Corps School at Quantico, Virginia, from June 5th through 10th.

Rockefeller's hope was that the experts, locked away from the world for a few days, could develop a program that would give the West the initiative at Geneva and exploit to the full President Eisenhower's great prestige. Anything less, Nelson feared, would allow the Soviets to promote their unacceptable disarmament plan before the world.

Naturally, this put Rockefeller on a collision course with the State Department. State was preparing its own position papers for Geneva and wanted no outside advice. Moreover, the Quantico meeting was set up under the inner planning group in the Operations Coordinating Board that Herbert Hoover, Jr., detested so thoroughly. But the panelists were former government officials, military men, university specialists and industrialists out of the very top drawer, and the Administration sent high officers as observers.

The Quantico panel devised a scheme later to become known for its most dramatic feature as the "open skies" plan. In essence, the plan called for an exchange of blueprints of military installations between the United States and Russia, with each country granting the other the right of unlimited aerial reconnaissance flights over its territory. The reasoning was that this "open skies" photography would give each nation accurate information on any military buildup by the other, thus minimizing the danger of a surprise attack. More than that, the idea was that the foundation would be laid for serious disarmament talks if the Soviets accepted this limited inspection in good faith.

Nelson presented the plan to President Eisenhower as a two-edged sword to be taken to Geneva: if accepted, it would cut away a lot of the vagueness surrounding the Soviet "peace" proposals; if rejected, it would undercut the Reds' propaganda claims. The President's first reaction was favorable. But, predictably, Dulles didn't think much of the idea. The President told Nelson sometime later that the Secretary called it a "public relations stunt" and wanted no part of it at the Summit Conference. Anyway, the Secretary argued, the State Department was working on its own disarmament proposal.

The President went along with his Secretary of State, but he showed his sympathy for Rockefeller's proposal by insisting on inviting him to a briefing on the Geneva Conference two days later.

Nelson refused to quit on the "open skies" idea. He kept pressing, he explained afterward, because there was nowhere any indication that the United States would have anything to offer to counter the continuing Russian "peace propaganda," which was pouring out day by day to the neutral and uncommitted countries. The West, he felt, had to put forward a positive program or the Soviets would use Geneva to put us in the wrong before the world.

The President, meanwhile, had some second thoughts, and instructed Harold E. Stassen, a newly named Special Assistant for disarmament, to try to work a mutual inspection proposal into a general disarmament paper he was developing. Rockefeller was dubious, pointing out to Mr. Eisenhower that drafting of a comprehensive peace plan would be the work of months.

And there things stood when the State Department began to make up the list of those who would go to the Summit Meeting at Geneva. Conspicuously missing were Rockefeller and Stassen, the State Department taking the position that "outside" experts might give a propaganda tinge to the American delegation. The President, however, decided the two and several others should go to Paris to be handy if they should be needed.

The Summit Conference opened Monday, July 18, at Geneva, and Nelson's fear that the Soviets had come to propagandize, not to negotiate, was promptly justified. After weeks of telling the world that Geneva was a sort of Cold War peace conference to end fear, the Russian spokesman, Premier Nikolai Bulganin, under the watchful eye of his boss and successor, Nikita Khrushchev, offered once again the often-rejected, long-stalled Communist proposal for immediate destruction of all atom bombs and a worldwide slash in armaments without verification. It was a proposition no Western nation could accept and survive, as the Reds well knew, but presented in the great international forum of the Summit, it had tremendous impact on the emerging countries.

That night in Geneva and Paris, worried men pondered the problem of how the West could salvage its position. In Paris, Rockefeller rounded up the group of other high government officials on standby duty for Geneva, and obtained a consensus that the situation warranted putting pressure on Dulles and the President to use the "open skies" proposal. One of those most importantly approving the plan was the chairman of the Joint Chiefs of Staff, Admiral Arthur W. Radford. Another was Deputy Defense Secretary Robert Anderson. On their own they sent a cable to Dulles urging him to adopt the scheme.

The next morning, Rockefeller and Stassen sent the coded text of the statement to Secretary Dulles at Geneva, and Rockefeller, on his own, duplicated the message to Colonel Andrew J. Goodpaster, the President's military aide. But Mr. Eisenhower also had been doing some thinking about mutual inspection, and within hours Rockefeller and Stassen were ordered to Geneva. In the meantime, the President took the matter up with British Prime Minister Sir Anthony Eden, who welcomed it enthusiastically. By the time the statement was whipped into final shape late the following day, even Dulles was all for it. A speech drafted by Rockefeller was accepted as the declaration of positions.

The President didn't read the statement to the Summit Conference. He had it with him at the plenary session on Thursday, July 21st, but, when his turn came to speak, he took up one of the routine position papers prepared by the State Department. Rockefeller, sitting directly behind him, wondered briefly if something new had come up.

Halfway through the prepared speech, the President laid down his papers. Surveying the ornate council chamber and the delegates and their staffs for a moment, he began to talk almost informally in the frank, open manner so familiar to television audiences. The world situation, he said, required the United States and Russia to exchange "a blueprint of our military establishments" and to "provide within our countries facilities for aerial photography to the other country to convince the world that we are providing as between ourselves against the possibility of great surprise attack."

This was strong, meaty stuff. The Soviets had been talking peace in a sort of never-never land; now the President challenged them to their teeth to take a single, concrete step toward peace and they were nonplussed. Bulganin, playing the role of statesman, liked it; but Khrushchev, whose official rank at the conference was that of a political observer on Bulganin's staff, was furious. As the meeting broke up, he confronted Rockefeller and the President and, ignoring Rockefeller, accused the United States of trying to sabotage the Summit. The President, Rockefeller said, in recalling the incident, came out better than even in the exchange.

"Khrushchev knew who I was, but he just looked at me and went on talking to the President," Rockefeller reminisced. "We weren't introduced."

The "open skies" plan, as the most dramatic aspect of the U. S. challenge, excited the imagination of the world and changed the mood at Geneva. There was an all-too-brief spurt of hope as the conference ended, with everybody applauding the "Spirit of Geneva," which nobody managed to define. In a few weeks even that would be dead. But Rockefeller has always felt that by taking up the Soviet challenge as he did, Mr. Eisenhower established himself as "the diplomatic figure at the conference," and saved the West from an ignominious propaganda defeat.

Back in Washington, Rockefeller had every reason to feel that his long fight for the mutual inspection proposal was justified. He was no hero to the State Department—he would never be that —but Secretary Dulles, mellowed perhaps in the afterglow of Geneva, was inclined to the view that everybody had done well at the conference. He told Nelson that the Summit Meeting had produced a moratorium in the Cold War, and he was inclined to think some progress could be made in the unification of Germany and other sensitive areas as a consequence.

It was a doomed hope. In November, at the Foreign Ministers' Conference to which all the problems of Geneva had been referred for resolution, the Soviets began their tactics of delay and obstructionism that in the end killed off all the Geneva proposals, including, very definitely, the "open skies" plan.

Rockefeller never shared Dulles's optimism. There'd been nothing at Geneva to change his profound conviction that you can't trust the Soviets. On his return to Washington, he was concerned that the United States hadn't imprinted on the Communist mind its absolute determination to use all its power and resources in the struggle for peace. He felt that only a declaration of a policy of strength could clear the air.

To get the ball rolling, he went to President Eisenhower, still in his role as planner for the Operations Coordinating Board, and got permission to convene a second conference of experts at

Quantico to try to define the components—economic, military and moral—of a long-term national policy.

The second Quantico conference was held September 25th to 29th. Again all the panelists were top men in their fields and in the government, and again all had to get security clearance to give them access to the top-secret material that comprised the working papers for the studies. But unlike the first meeting, which was concerned solely with preparing for Geneva, the later panel gave only incidental thought to the Foreign Ministers' Conference, then being planned by the State Department, and spread its concerns over nearly all aspects of national and international affairs. Although some ideas generated at Quantico II went into the State Department hopper for use at the Foreign Ministers' meeting, the complete, 41-page, unanimous report of the panel wasn't published until December when Nelson was clearing up his desk to resign. Its circulation was restricted to government officials qualified to receive classified material.

The Quantico II report was never acted on as a whole, perhaps because of its cost—a whopping $18 billion over six years to build up our military and economic strength around the world —but many of its concepts have since filtered into our policy. As an example, one may cite President Kennedy's buildup of conventional military forces to fight less-than-nuclear wars. The concept became commonplace by the 1960's, but in 1955, despite the lesson of the Korean War, our military strategy was keyed almost wholly to atomic deterrence. The panel was clearly ahead of its time in this and other matters.

The report also enunciated four precepts that Rockefeller continues to regard as the cornerstones of foreign policy. These call for: full disclosure of the dangers confronting the country to rally the national will behind the government; military spending on whatever scale is necessary to make sure our defense never becomes second best; economic aid to build up the free countries so they can eventually contribute to the defense effort around the world, and constant pressure on the Communists to unmask the true intentions behind their propaganda and so-called aid programs. As a corollary to the military buildup, Rockefeller, both as Special Assistant and as Governor of New York, has stressed the overriding importance of an adequate civilian defense program to impress on the Russians that our people will fight if forced to war.

Long before the Quantico II report was printed, Rockefeller had decided to resign by the end of the year. Back in August, at the time he set up the conference, he told the President that he'd return to private life as soon as he could get his desk cleared up and pending matters settled. It took a lot of clearing up. He was still chairman of the President's Advisory Committee on Government Organization, a post he'd continue in until he entered politics; he was consultant, at the request of Defense Secretary Wilson, in a second reorganization study of the Pentagon, and as Special Assistant he was involved in projects ranging from atoms for peace to helping implement the South American projects he'd initiated so many years ago as Coordinator of Inter-American Affairs.

The parting between Rockefeller and the President was cordial and personally warm. In a letter accepting Nelson's resignation, which was dated December 31st, Mr. Eisenhower wrote:

> The breadth of your service to your government has indeed been outstanding. You should have an especially great sense of satisfaction in the splendid contribution you have made during this administration to the advancement of human values, not only throughout the United States while you were Under Secretary of Health, Education, and Welfare, but also with respect to nations throughout the world in your capacity as Special Assistant.

Rockefeller for his part wrote the President: "Your leadership . . . gives hope and faith to people throughout the world. Being a member of your staff and working for you personally has been an association which I will always cherish."

The friendly relationship continued. Three months after his resignation, Rockefeller returned to the White House for one of the President's intimate stag dinners, and they corresponded on friendly terms. In the preconvention months in 1960, Mr. Eisenhower would show flashes of irritation over some of Rockefeller's statements, but his anger would fade quickly.

Rockefeller's stated reason for leaving the White House was because of "compelling personal responsibilities." That, of course, was nonsense. He has said he would have stayed on in government as Under Secretary of Defense if his way hadn't been blocked. The focus of his interest was still national and world affairs. But a year of frustration, illuminating though it had been, was quite enough. A conviction was growing on him that to make your authority stand up in government you need a political base of power. He was determined that the next time out he'd have such a base. How solid it would be he couldn't foresee. But he could dream and plan.

13

The Move to Politics

WESTCHESTER COUNTY LIES due north of New York City, its border running along the Bronx line from the Hudson River to Long Island Sound. In its upper reaches, which include Pocantico Hills, it is lush and rolling estate country. Its industry, in the main, is crowded along the shore lines of the Hudson and the Sound, while the central and northern parts of the county, despite the subdividers and developers, have the lowest population density in the New York metropolitan area. Its per capita wealth, long the highest of any suburban county in the nation, has remained near the top even though its population increased by nearly one-third in the 1950–1960 decade to the present level of more than 808,000. It boasts more private golf courses than any other county, and it probably has more private swimming pools than anyplace east of California. Sealed off, to a great degree, from working-class immigration by comparatively high taxes, living costs and land values, by inconvenient transportation and by limited industrial development, with a consequent scarcity of local jobs, it is solidly middle class in its orientation.

In politics, it is, and has been for more than fifty years, solidly Republican, dominated by one of the strongest county political machines in the country.

The Republican dominance is no happenstance of politics. It was contrived out of the ambitions of a remarkable man, the late William L. Ward, who decided around the turn of the century that only a strongly centralized organization could avert fragmentation of the political power potential of the county. It was a finding that required little prescience. At the time Ward moved in, many of the multimillionaires, employing scores to hundreds of servants, gardeners, stablemen and laborers on their estates—wages, after all, averaged out to only about a dollar a day plus board—were running private political organizations of their own with no liaison on joint problems.

It was a system that invited anarchy. The politically ambitious seeking advancement were compelled to scrounge for allies where they could find them because no overall alliances existed. Uncontrolled, this was trending toward a collection of Republican satrapies, often warring on each other, that would be politically powerless in larger affairs. Uncontrolled, also, the haphazard methods might have tempted the Democrats, who occasionally made forays north of the city line from their bastion in Tammany Hall, to make a serious try to take over Westchester.

In establishing effective political hegemony over Westchester, Ward's contribution was to provide a policy to unite the big contributors to the party and to bind the working politicians to the organization by setting up a system of promotions, using the township as the unit of political power, that tied the hopes of the ambitious to the overall accomplishments of the county machine. There was, of course, nothing new in this; it is as old as politics. Ward's achievement was that he built so well that sixty years later, and a generation after his death, the Republican control of the county is almost absolute. The GOP holds every office in county government, it elects all the Congressmen and legislators Westchester sends to Washington and Albany, and it fills the higher courts with the party faithful as they come up through the step-by-step grades of advancement first initiated under Ward.

From the outset, Ward's unification of the Westchester Republican Party was supported by the Rockefellers. Always generous contributors to the GOP on state and national levels, they began to kick in to the Westchester organization when they began acquiring the Pocantico Hills estate. Over the years they have continued to contribute as a family, individually, and through their various interests. How much the total amounts to can't possibly be determined. Reporting of political contributions is, after all, a relatively new legal requirement, and there is no way to go back into the records to add up the many individual gifts.

Aside from their contributions, none of the Rockefellers showed any interest in the Westchester County Republican organization, as Ward was acutely aware. He tried to draw the family into local affairs by arranging for Nelson Rockefeller's appointment to the Board of Health soon after his graduation from Dartmouth. Nelson served twenty-one years in the non-paying post, and came up, according to those who served with him, with valuable suggestions, but his primary interests lay elsewhere, so nothing came of Ward's stratagem.

By 1958, however, all this was changed. Nelson Rockefeller needed the Westchester County Republican organization. For nearly two years, he had been mulling over the idea of running for Governor; for a year, experts had been researching state problems under his direction, making more than a hundred separate studies. He heard nearly all the conceivable arguments for and against his running from his family, from his closest associates, including specifically his most trusted personal adviser, Frank Jamieson, who was distinctly bearish on the prospects, and from state-level politicians. Now time was running against him. Time in the absolute sense in that he was approaching fifty, and if he passed up 1958 he would have to wait at least four years for another chance, and the second chance might never come. And time in a more limited sense in that the Republicans were already beginning to choose up sides with the summer convention in mind.

To get into the game, even if he didn't follow through, Rockefeller needed a base of operations. And where better could he turn than Westchester County where his ambitions were certain to get respectful and serious considerations? Then, too, sponsorship by Westchester County would take some of the edge off the faint suspicion upstate Republicans always feel for those identified with New York City, as Nelson had been identified most of his life.

It wasn't a simple matter of asking and receiving, as Nelson soon found out.

Typically, he made the first sounding himself. The setting was the annual "victory" dinner of the Westchester Republican Committee in White Plains in mid-January of 1958. Chatting with the late Herbert Gerlach, then chairman of the county committee, Rockefeller remarked, almost offhandedly: "A lot of people have been talking to me about running for Governor; I'd like to get your views on it."

Gerlach couldn't possibly have been surprised. Rockefeller's increasing interest in state politics, as evidenced that night by his presence at the Westchester dinner, was apparent to nearly everyone. As a practical, county-level politician, Gerlach might have been expected to relish the idea of having a very wealthy and generous party contributor as a candidate. But while he gave Rockefeller the respectful consideration his statement merited, he didn't throw his hat in the air.

"I don't know what our position is just now," Gerlach told Nelson as the two looked over the merrymakers. "We might have a candidate already. You know Malcolm Wilson hasn't made up his mind what he's going to do."

"Let's talk to him," Rockefeller said instantly. The two hunted up Wilson and set up a meeting for the following Saturday in Gerlach's law office in White Plains.

Later both Rockefeller and Wilson were to insist that nothing important transpired at that first meeting in Gerlach's office. Certainly there were "no commitments made and none asked," as Wilson put it. They agreed only to wait and see what developed. But it led on Wilson's part to a very vital decision that was to have great bearing on the future of both men. For when the trio met a second time early in February, again in Gerlach's office, Gerlach urged Rockefeller to run and promised him Westchester's support. No mention was made of Wilson's never openly avowed state ambitions, but his presence backed up Gerlach's urgings.

The second meeting, like the first, was largely exploratory, but, as Wilson recalled, there was an extended discussion of the other possible candidates, with Wilson giving a rundown on their respective prospects. It was an enlightening session for Rockefeller because Wilson, one of the best-informed politicians in the state, demonstrated conclusively that he knew the score down to the meagerest detail. The meeting was important, moreover, because Rockefeller and Wilson found they could talk each other's language. Thereafter Gerlach dropped out of the picture.

But Rockefeller held back from an irrevocable commitment as March dragged by. Then on the first Sunday in April, in Wilson's office in White Plains, Wilson and Rockefeller met for the climactic session. The meeting began about 6 P.M. and ran into the early hours of the next morning. "We had a discussion in depth," Wilson said. The talk ranged over numerous subjects, from state affairs to possible rivals for the nomination to Rockefeller's political philosophy. "I had to satisfy myself that he really believed in Republican principles," said Wilson. "We talked it out very frankly, and at last he invited me to take charge of his campaign. I accepted."

It was a vital agreement to both men. What Rockefeller, who was being called a New Deal Democrat in Republican clothing, got out of it was the imprimatur of one of New York State's most widely respected Republican conservative spokesmen and an expert political ally. What Wilson got was a broadened role in the Republican Party and, eventually, election as Lieutenant Governor.

Wilson's political posture in 1958 was rather paradoxical. At forty-four, he was rounding out twenty years as Assemblyman from Yonkers, and, while his highest official position was chairman of the Codes Committee, he was quite possibly the most powerful individual in the Assembly with the exception of the Speaker, then Oswald D. Heck.

A hard worker, a tireless doer of political favors and intellectually superior to most of his colleagues, Wilson had built up over the years a personal following that gave him command of a bloc of about thirty Republican votes, give or take a couple because of local pressures, on showdown issues. This gave him what amounted to a balance of power in the Assembly, but he exercised it sparingly and only when it could be done without laying his adherents open to party discipline. It also gave him a unique political position for an Assemblyman, because many of his legislative followers, county chairmen in their own right, openly committed themselves to follow Wilson's lead in the coming convention.

On the other hand, Wilson's personal political advancement appeared to be stymied. He'd been aiming for the Speakership of the Assembly, but a complicated deal between Speaker Heck, who had gubernatorial ambitions of his own, and J. Russel Sprague, the important Nassau County leader, had moved Joseph F. Carlino of Long Beach into the line of succession over his head. That left Wilson in a bind in 1958. He was at an age when the logic of politics almost required upward movement. But his field of action was circumscribed. For, great though his influence was, he had no wide popular following as he was realist enough to know. Without a costly buildup that was beyond his personal means, he might be rebuffed if he tried for nomination on the state ticket. And such a setback at that point in his career might very well have ended it. Furthermore since all the putative gubernatorial hopefuls except Rockefeller carried impeccable conservative credentials, Wilson's support given elsewhere, although it would have been gratefully received, would have had only limited impact on the convention outcome.

Clearly, therefore, the Rockefeller-Wilson alliance was indicated. That the association developed into friendship was velvet on both sides.

While the Rockefeller-Wilson negotiations were going on, the nomination drive by Nelson was proceeding uninterruptedly on other levels. On the voting level, there were recognition polls to determine which of the likely candidates for Governor was most widely known in the hinterlands. Rockefeller won every test, but the question remained whether the recognition was of Nelson Rockefeller as an individual or, as his rivals claimed, merely of the family name. There was no way for the outsider to make this determination because the polls were privately taken, but the raw results were exploited for full value. On the state party level, Republican Chairman L. Judson Morhouse, officially impartial but long anxious to snare Rockefeller as a candidate for some office, was counseling wait-and-see to county chairmen who were under increasing pressure through the winter and spring to declare for one candidate or another.

And on the top levels of the party, careful soundings were made to find out whether the national Republican hierarchy or the Big Money contributors were committed irrevocably in advance (as two years later they were to be committed to Vice-President Nixon for the Presidential nomination) to any candidate. This was just a simple precaution and one that all prudent candidates take within their capabilities. For Rockefeller it was particularly important. In March, 1957, when Leonard W. Hall resigned as Republican National Chairman, President Eisenhower had wished him good luck in his campaign for Governor of New York, and many accepted this as a commitment on the President's part. But a year later, Ike carefully stayed out of the New York situation.

As for the financial and industrial communities, they clearly had no preference, and, while no hosannas were heard for Rockefeller, there was at least no concerted effort to block him, perhaps because they didn't think it mattered much. All signs that year pointed to a Democratic victory and the return of Governor Averell Harriman to Albany.

In fact former Governor Thomas E. Dewey, long a spokesman for the important financial interests and a self-designated youngish elder statesman of the GOP, bluntly told Rockefeller, "You can't win," when Nelson broached the subject of running early in 1958. Thereafter Dewey took no formal part in the preconvention campaign, but, when the counties started swinging to Rockefeller as the summer approached, it was noted that known Dewey followers were high up in the list of pledges.

A campaign for a nomination is, of course, totally unrelated to an election campaign. Although, ideally, a would-be nominee should be able to demonstrate some degree of voter acceptance, that isn't paramount or even necessary. For in seeking delegates, the prospective candidate must first enlist the support of a comparative handful of men who control the party machinery and who in the long run will select the delegates. And these men (lady politicians rarely crash these inner circles) are interested first and foremost in what any nomination will mean to their own particular situations. Their primary assessments are made on the basis of what they must do to preserve their own organizations and to advance their interests. Until this is determined, neither personalities, nor issues, nor even victory or defeat in the election can be given any attention. Such close focus on the local organization also involves, of course, sedulous respect for local prejudice. As a consequence, in upstate New York, at least, Republican leaders tend to bear down heavily on their conservatism, in many cases far more heavily than the voters themselves. And this imposes on Republican gubernatorial hopefuls the necessity of looking as conservative as possible in preconvention posture while keeping open the way to a shift after the nomination to the more liberal stances that are absolutely vital to anybody hoping to make inroads into the big-swing independent vote that is so often decisive in New York.

In April, 1958, with all indecision behind him, Rockefeller faced up to this problem. By this time he had gathered around him a group of advisers dedicated to his nomination and election. The group fluctuated in size, and the personnel changed from time to time as specialists were brought in for advice. But the core remained unchanged right through the convention and election. As always in Nelson's undertakings, the key men were his closest intimates, Frank Jamieson, architect Wallace K. Harrison and John Lockwood, with Louise Boyer, as usual, coordinating.

Other members of the group had worked with Rockefeller at various times in various capacities. These included a brilliant and tireless young lawyer, Roger (Rod) Perkins, whose acquaintance dated back to Rockefeller's days as Under Secretary of Health, Welfare, and Education; George L. Hinman, a Binghamton, New York, lawyer and local political figure, and Dr. William J. Ronan, a professor of government at New York University, both of whom had worked on the Temporary State Commission on a Constitutional Convention with Rockefeller; Stacy May, of the Rockefeller Brothers studies, who taught Nelson economics at Dartmouth and has advised him on Communism ever since; and Nancy Hanks, who'd worked on various Rockefeller enterprises in New York and Washington. The only newcomer to the group, and he was the only officeholder, was Malcolm Wilson.

It was this group, with Rockefeller presiding, that came up with the beautifully simple strategy that was to blitz the convention and give Rockefeller the nomination unanimously. The heart of the plan was to present Rockefeller as a candidate of upstate Republicans, resting on his "favorite son" approval by Westchester County and his residence in Pocantico Hills. Malcolm Wilson, with his intimate knowledge of upstate politics, was adamant about this. He made the point that Wall Street is as fearsome a devil to upstate farmers as to cotton planters in Mississippi, and that, operating from a New York City base, Rockefeller would be indissolubly tied to the devil. Overcoming any such handicap might be insurmountable.

The second technique was to delay the public announcement of Nelson's candidacy for the nomination as long as possible. This delay was vital. Politicians, while they frequently find expedient reasons for going back on their commitments, hate to be forced to withdraw their pledges publicly since that almost inevitably involves a loss of prestige, and prestige is one of the basic ingredients in their power. But so long as Nelson's position was officially uncertain, the professionals could turn back other candidates by saying, "Let's see what Rockefeller is going to do." And that's the kind of an answer a politician likes.

Of course by April the press was full of speculation about the Rockefeller candidacy, and before the end of the month individual newspapers and the wire services were running unofficial box scores weekly on the relative strength of the prospective candidates. At that point, the serious challengers aside from Rockefeller were Senate Majority Leader Walter J. Mahoney, the strong man of the State Legislature, who was in the process of welding together an alliance that would establish him as the spokesman for the so-called Taft wing of the GOP upstate; former National Chairman Hall, who never managed to get his drive off the ground, perhaps because he was thrown into the race too early by President Eisenhower's premature good wishes, and Assembly Speaker Oswald D. Heck, of Schenectady, whose failing health was blunting his ambitions and who would later step aside without making a real try. An official candidate was former U. S. Attorney Paul Williams, who was put up as a "favorite son" by New York County (Manhattan). No one but Williams took this seriously.

As part of the plan to give an upstate identification to Rockefeller, his strategists early in the proceedings shunted aside U. S. Senator Jacob K. Javits, who had been one of the early trumpeters of Nelson's virtues, because he was too patently a New York City Republican liberal. Javits dropped out of the picture until after the convention, and in the election campaign he confined most of his activities to New York City.

The informal polling by reporters in compiling their preconvention box scores on the candidates turned into a net plus for Rockefeller. For while the polls produced widely differing figures on the individual candidates (each reporter worked on his own list of leaders), they showed clearly that no hopeful, including

Rockefeller, was in anything like a runaway position. They also showed, beyond question, that the man to beat if the race went down to the wire would be Senator Mahoney, an unannounced candidate at this time. With the lack of any signposts pointing to the winner, party professionals found it easy to avoid commitments.

But Rockefeller had much more going for him in this formative period. He had his name, which, as he has always been aware, has a certain mystique for the American people. And he had his fortune. The latter is not mentioned in any invidious sense. But it is a political axiom that if you're going to lose an election it is better to lose it with a rich candidate than a poor one because the rich loser at least can be counted on to raise campaign funds that would help in local elections and perhaps cushion the lean years until the next time. And make no mistake, New York State Republicans were definitely defeatist in the spring of 1958. President Eisenhower's 1956 sweep of the state by 1.6 million votes was a purely personal victory, as evidenced by the fact that Senator Javits ran 1.1 million votes behind him, and in the 1957 municipal elections, Mayor Wagner won New York by an old-fashioned Democratic plurality of 921,000, and the Democrats gained substantially in upstate cities besides making gains in the suburbs. With Governor Harriman running ahead of everybody in the spring polls of 1958—specifically including Rockefeller—and with the long-standing tradition that the party in power loses influence in midterm Congressional elections, and 1958 of course was midterm, the Republicans had every reason for their gloom.

Rockefeller himself was acutely aware of this. He had faced the problem in making up his mind to run and decided to push ahead. But he was perceptive enough to give gloom full credit for the part it played in his success. Long after the election was won, he was to say of the nomination: "If they'd thought I was going to win they might not have given it to me." It is hardly likely he ever believed that, but it showed that he knew what was going on.

May passed without any significant changes in the situation.

The box scores showed Rockefeller and Mahoney gaining ground while the other hopefuls stood still, but positions taken in conversations with newspapermen aren't considered binding by those taking them in the framework of speculation, and besides many of the leaders faced fights in the June primaries and were more concerned with these contests than with the statewide picture. It became apparent, however, that no one was within striking distance of a first-ballot nomination.

By June, however, the groundwork was completed and the campaign moved out in the open. The first step was taken by Republican State Chairman Morhouse, whose leaning toward Rockefeller was one of the worst kept secrets in state politics. Morhouse began circulating around the state, showing county leaders and other important Republicans a whole series of polls indicating that Rockefeller was not only the best-known and most popular candidate for the GOP nomination, but that he would make the strongest candidate against Harriman. Even so, Morhouse's own polls showed in mid-June, 1958, that Harriman was leading Rockefeller by a wide margin as the choice of the voters in the coming election.

Morhouse's direct plug for Rockefeller stirred up the expected bitter riposte within the party. Supporters of Hall and Mahoney were particularly incensed, accusing the state chairman of trying to pick the candidate. Morhouse couldn't have cared less, although he made the *pro forma* disavowals that he was overstepping his powers. But by this time, the state chairman's future was tied to Rockefeller's star, and only by a Rockefeller nomination could he stay in office. He had no choice.

He found somewhat unexpected defenders in the editorial writers of the important newspapers in the state. Uniformly, they applauded Morhouse for putting the results of the polls before county leaders, and almost equally uniformly they revealed a bias in favor of Rockefeller, a bias that would be transformed in the fall to election campaign support for Nelson by the overwhelming majority of the state's newspapers.

The stage was now set for phase three of the preconvention campaign planned so carefully back in April—the actual nailing down of delegates to the convention. A great deal of quiet missionary work had been done, both inside and outside the party, and the Rockefeller people had reasonable expectations that they could bring off their coup. But the disclosure of the Morhouse polls had spurred supporters of Senator Mahoney, still an unannounced candidate, to call in county leaders to declare themselves for or against the powerful Senate Majority Leader. Through June, Mahoney's people were able to line up leaders representing a potential of nearly three hundred convention votes, enough if other candidates could hold their strength to prevent a first-ballot nomination.

Clearly it was time to act. On June 30th at a press conference in his office on the fifty-sixth floor of Rockefeller Center, Nelson Rockefeller formally announced his candidacy to a crowd of reporters. He gave the usual reasons. He had been urged to run by his friends and the "challenge" intrigued him. He thought New York State needed an infusion of "political courage." He had no panacea to offer. He thought the Republicans could do a better job of running the state and pulling it out of its doldrums, and he thought he was the man to do it. But he did not pretend there was any public clamor for his nomination.

And now began the open phase of the nomination drive: the first test of what skills Rockefeller could bring to the down-to-earth business of rallying support to his cause in direct contact with the people. The plan was subtle and ingenious. Professional politicians have a natural bias in favor of other professional politicians, all things being equal, and Rockefeller was opposing widely respected pros in Mahoney, Hall and Assembly Speaker Heck. The problem was to overcome this predilection of like for like by displaying Rockefeller as a likely winner with grass-roots support. Words wouldn't do it. Pressure was needed, but it was necessary to apply it delicately to avoid resentment that could backfire dangerously.

The device hit upon was disarmingly simple. Instead of setting up meetings with party leaders, alone, as the other hopefuls were doing, Wilson, exploiting Rockefeller's glamor all the way, set up luncheons and dinners which included Young Republicans,

women's organizations and various community leaders outside
the party so he could show Nelson off. The idea was to demonstrate to the leaders that the people of their own communities
could enthuse about Rockefeller and to make the point by calculated understatement.

For this phase of the campaign, Rockefeller and Wilson traveled alone, with Steven Rockefeller doing the driving. The for-
mat was always the same. Wilson would introduce Rockefeller
and then turn him loose to exert his charm and enthusiasm on
the audience. The spots were carefully picked, of course, to produce a maximum bandwagon effect, but the plan worked beyond
all expectations. The certain spark that Rockefeller was to surprise the Democrats with in the election campaign won him
warm receptions everywhere.

One county leader, known to favor Senator Mahoney, remarked after watching his wife and Republican women workers
flutter around Nelson, "Well, I guess we're for Rockefeller after
all." His delegation made it official without leaving the room.

The touring started within an hour after Rockefeller announced his candidacy, and, on the way up the Taconic Parkway
to the first meeting at Kinderhook, New York, to talk to Columbia County delegates, Wilson and Nelson passed a car in which
John D. Rockefeller, Jr., was returning home to Pocantico Hills
after an afternoon ride. The two cars stopped while Nelson introduced Wilson and told his father that the campaign was underway. The elder Rockefeller warmly wished him luck.

Before July ran out, Nelson had met and talked with leaders
of every county north of the New York City line except Erie,
which was bypassed out of deference to the ambitions of Senator
Mahoney, who became a formal candidate shortly after Nelson's
announcement. But Mahoney's move came too late. The Rockefeller drive picked up momentum day by day and when Oneida,
Herkimer and Madison counties, originally credited to Mahoney,
switched en bloc to Rockefeller late in the month, the race was
all but over. In New York City, Wilson lined up the leaders of
Manhattan and Queens for Rockefeller, the Bronx fell in step
a short time later and only John R. Crews, head of the Brooklyn

organization with the largest bloc of votes at the convention, remained outside the fold, still officially committed to Speaker Heck. But Crews was to show up at the Republican convention in Rochester wearing a large Rockefeller button.

Early in August all opposition collapsed. More than two weeks before the scheduled opening of the convention, Rockefeller was assured not only of nomination by unanimous vote but also that no name would be entered against his. It was a complete victory in the first straight-out political contest of Nelson Rockefeller's life, and it was notable that there was no public hard feeling on the part of the losers.

Not that there wasn't bitterness. Right up to the last minute before the convention, Senator Mahoney had to battle to keep his more fervent supporters from staging a march on the convention hall to stage a demonstration on his behalf. But there were no angry statements by any of the principals involved, and, while a number of county chairmen complained off the record of having their arms twisted to compel them to go along with the Rockefeller tide, no one was willing to come forward with a flat charge. The complaints, incidentally, were that financial or business interests allied with or sympathetic to the Rockefellers exerted pressure to swing delegates. In the Rockefeller case there was no evidence ever adduced to support the accusations.

In the aftermath there was also the accusation that Rockefeller bought the nomination by shelling out huge cash contributions to the various delegations he met with and promising them more during the election campaign. This was flatly denied by Wilson, who handled all the money on the delegate-seeking tours. Wilson said that no contribution was made to any delegation at any time although he conceded that he picked up the checks for the luncheons and dinners where Rockefeller spoke his piece. The biggest tab, Wilson said, was for just under $1,000 for the Monroe County dinner while others cost less than $100. The expenses of the trips were paid immediately on Wilson's check, and he was in turn reimbursed by the Westchester County Republican Organization which was the sponsoring agency for Rockefeller.

Westchester got its money back when the campaign contributions started coming in.

As for Rockefeller he found the campaign stimulating. As a neophyte getting his baptism in organization political fire, he'd handled himself adroitly and with a skill that surprised the newcomers around him. From start to finish he'd held final say on all decisions, although he listened carefully to the experts and deferred to their judgments when they convinced him they were right. He'd also shown a realistic approach to making needed concessions as they came up, a very heartening indicator to those who would help him in the coming campaign.

And he'd won the respect, albeit somewhat grudging, of those who found themselves outfought on their own grounds. That he had a flair for the difficult calling of politics was undeniable. Not that he was by any means an experienced politician. He had a lot to learn still, and he'd learn a lot of it the hard way in the coming months and years.

But his first fight had shown that he wasn't afraid of being unorthodox as a campaigner. He'd tackled with gusto the job of rounding up the delegates in person instead of leaving it, as most candidates do, to professional party workers who feel that they alone can handle this type of negotiation. And he'd proved that he wasn't at all afraid that his money or his name would beat him, thereby rejecting the belief of at least 90 percent of the Republican politicians of the state, including a substantial majority of those who'd joined his cause.

But for Nelson Rockefeller, caught up in the excitement of his venture into politics, there was no time to worry, even if there had been something to worry about—and he hasn't admitted to this day that he ever contemplated defeat.

He had the convention and the election ahead of him, and he would dive into the future with total absorption.

14

::

Winning a Nomination

New York Republicans run tidy state conventions. Under
what may be called the Thomas E. Dewey rule of unity—established
after Dewey assumed command of the party in 1938 when he
came within a fraction of 1 percent of displacing the formidable
Herbert H. Lehman as Governor—there are no floor fights. If
two or more hopefuls arrive contesting for an open place on
the ticket, the practice is for their managers and party leaders to
get together like the Chinese generals of legend and talk the man
in the weaker position into withdrawing without firing a shot.
He invariably does. For neatness, the method can't be faulted.
It is true that it severely limits the political scope of the dele-

gates, most of whom find out what backroom fighting is going on from the newspapers. But it avoids damaging intraparty recriminations in public, and it provides ample opportunity for the wheeling and dealing so dear to the hearts of convention managers. And while an arm twisted in private may hurt every bit as much as one twisted on the floor of a convention, the friends of the private sufferer are spared the spectacle of his humiliation and thus able to forget and forgive more easily.

The neatness also makes for dullness, a dullness compounded in New York because by law the Democratic convention meets at the same time, and the brawling Democrats usually make all the news.

No Republican convention ever looked tidier in prospect than that of 1958—and none ever shaped up as duller. As the delegates gathered in Rochester in the last week of August, the dominant mood was one of defeatism. They were ready dutifully to nominate Nelson Rockefeller for Governor on the first ballot and they expected that the incumbent Attorney General, Louis J. Lefkowitz, who was appointed to his office by the Legislature when Jacob K. Javits resigned to become U. S. Senator in 1957, would be named to succeed himself. The remaining three places on the ticket to be chosen—U. S. Senator, Lieutenant Governor and State Comptroller—were wide open, but this caused no excitement because nobody of any stature in the party seemed at all anxious to risk a beating in the statewide election.

The arrival of the ebullient Rockefeller did little to lighten the mood. He got a warm welcome as he arrived in the crowded lobby of the Sheraton Hotel, with his fast-expanding staff, but he went directly to his seventh-floor suite and the delegates who wanted to cheer him couldn't find him. Even the press found its work cut out for it. Richard Amper, who was handling newsmen, was tucked away in a single room down on the third floor with access to the Rockefeller suite only through the overcrowded hotel switchboard. Amper coped as well as he could with the situation, but, with reporters constantly thronging his room and using his phone, he was under severe handicaps.

The foul-up was admittedly minor. But when reports of it

appeared in the newspapers, one politician, who was something less than a Rockefeller idolator, growled publicly, "Well, what do you expect when you hand things over to a bunch of amateurs!" He couldn't have been more wrong; the Rockefeller operation was to develop in a surpringly short time into a smoothly clicking machine.

At the convention, however, there were more important matters to be taken care of, and the first of these was the completion of a state ticket. In New York it is a tradition of both parties that state tickets must be balanced by distributing nominations both geographically and ethnically. This generally means that the ticket should have at least one Jew, one Italian-American and a Catholic, usually of Irish extraction, while no more than two of the nominees should come from downstate. In 1958, the Republicans started out aiming for just such a balanced ticket.

With Lefkowitz slated for Attorney General, the key man on the ticket would be the Italian-American, and here the Rockefeller forces ran into a snag that not even Rockefeller's most strenuous personal effort could untangle. It was simply that the Italian-American deemed most fitting to be Rockefeller's running mate for Lieutenant Governor, Joseph F. Carlino, the attractive Majority Leader of the State Assembly, was not available. Carlino said so to Rockefeller and party leaders, and, equally importantly, Carlino's political mentor, J. Russel Sprague, said so in spades, bluntly turning down former Governor Dewey when he sought to change his mind.

Once it became apparent that Carlino wouldn't be available under any circumstances, the Rockefeller forces abandoned hope of getting a traditionally balanced ticket and came up with one that was shockingly unorthodox to old-line politicians. It consisted of Representative Kenneth B. Keating, of Rochester, for Senator; Malcolm Wilson for Lieutenant Governor; Lefkowitz for Attorney General and James A. Lundy of Queens for Comptroller.

It was a ticket that pleased very few. Keating was virtually unknown outside Monroe County, which embraces Rochester, and he angered many delegates by calling a press conference to announce that he was running only because he'd been asked by President Eisenhower and Vice President Nixon. There was also grumbling because Westchester County was getting two candidates in Rockefeller and Wilson, an unprecedented departure in nominating procedure, but the fact that Wilson was a Catholic of Irish extraction helped mute some of these complaints. The objections to Lefkowitz were that he'd been opposed by Senator Javits and that he was unknown outside New York City. But by one of the ironies of political habit of mind, no one seemed to care one way or the other about the selection of Lundy, probably because it was accepted as a practical political payoff to Queens leader Frank Kenna by the Rockefeller forces for switching the Queens delegation to Rockefeller. (Lundy turned out to be the only loser.)

And, of course, Italian-American pressure groups screamed that the GOP was cutting its own throat by denying them a place on the ticket.

But all this was taking place offstage in hotel rooms, across dining room tables and in corridors where the professionals could deal without being put on the record.

Meanwhile the convention opened routinely on Monday, August 25th in the War Memorial Auditorium, a few blocks from the headquarters hotel. The proceedings followed the tidy script so faithfully that it appeared certain that the delegates would go home asking themselves, "Was this convention necessary?"

When Rockefeller's name was placed in nomination, the traditional demonstration was made on the floor, but it lacked fire. It was all too expected and the appearance of the Rockefeller girls, nicknamed the Playtex parade, who wore blue sweaters spelling out Rockefeller on their well-developed bosoms, seemed somehow only to emphasize the air of artificiality. The delegates themselves dutifully marched around the hall, waving their banners and shouting their slogans just long enough to satisfy the decencies and the television cameras.

Rockefeller himself spent the afternoon of his nomination in his hotel suite, seeing an endless string of visitors and going over his acceptance speech.

But for his acceptance speech, it was impressed on Nelson that he must follow the script. The speech was the product of many hands—Rockefeller had no regular speech writer at the time, relying mostly on Frank Jamieson to pull it together, with Dr. Ronan making substantial contributions. But it was essentially a political speech, designed to please as many people as possible, to salve the sting of defeat for the losers and to arouse the seemingly lethargic delegates. A great number of politicians had made suggestions, and it would have been downright stupid to omit any of these ideas, no matter their content, at the outset of a tough election campaign.

At last Rockefeller and his family reached the convention hall, surrounded by a veritable phalanx of Rochester cops. (The police had become excessively security conscious after a completely unfounded rumor of a plot to kidnap Nelson swept the city.) Rockefeller was very obviously at the top of his form. He smiled and waved to the audience, which gave him a welcome that was more respectful than enthusiastic, and he chatted easily and gaily with those around him while waiting for the formalities to start. Seated in the front row on the platform, Rockefeller winked and nodded to acquaintances in the press section while being introduced.

He stood up with the traditional introductory phrase, ". . . the next Governor of New York," ringing in his ears. He looked over the audience as the conventional cheers died down, exuding a confidence that seemed out of place among so many doomsayers. Then he adjusted his manuscript on the lectern, gauged the distance from the microphones arrayed in front of him and began to speak.

And, suddenly, it was a brand-new convention.

Now Nelson Rockefeller is no orator. He lacks the true gift of eloquence that builds to a climax and twists the heart with a phrase. His presentation, when stacked up against that of spellbinders like Senators Dirksen and Humphrey, for example, is almost pedestrian. But he has some spark of communication that seems to leap from him to his audience, a spark that invests his words with sincerity and warmth and that can, when he is at his best, win him the instant sympathy and good wishes of his listeners.

He was at his very best that August night. There he was with a contrived speech, a document with no claim to literary merit, addressing an audience conditioned to the idea of defeat, and before he'd spoken half a dozen sentences the ten thousand people in the War Memorial Auditorium (the local organization had thoughtfully and efficiently packed the galleries) were his. A kind of electric excitement seemed to crackle around the arena. On the platform behind Rockefeller, the hardened professional politicians looked at one another with dawning discovery in their eyes and whispered their surprise. In the press section, typewriters staccatoed into action as reporters, who'd already filed the speech, tried to catch their editions with this new element in the convention.

Rockefeller himself seemed to expand. His delivery grew crisper as the bursts of applause interrupted him time and again. He was tasting the heady wine of mastery over a large audience, and the excitement of the crowd urged him on to give it everything and a little bit more. He rose to the moment exuberantly.

"My fellow Republicans," he began, "you have placed your trust in me and I stand before you with a deep sense of humility. I thank you from the bottom of my heart.

"You have offered me the greatest challenge of my life and the highest opportunity to serve the people of our Empire State.

"I proudly accept your nomination."

As the speech progressed, the excitement in the hall mounted although he was saying the same old clichés. County leaders scurried from delegation to delegation, comparing notes and reporting on the reactions of their varied groups. At the speech's end, the huge audience rose in a spontaneous, almost hysterical burst of applause. Behind Rockefeller on the platform, the surprised professionals were shaking hands with each other and with every member of the Rockefeller entourage they could reach. Tom Dewey in his excitement publicly embraced his sworn political enemy, Arthur Wicks, whom Dewey had driven out of the Senate Majority Leadership and out of politics. Mrs. Rockefeller and the five Rockefeller children were surrounded by well-wishers. And from the floor of the convention, delegates swarmed toward the platform to try to shake Rockefeller's hand and offer their congratulations.

Backstage and back at the convention hotel headquarters, the phones rang constantly. The radio and television audiences, sitting at home, had felt the impact of the speech, and people all over the state were calling up to let Rockefeller know.

As the press from one end of the state to the other reported the next morning, the speech definitely changed the whole attitude of the convention. The delegates had arrived scenting only defeat. After listening to Rockefeller, they began to entertain hopes of victory. Here was a new, forceful and attractive personality whose appeal was undeniable and who just might bring off the impossible. The victory hopes weren't very strong, but just the fact they had been aroused would make it easier for the Republicans to recruit workers once the campaign breaks started going Rockefeller's way.

That was for the future. Returning to the hotel after his acceptance speech, Rockefeller was besieged for hours by people calling on him to offer campaign services. But he also had a lot of work to do. The matter of getting Keating to run for Senator was still up in the air, and the phones to Washington were busy setting up a call to be made to Keating in the morning by the Vice President.

At any rate, leaving the Rockefeller suite around 2 A.M. after the speech, Dewey advised reporters, who were hanging around to get the final word on Keating, to go to bed. "Nothing will happen until the morning," he said. The advice was good. Nothing did happen, and the next morning Keating fell into line.

It would be too much to say that the high point reached when Rockefeller made his speech was sustained for the rest of the convention. It wasn't. But neither did the delegates drop back into the defeatism that marked the opening session. Rockefeller made one last appearance before the convention when the full ticket was introduced to a half-empty auditorium.

That night as Rockefeller sat with his advisers talking over the immediate campaign arrangements that would have to be made, someone tuned in the Democratic convention in Buffalo where Tammany leader Carmine G. De Sapio was humiliating Governor Harriman by forcing the nomination of Manhattan District Attorney Frank S. Hogan for U. S. Senator against Harriman's commitment to Thomas Finletter.

"That's it," Frank Jamieson said. "There's our campaign issue."

The professionals looked at him in consternation.

"We said to ourselves 'Oh, no, not again,' " Malcolm Wilson recalled long after the election. "We'd been beating Tammany to death for as long as we could remember and where had it ever got us? If Jamie was going to push for that, we'd have our work cut out for us."

Jamie did push for it. He pushed hard, and Rockefeller went along with him in the face of considerable opposition. And gradually, the pros came around. "It was the one big issue we had," Wilson was to say later. "Jamieson was right all along. We were thinking of the standard Tammany attacks; we couldn't attack Frank Hogan on this thing. But Jamieson saw immediately that we could turn the convention on the Democrats without even mentioning Hogan. It was the best thing we developed."

There was a certain irony in this. More than one hundred reports and over thirty position papers had been prepared to equip Rockefeller with campaign material, only to have the best material handed to him by the Democrats. That Rockefeller was flexible enough to switch to the new issue after Jamieson spelled out how it could be used was an early indication that he was going to run his own kind of campaign. And the postelection analyses of most experts sustained Jamieson's intuitive choice of "bossism" as one of the most effective campaign arguments.

But on the night that Jamieson picked the issue, the campaign was still ahead. Rockefeller had been setting a grueling pace for himself for months, and rougher days were ahead. He took off for a brief vacation at Mount Desert Island to get ready.

15

An Election Upset

On the basis of Rockefeller's acceptance speech at Rochester, the Republican Party managers knew they had a "live" candidate going for them in the 1958 election. What they couldn't know was that as a campaigner, Rockefeller would prove a "natural"—one of those rare men, even among politicians, who actually enjoy the campaign trail with all its hardships and sleeplessness and who can communicate to the voters some sense of their excitement.

This talent, plus Nelson's undeniable flair for handling people, set the tone of the campaign. It was apparent that the best card the GOP had was Rockefeller himself, and all agreed, including the Madison Avenue advertising agency that was advising on media, that Nelson's personality must be exploited to the utmost. To this end, a fortune was spent on taped television shorts of one to five minutes to saturate the state's TV stations, and Rockefeller undertook a grueling schedule of campaign trips that took him into every one of the state's sixty-two counties, a gesture more symbolic than useful because he could gain nothing by going into the smaller upstate areas where commitment to the GOP was total, and the trips put an additional physical strain on Nelson and his overworked staff.

But while Nelson put himself in the hands of the party pro schedule makers—R. Burdell Bixby, an old Dewey lieutenant, was brought in to lay out the campaign tours—he reserved to himself the final decision on all major matters of policy, and some of those decisions, hammered out in long private talks with Frank Jamieson after the technical experts had had their say, angered and worried the professionals. Rockefeller listened courteously to complaints and fears, but usually wound up going his own way.

As is customary with Republican candidates for Governor, Rockefeller set up his own campaign headquarters in the Hotel Roosevelt in New York City, taking over the whole seventh floor. Offices were provided for each of the other candidates and their staffs, and, under the general supervision of Jamieson, who divided his time between Rockefeller Center and the Roosevelt, the campaign got going. Dick Amper, who would become Rockefeller's press secretary, was in charge of the day-to-day contacts with the reporters, and Carl Spad, a graduate of the Young Republican movement, functioned as transportation officer and general factotum. A few blocks away at the Hotel Lexington, Oren Root, Jr., a veteran of the Citizens for Willkie campaign of 1940 and a onetime schoolmate of Rockefeller at the Lincoln School, set up an Independent Citizens Committee for Rockefeller. And down on 42nd Street, the Republican State Committee handled the strictly organization phases of the election drive, although State Chairman L. Judson Morhouse and his press aide,

Harry J. O'Donnell, spent most of their time at quarters assigned
to them at the Roosevelt for better liaison and to coordinate
their work. O'Donnell, a veteran campaign publicist, also proved
a fertile source of suggestions for news stories.

A certain amount of excitement was generated by the organization of the campaign machinery, but by the time that was completed the high mood of Rockefeller's convention appearance
had worn thin. The expert consensus was still that Governor
Harriman would win going away.

A break was needed to lift campaign morale and to get the
rank and file working. Rockefeller himself supplied the break
with his first campaign appearance. From the outset he pulled
the crowds, and from the outset the crowds were friendly. Political observers, mindful that they'd overlooked the significance of
the crowds that turned out for President Truman in his surprise
election in 1948, began to take a closer look at Nelson's prospects.

Throughout the campaign, Rockefeller clung to two principles
that outraged old-line Republicans and anguished a lot of influential people outside the political community who would of
necessity support him. He refused adamantly to promise a tax
cut, or even hint at the possibility of reducing taxes. And he
steadfastly spurned all offers by the national Republican organization to help out in New York. In the view of the many Republicans who expected Rockefeller to lose—and their name was
legion—both attitudes were capricious. They reasoned that Rockefeller could afford to promise a tax cut and give minor candidates something to offer their people in local campaigns since he
wouldn't have to do anything about it in the long run. And
there was considerable sentiment upstate for inviting Vice-President Nixon, already the front-runner for the 1960 Presidential
nomination, to show himself off to the troops.

On one occasion, lunching in a private dining room with an
influential newspaper publisher, Rockefeller was put on the spot
on taxes. The publisher aggressively advanced arguments for a
tax cut, both as a campaign tactic and as a practical policy.
Rockefeller tried to keep the dialogue on the subject of sound
fiscal procedures, but the publisher was insistent.

"Then there won't be a tax cut at all," he said almost angrily.

"I'm afraid not," said Rockefeller. "The way I see it we'll be lucky if we don't have to raise taxes. We're going to need a hundred and fifty or two hundred million more just to keep up."

At this point, the engaging Wallace K. Harrison, who, with Jamieson, accompanied Rockefeller to the luncheon, intervened and turned the conversation to pleasanter topics.

But Rockefeller wasn't in the least confused about the outcome.

"Well I didn't do myself any good over there," he remarked to Dick Amper when he returned to the Hotel Roosevelt headquarters after lunch. He was right.

The exclusion of the national Republican organization required more delicate handling. The first crisis rose late in September when President Eisenhower was booked into New York for a nonpolitical speaking engagement made many months in advance. Word was sent up from Washington that Ike would be available to do anything asked of him in Nelson's behalf. It was a tough spot. Nobody snubs the President of the United States, and Rockefeller had no wish even to appear to be doing so. On the other hand, if Ike directly took part in the election drive, Rockefeller, who had been refusing to discuss anything but state issues, would of necessity find himself forced into the position of defending the National Administration's domestic and foreign policies, a posture that Harriman was trying desperately to force him into. The compromise worked out was to shuttle the President from the Hotel Astor on Broadway where he was staying to the Hotel Roosevelt to talk to Republican workers at a private gathering and then down Park Avenue to the Hotel Commodore where he spoke to a couple of hundred Rockefeller volunteers and so back to the Astor. The trip was conducted without fanfare; there was no public rally, and there was no statewide broadcast. But Eisenhower apparently went along with the scheme, and, although it was probably the only time Ike's help ever was spurned by a Republican candidate, the incident passed almost unnoticed by the voters at large.

More publicized and more embarrassing in its outcome was

the flying visit to New York by Vice President Nixon in October after Rockefeller's outlook had improved considerably. Nixon had taken on himself the burden of representing the National Administration in the Congressional campaigns in 1958, and, when it became apparent that Rockefeller didn't intend to invite him to New York, the Vice President arranged to make a statewide broadcast for Congressional candidates under the aegis of the New York State Committee.

Rockefeller was off on one of his upstate trips when Nixon arrived in town, and there was no one on hand to greet the Vice President, whose feelings apparently were ruffled. At any rate he sent out word that he was busy on his speech when Rockefeller phoned later that night after his return to New York.

The two men did get together the following morning for breakfast at Nixon's hotel, but they looked self-conscious and unhappy as they shook hands for the photographers. Both, of course, insisted to reporters that they were the best of friends and that the whole thing was a misunderstanding. That closed the incident so far as the public was concerned, but it by no means stilled criticism of Rockefeller among Nixon's admirers and would-be bandwagon riders. And it provided a guidepost to the "misunderstandings" that would crop up between the Vice President and Rockefeller over the next two years.

That Rockefeller, in the first political campaign of his life, was able to shrug off the intraparty criticism, some of it quite patently motivated by malice, and go his own way is a measure of how fast his political knack developed. Far more experienced campaigners have found themselves immobilized by sniping from supposedly friendly quarters: for Rockefeller it was just part of the game. He accepted criticism he found valid, but he wasted no sleep worrying over complaints he considered malicious or trivial.

As a campaigner, Rockefeller had going for him one priceless asset: his name. The Rockefellers have been part of the American folklore for three-quarters of a century at least, but relatively few Americans have ever met a Rockefeller in the flesh or shaken the hand of one. Everywhere Nelson went, people turned out to see him, and those turning out included the political sophisticates as well as the just plain curious.

In the early days, this curiosity factor led a lot of people to downgrade the significance of the crowds Rockefeller drew. That soon passed. Because time after time, the curious who merely came to see a Rockefeller wound up clamoring for him to stay.

"They come out to see whether he's for real," one upstate politician remarked as he stood looking over a rally, "and then, Bang, he's got 'em. I don't know what's doing it, that grin or the winks he throws around or just that he looks so goddamn regular they believe in him. I guess he surprises them. Whatever it is, it's dynamite."

The assessment was not an isolated one. All over the state, party leaders reported that enthusiasm picked up after a visit by Rockefeller and that more volunteers were turning out. The demands for his appearances grew until they got out of hand and had to be filed away for future reference. One thing is certain: the upstate GOP got a shot in the arm from Nelson's campaigning.

Whatever his magic was it worked just as well in Democratic New York City. Whether on the Lower East Side where Republican is almost a dirty word, up in the Bronx or in a crowd of 300,000 on the boardwalk at Coney Island, people flocked around Nelson as soon as he appeared and seemed pleased to meet him, even when they told him pointedly they didn't intend to vote for him. Such remarks never ruffled him.

His style was always the same. He would approach a prospective voter with his hand outstretched and say, "I'm Nelson Rockefeller," by way of introduction. Occasionally the proffered hand would be refused, but most people reached for it eagerly, and Nelson, unlike some politicians who consider the handshake enough, would go on to explain that he was running for Governor and chat briefly. Additionally, he gave gray hair to some of his staff by his inability to pass up children. It was not unusual for him to stop everything while he talked with a group of youngsters, not infrequently passing by adult voters standing around to shake his hand.

"I don't know what we're going to do with him; he actually *likes* this stuff," Dick Amper commented despairingly at an up-state airport as he tried to hold a plane while Nelson visited with a batch of kids at the loading gate.

Of course nothing was ever done. Rockefeller stopped and chatted and gave as much time as children wanted right to the end of the campaign. And while this frequently caused him to fall behind schedule, he never fell so far behind that the people at the next stop didn't wait for him. He enjoyed the kids—and, besides, the publicity pictures, made by his own photographer if there were no news cameramen around, had a very high accept-ance rating with editors.

For Rockefeller was very conscious of the value of pictures. Jamieson, who had a healthy skepticism of the vote-getting ap-peal of campaign speeches, had added a still photographer and a motion-picture cameraman to the staff at the beginning of the campaign trips and had impressed on Nelson that cooperation with news photographers was a must. The staff-made stills were circulated to newspapers, and the movie film was processed and furnished to TV stations for use in newsreel clips.

The cameras proved invaluable on Nelson's celebrated gas-tronomical tours through New York's neighborhoods. Pictures of him eating blintzes—a delicacy hitherto unknown to him—in the Lower East Side, pizza in what used to be Little Italy and hot dogs in Coney Island hit the newspapers across the country. What it all proved, except that Rockefeller has a cast-iron stomach, is hard to say. But the campaign managers called it a plus, claiming that it humanized Rockefeller. They may have been right.

Be that as it may, there was no doubt at the close of the cam-paign that the photogenic Rockefeller won the battle for picture space easily over Governor Harriman, whose tall gauntness and harried expression rarely made page one. (Later anti-Rockefeller Republicans on the national level were to scoff, "What's he ever done but eat blintzes?")

On the more routine campaign level, Rockefeller got the breaks from the start. Jamieson's hunch that there was Republi-can gold in the fight between Tammany leader De Sapio and

Harriman over the nomination of District Attorney Frank S. Hogan for U. S. Senator paid off beyond expectation. The key was found in the late Governor Alfred E. Smith's battle to block the nomination of William Randolph Hearst for U. S. Senator in 1924 when Smith locked himself in his hotel room and refused to accept renomination until Hearst's name was withdrawn. Under Jamieson's direction this was incorporated in a speech contrasting Harriman's "surrender" to De Sapio with Smith's courage.

The most important thing about this attack was that it threw Harriman off balance. The Democratic Governor, who'd laughingly proposed Rockefeller as a possible GOP opponent at an Albany correspondents' dinner in 1957, was completely unprepared for a Rockefeller punching out at the political courage of a fellow millionaire. And since Rockefeller used the bossism issue as a jumping-off point for implying that the Harriman administration was somehow responsible for the notorious gangsters' meeting at Apalachin, New York, that was broken up by state troopers in 1957, and went on from there to describe all the ancient evils of Tammany with its long record of corruption, Harriman was forced over on the defensive. He never recovered the ball.

Actually the area of attack by Harriman was, in any case, severely limited. With Rockefeller adamantly refusing to debate or defend the policies of the National Administration, Harriman was unable to capitalize on what appeared to be the growing public discontent with the way President Eisenhower and the Republicans were running the country.

As for Rockefeller, he charged Harriman with bungling and inefficiency, availing himself of political license to accuse the Governor of putting the state in a financial hole, although he was well aware that the Republican Legislature had thwarted every Democratic effort to increase revenues. But Rockefeller also was subject to special pressures in his quest for New York City support. As a liberal Republican, he sympathized with the aspirations of minority groups seeking their place in society; he was devoted to the belief that public education should be expanded and improved, and he favored welfare and labor policies that were at the very least somewhat to the left of the Republican center. He spelled out these positions circumspectly before appropriate audiences.

"Sometimes I listen to him and I forget myself and think he's our guy," one Democratic politician remarked, only half-kidding, as he watched Nelson evoke cheers at a garment district rally. "Anyway he's running on our platform."

A number of Republicans shared this view, but they quite definitely weren't kidding.

Rockefeller was aware of the dichotomy in the Republican Party over the informal way he rewrote the GOP platform, but he paid no attention to the grumbling. He believed, both as a practical political tactic and as a matter of principle, he was on the right course, and he was, as always, prepared to follow his star.

Nelson, of course, was not the only Rockefeller campaigning. His brothers prudently stayed away from the public eye, although their influence was exerted on other political levels. But Mrs. Rockefeller, the twins, Mary and Michael, and slender, serious Steven put in long hours working for votes. The twins worked mostly at the campaign headquarters in the Hotel Roosevelt, but had to go back to school several weeks before Election Day. Stevie was marking time waiting to serve a six-month army hitch, and he constituted himself an aide-de-camp to his father on his frequent trips, taking over all the petty chores that the professional campaign workers disdained.

But the secret weapon proved to be Mrs. Rockefeller. Slender, aristocratic of feature, elegantly but quietly turned out, she had a glamor for lady Republicans and other women that carried a special cachet. For while the ladies were impressed and intrigued by Nelson, he was, after all, a candidate and by the rules of the game was expected to charm them. Mrs. Rockefeller, on the other hand, was clearly apolitical, an embodiment of capital S Society, and meeting her had a status value peculiarly its own. She drew capacity crowds at every one of the endless tea parties and women's club meetings she attended.

In upstate New York, it is customary for candidates for Governor to tour by bus. One bus is for the staff and the second for the press. A limousine is provided for the candidate and his wife, but usually the wife rides alone because her political hopeful spends most of his time between stops getting briefed on what's ahead or chatting with reporters in the press bus to sound out their reactions. (Rockefeller's managers briefly tried airlifting the staff and press to major cities and then using fleets of cars, but it proved unsatisfactory all around and was abandoned.)

Mrs. Rockefeller was introduced to this life in September, 1958, about the time the polls first began to give Nelson a chance to make the election a contest. The excitement was high among the people around Nelson, and in the novelty of the situation she seemed to enjoy the baptism. But repetition brought disillusionment. One thing she couldn't get used to was the ever-present press. After a lifetime spent avoiding publicity, it was slightly unnerving to find reporters everywhere ready to report her every phrase and to note every detail of her dress and behavior. Her principal difficulties arose, of course, not from the political reporters covering the tour—they left her pretty much alone—but from specials and local feature writers anxious to develop exclusives. She coped with the situation, cooperating when she could, but making it clear when questions invaded what she considered private matters that she wasn't intimidated.

At teas, suppers and receptions, she was an instant hit. Her unpretentious little speeches urged the election of her husband and others on the ticket, but they could hardly be considered political. And when questions of policy were thrown her way from the floor, she turned them back with, "I leave the political decisions to my husband." It was an answer that pleased many women in her audiences. But what really won the lady Republicans and their friends were her poise and warmth. She would listen carefully and with evident interest to a mother boasting about her children, and that quite possibly was a contributory factor in the voting turnout for Nelson.

In New York City, Mrs. Rockefeller made a couple of campaign trips on her own, inspecting hospitals and housing projects.

The high point of her city campaigning was a trip through the garment district where she posed for photographs at a sewing machine and discussed sewing problems with the girls. Of course, the garment district is considered Liberal-Democratic "country," and it is doubtful if this trip produced any votes.

Stevie also did his bit in putting across the family portrait, mostly by standing and shyly taking a bow when his father introduced him from time to time at appropriate gatherings.

The upstate campaigning was aimed primarily at convincing Republicans that the state ticket had a chance to win if they would turn out and do a job on Election Day. The real battleground was New York City, and in mid-October, when State GOP Chairman Morhouse was at last able to produce a poll showing Rockefeller running ahead of Harriman, the campaign shifted to the city for the windup drive.

The Morhouse poll, which assigned 44 percent of the vote to Nelson and 42 percent to Harriman, with 14 percent undecided, wasn't taken too seriously by the Democrats, but the crowds Nelson drew and his almost complete domination of the news during his windup drive had their impact. The odds-makers reported there was almost no action on election bets and refused to establish a betting line.

The crowds turning out to see Nelson had the effect of helping create a bandwagon psychology, although it is doubtful that his two most spectacular appearances—in Harlem where he spoke to thousands at a street rally from a platform he shared with Count Basie and in adjoining Spanish Harlem where police had to intervene to save him from being mobbed by enthusiastic Puerto Ricans—won him more than a handful of votes.

But the turnouts in a campaign that was fast running out of steam were remarkable enough to alert Democratic district leaders to recheck the public sentiment. Their individual survival depended in many cases on making a good showing on Election Day, and, while the overall consensus was that Harriman was safe, local politicians are judged strictly on the votes they deliver. The cumulative results of their surveys were dismaying. District after district reported that the split in Democratic ranks, which had been abundantly in evidence since the De Sapio-Harriman fight at the convention, was reaching down to the precinct level. Revised assessments indicated that the Democrats needed a big break to enable them to carry the city by 500,000—a plurality which, by rule of thumb, is considered the absolute minimum that a Democratic candidate must take to the city line if he is to have a chance of winning a statewide election.

The difficulty was to find a new issue. By mid-October in any election all campaign speeches are reruns; the so-called "big" questions have been explored and discussed *ad nauseam.* Any new issue to be effective must be electrifying: either so scandalous that it can't be ignored or so direct a raid on the pocketbook that the voters will rise. At Democratic headquarters, some strategist came up with the idea of charging that Rockefeller's election would mean the end of rent control.

That Rockefeller had promised to continue rent control cut no ice. The charge could be given an aura of plausibility because the Republican-controlled Legislature was definitely hostile to rent control. The Democrats threw in a suggestion that the Rockefellers had vast real-estate holdings in New York, directly and indirectly, and presumably would benefit by ending controls. And the Democrats noted that the powerful real-estate lobby was supporting the GOP.

This was a "gut" issue. There were about two million rent-controlled residential units in the state and about 90 percent of them, involving an estimated four and a half million people, were in New York City. Decontrol would threaten most, if not all, with immediate rises in the cost of living. A mere rumor, pressed forcibly enough, could produce serious trouble.

At Rockefeller's headquarters somebody hit the panic button.

A massive advertising campaign to knock down the charge was undertaken, somewhat to the dismay of the professional politicians who argued that the election was won and that the proper tactic was "don't rock the boat." Whether they were right can never be determined. But the "separate shop" that Rockefeller was running at the Hotel Roosevelt wasn't taking any chances. Radio and television spots were bought in wholesale

lots to preach the message that Rockefeller promised to continue
and improve rent control. To make sure that nobody missed the
message, ads appeared even in the sports pages of the New York
City papers. Precisely how much was spent in this effort was
never sorted out, but the outlay was considerable.

It was an ironic windup to the campaign. After holding the
initiative from the start with a "bossism" charge that was largely
synthetic so far as Harriman was concerned, Rockefeller ended
defending himself from a charge no better grounded. But his
swift reaction, or overreaction as some Republican politicians
insisted, was a hint of things to come. Repeatedly as Governor,
he would charge into situations that seemed to endanger his
position without waiting to see whether the challenge was real or
a feint. His impetuosity would frequently worry those around
him, but constitutionally, he seemed to find it necessary to face
up to every challenge as soon as it appeared, often, it may be
noted, building up situations that might otherwise have disappeared from lack of substance.

The last outside development of the campaign had a bizarre
touch. The *New York Post,* which had been Harriman's strongest
supporter in the state, switched its allegiance to Rockefeller in a
signed editorial appearing in its last edition on election eve.
Dorothy Schiff, the publisher, said she was changing candidates
because Tammany Hall tried to label the Rockefellers as "anti-
Semitic." It was a charge that nobody had taken seriously.

And so the campaign ended. As an exercise in public education via a dialogue about the issues, it produced more heat than
light. At the close, as at the beginning, no meaningful difference
had been developed. The question the voters were going to decide came down in the payoff hours to one of personality. On
the one hand there was Nelson Rockefeller, new, exciting and
stamped with the glamor of his family name. On the other there
was Averell Harriman, an able but frustrated Governor, trailing
the glories of a New Deal past that should have earned him more
consideration than he got from New York City voters. Harriman's
dedication to the New Deal and the very real contribution he

made as Ambassador to Moscow had given him every reason to expect their support.

November 5, 1958, Election Day, dawned fair—"Republican weather," according to an ancient political tradition that bad weather keeps the farmers at home and helps Democratic chances. Nelson, Mrs. Rockefeller and Steven were at the family enclave at Pocantico Hills. They voted at 9:20 A.M. in the Pocantico Hills fire headquarters, and Mrs. Rockefeller, with her usual graciousness, apologized to the half-dozen voters in line behind them when the family had to hold up operations for the benefit of the news photographers and their inevitable, "One more please."

Reporters noted that Rockefeller was tired and seemed a bit drawn as might be expected after his strenuous weeks of campaigning. But he was still the campaigner.

"I've kept myself in balance," he told reporters, "so whichever way it goes, I'm relaxed."

It was quite possibly the most specious statement he ever made. With his future at stake—he disdained the suggestion that a good run as a loser would give him claims on Republican loyalty in the years ahead—he was keyed to a nervous pitch that was almost insupportable as those closest to him realized. But he carried off the long day without giving himself away.

After motoring into the city with Mrs. Rockefeller and Stevie, he went to his headquarters at the Hotel Roosevelt where he spent the afternoon hashing over the campaign. It was a fruitless visit. A more experienced candidate would have known that campaign headquarters is the most discouraging place to be on Election Day; there are too many "might have beens" to be worried over. Nelson weathered the wearying hours, and went home for dinner.

Rockefeller returned to his headquarters in the Hotel Roosevelt to get the election returns and ran into the heady air of expectant victory. What creates this atmosphere is a mystery. By some arcane alchemy, political hangers-on, who never commit themselves during a campaign, seem to sense just before the voting machines are locked the identity of the winner and they flock to his headquarters. Professional politicians, who are themselves bemused by this divination, invariably relax once they see which way the freeloaders are jumping.

On election night, 1958, their one goal was the Hotel Roosevelt. Before the first returns were flashed, the ballroom was so crowded that movement was impossible. Campaign workers drifting down from the upper floors to share the excitement found themselves pushed out into the corridors, so they drifted away to the bars around the hotel to get the results by television.

Rockefeller got the returns in his suite, surrounded by his top campaign advisers, with the imperturbable Frank Jamieson scanning and evaluating the figures as they came off the computers. Shortly after 9 o'clock it was all over. Every reasonable projection indicated a landslide, and it remained only to await the official canvass to decide just how big it would be. Rockefeller was jubilant.

But he refused to go out on a limb. Down in the ballroom, the well-wishers, party workers and hangers-on were clamoring for his presence. He remained in the suite until 10:45 P.M. when the telegram conceding the election arrived from Governor Harriman.

Then and then only, the Rockefellers and their five children rode down to the ballroom to receive the plaudits of victory. They ran into a scene of indescribable confusion. Standing room had long since been exhausted. People were jammed together in unyielding walls of humanity, unable to move without shoving their neighbors, and screaming victory slogans. To get to the platform the Rockefellers linked hands and were, almost literally, hauled through the crowd. It was a long time—nobody held a stopwatch on it—before Nelson could make himself heard.

Rockefeller, whose complexion normally tends to the sallow, was ashen with fatigue, but he was also unashamedly, almost boyishly elated. He thanked everyone, as many as he could remember by name and the rest with apologies for not naming them. And he addressed himself seriously to the tasks ahead.

"We'll give it everything we've got," he promised.

And so, early on the morning of November 6th, he got to bed

at last, having scored a famous victory—"A Republican oasis in a desert of defeat," Roscoe Drummond called it in his syndicated column. How famous the victory was would become apparent on the following day as the returns from around the country were tabulated.

The scope of the Rockefeller victory became apparent when the afternoon papers came out. The Democrats swept the Congressional and Senatorial contests across the country, and they scored spectacularly in the state houses; the one notable exception outside New York being far-off Oregon where Mark O. Hatfield won in an election that got little publicity in the East.

In contrast to the debacle, Rockefeller had done the impossible. The official canvass of the vote eventually gave him a plurality of 573,034, and he carried in all the candidates on the state ticket except James A. Lundy, whose nomination had been a political payoff and who was beaten for Comptroller by the Democratic incumbent, the formidable Arthur Levitt who'd spent four years building up a following in Parent-Teacher Associations and small taxpayer circles.

And just to frost the cake for Rockefeller, the other election statistics proved that Nelson was the only draw the GOP had. For three New York Republican Congressmen and six members of the State Legislature were among the casualties. Furthermore, reports from the boondocks gave Rockefeller's pulling power the credit for "saving" at least half a dozen legislators who got in on margins of a few hundred votes or less.

On November 6, 1958, Nelson Rockefeller was a full-fledged national political figure.

The scope of Rockefeller's election victory of course brought the charge that he "bought" the election. As a matter of practical politics, the charge was ridiculous. Nobody, not even a Rockefeller, has enough money to buy an election involving nearly 6,000,000 people. To buy a plurality of nearly 600,000 in a sophisticated state like New York was obviously beyond human reach.

And, in the final count, the spending was just about in line with what any state campaign costs. The Republican State Committee reported spending just over $1,250,000 and had a deficit of $175,000. The best evidence indicated that the independent committee headed by Oren Root—an "average effort" by his standards—spent another quarter of a million. This added up to something over $1.7 million in acknowledged expenditures—a truly massive effort, but only about routine for a state election in New York. (The Democrats spent almost as much, but their deficit was larger.) On this basis, however, money qua money didn't win the election—although it helped. The election was won by Nelson Rockefeller.

The fortunate circumstance of the outcome delighted Rockefeller. Overnight he became a national political figure. The political columnists who'd had a lot of fun kicking around Rockefeller as a playboy found themselves compelled to get serious. A new power had arisen in the international wing of the Republican Party, and, while it was still fashionable in the National Press Club to downgrade Nelson, he couldn't be quite ignored.

In the coming months as he wrested control of the New York State Republican Party from the grip of the old Dewey organization and asserted his own distinctive style, his stature would increase.

16

The Governor

EVERY ADMINISTRATION HAS a style of its own. When the
Democrats stormed into Albany on New Year's Eve, 1954, to take
back the Executive Mansion after twelve long years of Thomas
E. Dewey, they arrived as conquerors, trailing the laurels of victory and anxious for the division of the prizes. At the principal
hotels, cocktail parties were continuous—one party in a lounge
at the De Witt Clinton, known generally as "The Shelf," ran
from early afternoon deep into the night with the hosts and
bartenders changing every few hours, but the guests remaining
and more coming. How the bills were sorted out is a mystery.

And some more exuberant Democrats, unable to get into the larger parties, staged private celebrations at one of which the enthusiasm got so out of hand that the Albany police, Democrats all, had to be called to remind the celebrants politely that it was forbidden to throw empty beer cans into the street from high up in the hotel.

On New Year's Eve, 1958, there were no Republican celebrations in Albany, and for that matter few Republicans. Several floors were reserved at the hotels for assorted Rockefellers and their friends, and the fortunate few invited to the private swearing-in ceremonies at the Executive Mansion checked in quietly and slipped away for a decorous dinner with the new Governor. He took the oath at 10:30 P.M. for the first time from Chief Judge Albert Conway, of the Court of Appeals, in a traditional New York ritual that requires the incoming Governor to qualify before the legal ending of the term of his predecessor to ensure there will be no break in the continuity of the office. After the rite, the party wound up swiftly, and everybody was tucked safely in bed by 1 A.M. The reporters assigned to Rockefeller went out to celebrate the coming of the New Year with Democrats, who had nothing in particular to celebrate.

Nelson Rockefeller was publicly sworn in as the fifty-third Governor of New York at 1:45 P.M. on New Year's Day, 1959, in the Assembly Chamber of the State Capitol, with Judge Conway again administering the oath. The room of course was inadequate to the occasion, as it is for all inaugurations. With most of the 208 members of the Legislature occupying choice seats, a long row of Rockefellers sitting just to the left of the Judges of the Court of Appeals, and with the more important party officers duly provided for, the smaller-fry politicians who gain status by getting into such ceremonies of pomp and power found themselves squeezed into the narrow galleries at either end of the boxlike room while various VIP's, with social and financial, but certainly not political credits, took over the remaining floor seats. It was a situation that caused some bitterness because the "strangers" had connections with the party hierarchy, connections that almost invariably involved substantial campaign contributions, and if they wanted in, no one could really deny them. And because it was "chic" in certain circles to attend the Rockefeller inauguration, the little fellows had to be content with invitations to the semipublic ball that was to follow that night, an alternative with small prestige value.

The new Governor was solemnly buoyant on the day of his inauguration. He approached the ceremonies in a mood of elation tempered by the certain knowledge that there were troublous days ahead. He was far more knowing about the state than he had been only a few weeks ago, and he was already getting hard lessons in a kind of politics that had up to then been beyond his experience—the delicate give-and-take necessary to develop support for programs. This hadn't obtruded itself into the campaign, but election had brought him into the arena where every slightest appointment was a matter of contention to practical politics and every idea advanced brought attacks, not only from the opposition but from within his own party. It was something most politicians learn over the years; Nelson's lessons were telescoped in a few short weeks.

For his inauguration, Nelson chose a blue business suit rather than the morning coat and striped trousers of tradition—a personal preference that he insisted on "because I've got to be myself." He also insisted on preparing his inaugural address.

It was, as might be expected, optimistic. It was appropriately grave. But the big thing about it was that it was more international than domestic. Its goals were soaring; its programs lofty. And it wasn't until he was halfway through that he mentioned New York for the first time. The papers the next day would compare the speech to a Presidential State of the Union message rather than an inaugural address, but it was a speech that Rockefeller felt it was necessary to make and he plowed ahead.

"As this sixth decade of our 20th Century nears its end," he began, "we are nearing, too, what could be a fatal testing time for free men and freedom itself—everywhere."

Rockefeller noted that while many generations think their own age is the "moment of historic decision—we know it.

"We know it because we have witnessed—for more than 25

years now—the tragic ordeal of freedom," he went on. "We have seen the tyrant—first Fascist, then Communist—strike down free nations, shackle free peoples, and dare free men everywhere to prove they can survive."

Defining the problem as a struggle "between those who believe in the essential equality of peoples of all nations and races and creeds—and those whose only creed is their own ruthless race for power," the new Governor keyed his program for New York to its function within the larger problem of building up the economic strength and raising the living standards of free peoples everywhere.

"We cannot hope to spur economic progress and prosperity in the world unless such a state as New York can itself help to lead America herself toward new horizons of well being and equal opportunity for all our people," he declared. "We cannot pretend to help inspire new young nations in the ways of freedom and its institutions if our schools do not enable our own youth to be enlightened citizens. We cannot hope to serve the cause of peace among nations if classes or factions in our own society war among themselves."

He specifically promised for New York a program to "put the state's fiscal house in order," improved and expanded programs of social and health insurance, better housing, improvement of all programs for the aged and a general rise in the physical and vocational rehabilitation procedures. He also committed himself to an ever-expanding educational plan, a project that was to give him severe political headaches in the months and years ahead. But it was a commitment deeply involved in his beliefs, and he went all out in his pledge.

"We must work, perhaps hardest of all, on the field where the future can be won or lost: in our schoolrooms. We must attack the problems of juvenile delinquency. We must continue urgently needed state aid to our schools. We must plan—years into the future—expansion of our state institutions for higher learning. For what we do not teach we cannot save—and this is true of freedom itself."

The scope of Rockefeller's plans dismayed many Republicans,

but on Inauguration Day, 1959, most of them dutifully praised his speech, assuming the new Governor would come to them for guidance when he got down to actual governing and would be steered by old hands. They had some surprises coming.

The inaugural activities did not of course end with the address and oath-taking. Governors of New York usually hold open house at the Executive Mansion on New Year's Day, and Rockefeller put in the afternoon receiving visitors.

And then he topped off the day with a typical Rockefeller gesture. He imported the New York City Ballet to dance at the Inaugural Ball in Albany's State Armory. It was the first open move in the program for culture that Rockefeller would press for the rest of his years as Governor, a drive that would make New York the first state to set up an Arts Council to bring good music and drama to the hinterlands with the help of state subsidies.

Throughout the long day, Rockefeller's energy never flagged. He shook hands with thousands in what must have seemed endless hours on reception lines, but for every well-wisher he had a warm smile, a firm handshake and a few words. "It's so nice of you to say so," he told one little old lady who told him at the Inaugural Ball that she was sure he'd be a great governor. "I will do my best."

It was a day of unalloyed triumph, and when Rockefeller at last returned to the Executive Mansion he savored its high points. In the next few weeks, as he got more deeply involved in day-to-day politicking, with its major and minor headaches, he was to refer to it frequently as his best day in office. Not that he complained. As he remarked time and again, he was "having the time of my life" as Governor. And he would add, if someone tried to sympathize with him during the rough going: "Nobody twisted my arm. I went looking for the job and I was damn glad to get it. It's a great challenge."

Rockefeller quickly proved the most peripatetic of governors. In the State Capitol at Albany, the second floor is "executive country," ruled entirely by the Governor, while the third floor is in the legislative domain. Most governors remain on the second floor throughout their terms, going upstairs only to deliver annual messages and, very occasionally, to read budget messages. When they want to see legislators, they summon them down to the second floor.

This, of course, was foreign to Rockefeller's nature. A direct actionist, he refused to stand on protocol, and, before the Legislature was in session for a week, he'd fallen into the habit of walking up to the third floor—he was often too impatient to wait for the elevator—to stroll around and talk to anyone he met. A number of young Assemblymen, meeting him for the first time on his corridor strolls, made hay for themselves by interesting him in their problems—interest they couldn't arouse by memo.

In time, of course, Rockefeller had to curtail these strolls. He never gave up entirely the practice of rushing up to the third floor to congratulate his leaders after they won particularly important votes, but he found that he was being besieged by favor seekers, some of whom had private legislative projects that couldn't survive analysis.

Rockefeller's enthusiasm, his drive, and, above all, his sincere interest in fitting himself into his role as Governor created a new tone around the Capitol. Even those who remained suspicious of him as a "millionaire New Dealer" felt his charm and often joined him in supporting programs that were far out from their usual positions. For the first few weeks, at least, everything seemed to be going his way.

Those were weeks of hard work for Rockefeller. Despite his professed longtime interest in politics and despite his occasional encounters with the Congress during his Washington period, he knew very little about the practical workings of the legislative process and, at the outset, realized perhaps less than most governors the multifarious factors that figure in a decision on even the simplest piece of legislation. Trivial as some of these considerations are, Rockefeller soon learned to go along with the intricate and often pettifogging maneuvering entailed. But compromise was one thing. Rockefeller knew that, before he could master the political process of making laws and running the state, he would have to train himself to understand the motivations behind the various questions brought up on any given bill and to anticipate them.

This it what he set out to do and he put in long hours in the learning. No early bird—he prefers to sleep until between 8 and 9 unless compelled to get up earlier because of commitments— he customarily reached his desk about 9:30 and worked steadily through the day, sending out for a sandwich for lunch. Almost invariably he still eats at his desk. At night, he continued a Washington practice by taking staff members, political leaders or whomever he happened to be working with to the Executive Mansion for dinner and several more hours of work. It was a taxing routine, but Nelson, who has been seriously ill only twice in his life (a bout of pneumonia and a touch of appendicitis, both in his youth), never showed fatigue.

Rockefeller later acknowledged that he had a lot to learn in those first few weeks in Albany, and the record shows that he learned swiftly and well. Before his first month in office was over, he established himself as a "take-charge guy," and those who'd hoped to steer a neophyte found themselves, instead, looking to the new Governor for leadership. He was ready to supply that in abundance. His own wide-ranging interests and the many studies of state government he'd commissioned equipped him with a series of programs which he sent up to the Legislature with special messages—and he was always receptive to new ideas.

As he acknowledged later, Rockefeller faced two problems of overriding importance when he took office as Governor. On the political level, his task was to unify the Republican Party, which was badly split in the upper echelons even though all factions had joined forces to elect Nelson in November. And on the government level, he had to straighten out the state's finances, because until his money base was secure all other sectors of his programs would remain meaningless.

Both were make or break problems. Although he turned aside all questions about the Presidency, he was pointed in that direction, and he needed full command of the Republican Party before he could show even the slightest interest. And the groupings that rallied behind Nelson for Governor included elements of the strong conservative wing of upstate Republicans who wanted no part of him for higher office.

He also needed command of the party to put over his program and establish a record against the day when he might strike out openly for the Presidency.

When he was elected Governor, few people knew what Nelson stood for. His campaign speeches had promised economy, efficiency, school aid and all the usual things that politicians promise—with the single exception of a tax cut—but he avoided specifics. His tours of duty in Washington had been largely unpublicized. He had made an impression only among circumscribed groups because in his first stint the nation was at war and Latin-American affairs got little play in the papers, and in the Eisenhower Administration because his jobs in government reorganization, as Under Secretary of Health, Education, and Welfare and, particularly, as White House adviser on international affairs were all one step removed from the spotlight. He couldn't be clearly identified with any single cause or faction. although the assumption that he was internationalist and liberal by Republican standards was a factor in his election.

But unlike most governors who reach the Executive Mansion already identified in the public mind with policies and programs, and thereby limited somewhat in their freedom of action, Rockefeller had no political personality to live up to. He'd stated noble goals in his campaign, but he had no commitment to any specific course of action or to any group. He would fashion his public image as he made his public record, and this placed on him an added burden to master the legislative process so he could make the record.

The foundation of this record, in his first year in office as it is today, would be his tax program. Rockefeller knew, as he has often remarked, that a considerable section not only of the Republican Party but of business regarded him as a far-out liberal New Deal "spender" and was deeply distrustful of his economic ideas.

Trained from childhood to regard sound financing as the *sine qua non* of any undertaking, Rockefeller realized that his first step must be to straighten out the finances of the state, which had been slipping into *de facto* deficit financing for several years by raiding reserve funds, although meeting the technical constitutional requirement for a balanced budget. The bookkeeping juggle couldn't go on indefinitely. Rockefeller knew, as every sophisticated observer of state affairs knew, that it would be almost impossible to cut state spending in the face of the rising demand for schools and education, for hospitals and for other services falling within the province of the state.

But intellectual acknowledgment of a need and its political acceptance are two different things. Even before Rockefeller took office, official "leaks" indicated that a new and sweeping tax reform program was in the making. The Republicans were definitely apprehensive. Fiscal logic plays a small part in the emotions of the average taxpayer, and in upstate New York where antitax sentiment was running high in 1959, there was political danger in increasing taxes.

In his first message to the Legislature, Rockefeller did nothing to alleviate the Republican apprehensions. He gave no clue to just what he had in mind, but he warned that "our steadily rising population will, under the terms of State aid laws, already in effect, result in constantly increasing State expenditures.

"The time is overdue for facing fiscal realities and making hard decisions," he continued. "It is imperative that sufficient revenues be collected to meet the expenditures of State government. . . . The situation confronting us calls for forthright action."

Within two weeks he slammed through an increase in the gasoline and diesel fuel taxes in a spectacular blitz conceived in cooperation with Senate Majority Leader Walter J. Mahoney.

The blitz, perfectly timed and adroitly handled, caught everyone flat-footed. The oil lobby, which only a few years earlier had forced the Legislature to put a gasoline tax rise on the ballot rather than simply pass a bill, and then beaten it down on Election Day, didn't have time to get the mimeograph machines warmed up before the bill became law. And the Republicans, who'd been wondering what kind of Governor they'd elected, got the answer all at once.

For Rockefeller it was a political coup of the first magnitude. In one stroke he'd put across an important part of his fiscal program, demonstrated that he was prepared to move swiftly and take risks for what he wanted, and put the lobbyists, who constituted themselves the guardians of the tax rolls, on notice that he was going to make tax policy without prior consultation with them. He also demonstrated to the Legislature that Mahoney, whose friends were still bitter that Rockefeller had beaten him for the nomination, was going along solidly with the administration. This alliance would deepen with the years, but in his first month in office Rockefeller was rightly apprehensive about Mahoney's role.

The gasoline tax bill represented a blitz because it was called up even before Rockefeller presented his budget, an unprecedented procedure in New York State and one that roused deep grumblings of discontent among the professional money-savers in both houses. They were also a little shocked that Rockefeller whom they identified as the Standard Oil heir—not knowing that the family has largely divested itself of its active oil interests—would slap his first tax rise on gasoline.

Rockefeller was jubilant. He waited up the night the gasoline tax bill passed to sign it.

He was perhaps a little too jubilant. The coup was an important one for the lift it gave the entire administration. It established Nelson's stature with the political professionals. But it was, after all, merely the first and brilliantly conceived step. And it put the economy-minded legislators on guard for the bigger fight that was to come.

The danger signals were already flying by the time Rockefeller had his first budget message ready for the Legislature. The rumblings had grown so loud that informal alliances were being lined up to fight a tax program that hadn't even been proposed.

But Rockefeller disregarded the cautionary advice showering in on him from all sides. As Frank Jamieson said, "he had to be his own man," and on February 2nd he went upstairs to read the budget message in person to a joint session of both houses.

The tax program was a blockbuster. Rockefeller called for a rise of $277 million in taxes, more than half of it to come from the detested personal income tax which was budgeted for an overall increase of nearly 35 percent. He also proposed increasing other major taxes, including an added two-cent levy on cigarettes to bring the tax up to five cents a pack.

The message was coolly received. Rockefeller got only the most perfunctory applause as he read the message, and at the conclusion there was only a spattering of handclapping. The Legislature's dislike for the program was apparent to everyone.

Rockefeller, of course, was aware of the mood. As he finished reading the message, he put his manuscript aside and made a direct appeal to the legislators to "have the courage to face this situation."

The appeal, coming from a man who had just proposed New York's first $2 billion budget and the biggest tax rise in the state's history, was received in a chill that matched the reception of the budget message itself. But Rockefeller was not about to give ground in the face of hostility. He defended his appropriations, and he bluntly laid his challenge on the line to members of his own party.

"I should like to say to those of you who do not want to vote for these taxes, that I recommend that you then have the courage to propose a cut in the statutes for expenditures of aid to localities of 10 or 20 percent, or in aid to education of 20 percent, or a cut in the expenditures on highways and other construction of 50 percent, but let all of us stand up and be counted to bring this budget into balance," he said.

It was a brutal challenge, perhaps too brutal from a man who wouldn't have to face the voters for four years to those who would have to seek their sufferance in just over a year, but it expressed Rockefeller's determination in terms beyond mistaking. Nelson was staking his future on the tax program; there would be no retreat. If the program failed, Rockefeller would have a bleak term ahead, and an even bleaker political future.

Even so, Nelson was somewhat dismayed by the virulence of the antitax sentiment that spread through Albany. It was a measure of his political immaturity that he didn't anticipate the bitter kickback when he hit the legislators where they lived—in the pocketbook issue that could mean the difference between holding their jobs or being retired to private life. And he had failed signally to do enough advance missionary work for his cause, possibly because, in his own administrative experience, decisions were made at the top and carried out by other levels. He clearly didn't appreciate that the legislators, each holding his mandate from the voters, prized highly their prerogative of being consulted.

Politically, the tax program was peculiarly unpalatable to the Republicans, even to those who wanted tax reform badly. For what Rockefeller proposed was to put income taxes on a current basis with withholding by employers, with dependent exemptions cut to a uniform $600 for each member of the family. Rates were to be stepped up, and the entire structure was to be brought into "conformity" with the Federal income tax system. In the process, hundreds of thousands of small wage earners would be added to the tax rolls, because under the previous New York system basic exemptions were $1,000 for a single person and $2,500 for married couples and heads of families, with dependent deductions at $400.

As it worked out, the low-income groups were provided with safeguards and higher bracket taxpayers actually got a break, because they were able to deduct their increased state taxes on their Federal returns. Rockefeller himself, paying Federal taxes in the 92-percent bracket, acknowledged to reporters that the net effect of the tax increase would be to reduce his Federal taxes.

But for the middle-income group, earning up to $20,000 a year, the boosts were savage, and it was precisely this group that represented to Republican politicians the backbone of their strength. As Senator Mahoney remarked when tinkering with the tax bill began, "We've got to salvage something for the people who sent us here."

In the fight over the tax increase, Nelson was blooded politically. Up to that point, he'd been playing at politics. Even his gasoline tax blitz, spectacular though it was, had been only a skirmish. But in seeking the income tax rise, he was playing for high stakes—"This isn't for one year, it's for all the years we'll be here," remarked Rockefeller's press secretary, Dick Amper.

Nelson was well aware of the risks. He worked tirelessly to line up votes for his program, cajoling and charming the legislators. But he also proved that he could wheel and deal when forced by necessity to use all the weapons at his command. Chairmanships were traded for votes, and recalcitrants were isolated and threatened with defeat of their local bills. On occasion, the embattled Rockefeller forces went over the heads of the legislators to the powers-that-be back in their home communities to bring the needed pressure.

The big battle was waged in the Assembly. Mahoney had the Senate well in hand—in the showdown only two Senate Republicans voted against the tax bill, and they were especially exempted from party discipline because they were being squeezed by newspapers and by extremely vocal and effective taxpayer groups back home.

In the Assembly, it was a different story. For years, a group of rural Republican Assemblymen had resented what they considered big-city domination of major Republican decisions, and they were quick to jump on the tax bill as an issue. But they miscounted grievously on one count; they had no strong leader. The one apparent leader who might have been effective was Charles Schoeneck, of Syracuse, who was won over to the administration side and rewarded by advancement to Majority Leader a short time later. But he paid a high price. In 1960, he was defeated for reelection to the Legislature strictly on the tax issue.

Not that Rockefeller got everything he wanted. At the suggestion of Senator Mahoney, a $25 tax rebate for married couples and heads of families was written into the bill, restoring the old balance between single and married taxpayers.

Rockefeller also was forced to yield on his proposal for forgiveness of all 1958 income taxes. Since his program called for putting 1959 tax collections on a current basis via withholding, the tax bill waived collection of the 1958 taxes—a "forgiveness" Rockefeller called it, although of course nobody was forgiven anything. But the bill also would have waived taxes for 1958 on dividends and interest, which would not be put on withholding, thereby creating a windfall for a privileged class of stock- and bondholders. This could have been extremely dangerous not only to the tax program, but to Rockefeller's political image. In the face of Democratic charges of "windfall," the dividend forgiveness was dropped. There was no lasting damage.

The victory on the tax bill stirred Rockefeller to an outburst of enthusiasm. He got the good news on a sunny afternoon in late March, and with Frank Jamieson at his side dashed up from the second floor to the office of Assembly Speaker Oswald D. Heck, his old opponent for the nomination, to congratulate and thank him. It was a gesture he was glad later to have made. For within a few months, Heck, who'd left a sickbed at the Lahey Clinic in Boston to manage the fight for the tax bill in his house, was dead. In less than a year, Jamieson also would be dead. But on the day of triumph, neither quite realized how close they were to the end, and both savored the victory with Nelson.

Strolling through the vaulted corridors of the Capitol, Rockefeller accepted congratulations and cheerfully exaggerated the fears he'd had over the bill. And he also made it clear that the tax fight was over so far as he was concerned. As he remarked to a staff aide that evening, "We can go ahead now with our program. This should give us what we need to work on."

The tax struggle got national coverage. Rockefeller as Governor would have been newsworthy in his first year if he'd done nothing. But that he undertook a bold program to raise taxes substantially while the economy was slumping off made him unique among governors. Albany was filled with Washington correspondents, columnists and magazine writers from all over, dropping in to have a look at the multimillionaire Governor whom many had classed as a dilettante at best. The consequence was that the country got a lot more information about Rockefeller than it gets normally about a freshman Governor of New York. And, by and large, national reaction was good. Newspapers outside the state when they commented on the tax program also invariably praised Nelson for his courage in facing up to the economic facts of life and for insisting to the people of New York that they must pay for the kind of government they were demanding.

Rockefeller read these comments avidly, but he studiously stuck to strictly New York affairs. He refused all invitations to speak outside the state to emphasize that he was devoting his energies to learning his new role, and, although visiting reporters badgered him at nearly every press conference about his political future, he insisted, "I have my hands full as Governor."

And, of course, he had his hands rather more than full. Besides learning his way around in precinct-level politics, a field totally foreign to his experience, and in the handling of a Legislature, Rockefeller felt impelled to press a broad variety of programs, which aroused little or no enthusiasm in a Legislature still fearful of the outcome of the tax vote.

It was an all-things-to-all-men program as sent up to the Legislature in a series of special messages, sometimes with implementing bills, but almost as often merely for study, and it promised material goodies for young and old—more schools, more hospitals, more roads, better housing for everybody, particularly the aging, and more sympathy for the businessman. It proposed to stimulate business. It promised the unemployed expanding "job opportunities"—a latter-day political cliché that nobody from Rockefeller to John F. Kennedy has satisfactorily defined, but that is supposed to mean something more than simply providing jobs. It looked forward to stamping out juvenile delinquency and dope addiction; to throttling illegal gambling and "big crime" by turning the paramilitary State Police into a sort of little FBI whenever troopers could be spared from traffic duty.

The outpouring of bills, programs and studies also had important political effects for Rockefeller. Nominated and elected largely on trust, so to speak, he moved into focus as a public man as his proposals outlined what he stood for. The political personality that emerged was by no means sharp. With the same enthusiasm that marked all his undertakings, Rockefeller rushed ahead pell-mell in his first session with the Legislature and sometimes blurred just what he was striving for by offering so many programs that at times he seemed to be in doubt as to just where he stood. The conflict proved, on analysis, more apparent than real; the central aims were rather closely coherent, but in the proliferation of plans the details often weren't spelled out with a nice exactness.

Yet out of the welter of ideas there emerged the framework of a Governor considerably broader and more complex than the candidate had seemed. The candidate had dutifully accepted the shibboleths of his party; the Governor patently was intent on giving a new tone to the party, on refashioning its style to provide a broader base for its appeal. His view was long term. Although he was scrupulous in carrying through the day-to-day duties of his office, it was obvious that the necessities of provincial politics bored him. He would give due attention to the needs of county leaders, but, after talking over their problems, he would more than likely launch into extensive disquisitions on what must be done for the state in the next decade or generation. As in his tax program, he was always looking to the future. To the bread-and-butter politician whose terms of reference are immediate problems and the short-term goal, this predilection was almost aberrant. They were inclined, at first, to brush off the Governor's talk as do-gooder enthusiasm. But most of them left his office convinced that he was deeply sincere in his concern, and determined to use his growing grasp of politics to accomplish his ends. To the politicians, of course, those ends encompassed ambition for higher office.

By the time the Legislature adjourned its 1959 session, Rockefeller had undergone a public metamorphosis. The glamorous millionaire who'd charmed his way to election eating blintzes and smiling his way around the state had fleshed out as a political personality with undeniable outlines. The voters had picked him at least partially because he brought a new face and new excitement to the rather dreary political scene. They found by the spring of 1959 that he carried the same excitement with him into office.

His broad humanitarian drives, always a controlling factor in his life but hitherto obscured by his glamour, were shown clearly in much of the legislation he sponsored and pushed through to law. To his campaign flair he had added a definite political flair, gaining a large measure of control over the party organization and revealing a grasp that would give him complete control within a year. His political courage was proved. He'd established his increasing identification with the Republican Party, although his detractors still called him a reformed New Dealer, and he was developing skill in reconciling divergent political viewpoints.

Not that a new Rockefeller impinged suddenly on the public consciousness. On the contrary, his name and his great wealth remained the things that brought the people out to see him. But his performance in his first legislative session revealed other dimensions of the man, and the word spread slowly that there was more to him than just his millions and position. Just how much more was the question.

Rockefeller himself was aware that changes had been wrought. He knew that he'd compiled a remarkable record in his freshman year as Governor—knowledge that was reinforced by the favorable comment appearing in the state's press and in magazines across the country.

As the legislators packed to go home, Rockefeller was elated. He'd come through unscratched in the face of predicted hostility that could have left lasting political scars. He'd fashioned a record by mastering a Legislature that had bedeviled poor Averell Harriman for four years, and he was in position to consolidate his power. He might have been smug if he hadn't been rushing so headlong into the future.

17

National Soundings

THE CONSTITUTION of the State of New York sends its Governor into virtual imprisonment in the State Capitol for one month every year. This is the so-called thirty-day bill period, starting with the adjournment of the Legislature and continuing until the Governor has signed or vetoed all the bills sent to his desk in the final week and a half of the session. Within the thirty days allotted, the Governor handles upward of thirteen hundred bills. Important legislation represents a small fraction of this stack, and those bills can be disposed of with a minimum amount of trouble. But the local, private and even niggling little matters that make up the great bulk of the closing-rush legislation are a different matter entirely. Most of the bills are harmless, affecting only local interests or situations. But tucked away among them is bound to be a number of sleepers—bills slipped by the jam of last-minute voting that won't stand exposure to daylight. These bills get by despite the vigilance of legislative leaders who are supposed to protect the Governor when he is of the same party and nothing can be done about it because of the nature of the legislative animal.

But the Governor is on a spot. He must distinguish between the special-interest bills freighted with possible windfalls and scandals and the legitimate minor legislation that is essential to the reelection of his followers and needful for local government.

In this job, the Governor relies on his own counsel, the Attorney General, the legislative leaders, county chairmen, experts drawn from the various state departments, and such outsiders as may have special knowledge of or interest in the situations involved. It is slow, boring paper work. It is also a very great necessity in the education of the Governor.

It was a particular necessity for Nelson Rockefeller. He was taking a crash course in grass-roots political organization and the bill-signing period provided a laboratory for examining what makes state- and county-level politicians tick. The countless talks necessary to dispose of thirteen hundred bills in a limited time also helped the Governor get direct knowledge of what was going on throughout the state and what was making legislators act as they did.

There was also the necessity for developing skill in the use of the veto. Although the State Constitution provides machinery for overriding a gubernatorial veto, as a practical matter no veto has been overridden in New York for more than a century—the precise date is lost somewhere in antique records—and the veto therefore is a very potent weapon in the hands of a governor in controlling the Legislature. But it must be used boldly, imaginatively and sparingly.

Rockefeller knew all this, and like a true Rockefeller he did his homework well and thoroughly in his first bill-signing period. Yet he fretted through the thirty days that tied him to his desk.

For more than a year he'd been self-gagged on national and foreign affairs. Aside from hurried flights for short vacations in Venezuela, he'd stayed close to the state since his possible gubernatorial candidacy became a matter of serious political consideration in the winter of 1958. With the legislative program on the books, he wanted to get on with other things. He was restless.

His restlessness was agitated by nationwide speculation over whether he would make a bid for the Republican nomination for President in 1960 as the glamour boy of Republican governors and guesses about his chances of wresting the nomination from Vice President Richard M. Nixon who, even then, seemed to have the contest sewed up.

His interest in the national scene was very apparent. He'd converted two brownstone houses he owned at 20–22 West 55th Street, in Manhattan, into a New York office, and there, through the spring of 1959, a staff of researchers, political scientists, speech writers and various technicians of politics was hard at work. Studies were made of national problems of special interest to Rockefeller, speeches were prepared and speaking invitations were carefully weighed to choose the best kind of audiences.

And from early May until the day after Christmas, 1959, Nelson Rockefeller acted, spoke and barnstormed the country exactly like an all-out candidate for the nomination.

It was a long exercise in frustration. In the eight months of his "campaign"—which Rockefeller never acknowledged as such—he got enthusiastic public welcomes everywhere as he swept back and forth across the country, trailed always by full election campaign complements of political correspondents. But whenever he met with party leaders and the Big Money men who control the destiny of the Republican conventions, he ran into insurmountable roadblocks. At private meeting after private meeting, he was told that commitment to Nixon was total; that all he could get out of rocking the boat was a fight that he couldn't win. Somewhat to his surprise, he found the financial community in city after city opposed, if not downright hostile, to the idea that he should entertain any hope of contesting for the presidential nomination. And he found lower GOP echelons stooping to such tricks as artificially limiting tickets to luncheons at which he spoke in order to deprive him of opportunities to ignite the enthusiasm of the rank and file.

It was a trying period. As a Rockefeller, Nelson was a little dismayed to find such open hostility to him among the oligarchs of the Grand Old Party, for the Rockefellers themselves stood at the top of the oligarchy.

But as a neophyte practicing politician he lacked the experience to realize that to the working party official the "devil you know" is always to be preferred. The Rockefeller way was to take the long-term view. He'd come to know that on county levels this wasn't possible. But to find men who planned for their business and private interests in terms of years and decades refusing even to consider a new idea in their political thinking was something new.

Further complicating Rockefeller's situation was the absence of his aide, confidant and friend, Frank Jamieson. Stricken with the lung cancer that was to cause his death in January of 1960, Jamieson was forced to take a long rest in 1959. And Rockefeller, for the first time in nearly twenty years, was engaged in a major undertaking without Jamie at his side to argue and talk things out with. He had other advisers, able men, knowing in politics, but Jamie had been, as Isabel Savell put it, the "millstone" on which Nelson ground out his ideas, and he missed the sure, intuitive feel Jamie had for politics. In the critical period when he was making his first tentative moves in national politics, this constituted a handicap of significant proportions.

None of this uncertainty ever surfaced. From early May when he began staking out his own position on national and foreign affairs right up to the windup of his last barnstorming swing in Miami, Florida, on December 18th, Rockefeller never gave the slightest indication that he was encountering top-level difficulties. On the day he parted with the press in Miami to fly home, the consensus among the forty or so reporters who had traveled with him over the months was that his next announcement would be that he would enter the New Hampshire primary in February, 1960.

Instead what Rockefeller next issued was his withdrawal statement of December 26, 1959—a statement that shocked and confounded some of the men closest to him, and a statement that may achieve a footnote in political history as the most unnecessary and damaging by any putative candidate for a nomination.

For in the months leading up to the withdrawal, Rockefeller had been fashioning an alternative to Richard M. Nixon as the Republican candidate for President. The alternative wasn't fully fleshed out, but the reception the New York Governor got from the Republican rank and file in his various trips around the country indicated that many of the party faithful found attitudes they could applaud in the international-liberal views Nelson propounded. These views were neither radical nor original, fitting on the whole within the framework of the GOP Eastern wing which dominated the GOP from the days of Wendell Willkie.

Rockefeller had proceeded cautiously in moving onto the national scene. After the 1959 bill-signing period he spent May and June in New York State, sharpening up his techniques and mending fences in areas where his tax increase program had caused resentment. This required considerable mending.

There was reason in all this. Late spring and early summer are hardly propitious times for political speeches in an off year, and Rockefeller who would make his national political debut, so to speak, at the Governors' Conference in San Juan, Puerto Rico, early in August was content to wait until then before kicking off any serious testing of his reception outside his home state.

Deeply interested in civil defense, Rockefeller in his first weeks in office had assigned the State Defense Council to study the problem of radioactive fallout shelters and devise a program to protect those removed from the immediate blast area in the event of a nuclear attack. The result was a report recommending mandatory construction of fallout shelters in all homes, schools, public buildings, stores, factories, theaters and other gathering places in the state. The council figured that such shelters could be built in private homes for an average of about $400.

Rockefeller embraced the program enthusiastically. He simply couldn't understand why anybody would object to spending $400 to protect his family, and he indicated that he would press for legislation at the 1960 session of the Legislature. The statement, tried out in upstate meetings, was hooted at by politicians of both parties as impractical. It also aroused the antibomb groups to new pitches of frenzy.

Nevertheless, Rockefeller stood by his commitment. His staff, which had been preparing for several weeks for the 1959 Governors' Conference, was instructed to whip the plan into shape for presentation to the governors as a national program. Rockefeller, as chairman of the Civil Defense Committee of the Conference, clearly expected to win wide support.

He was quickly disillusioned when he arrived in San Juan in August for the Conference. As the surprise winner of 1958, as a millionaire glamour politician and by virtue of his charm, he was the lion of the meeting, but the governors, mindful of the storm Rockefeller kicked up for himself in New York with the fallout shelter program, weren't buying. Out of courtesy, they authorized Rockefeller to persuade the National Administration to set up a civil defense conference; beyond that not a single governor made a commitment.

But a private party for a small group of correspondents covering the conference turned the spotlight on Rockefeller's candidacy. The party, the only outside social event Rockefeller allowed himself at the conference, was held the night of Puerto Rico's official reception for the visiting governors, and Nelson arrived at the downtown hotel late, hungry and tired.

Rockefeller shucked his heavy jacket (he was wearing a winter-weight suit in Puerto Rico's sweltering midsummer), ate a couple of sandwiches and for the next two and a half hours talked freely and frankly about his political situation. His listeners were fifteen top correspondents, most of whom he'd never met before, and the background stories they wrote after the guest of honor left put Rockefeller in the national picture beyond question.

This was reinforced when Rockefeller after his return to Albany found that one or two of the background stories had misinterpreted a remark he made about polls to write that he would base his decision whether to become an active candidate on a study of the polls. The Governor called a press conference to deny this point. The denial, of course, only had the effect of emphasizing Rockefeller's interest.

In the fall, Rockefeller hit the road in earnest in sounding out sentiment. His first foray was into New Hampshire where the first presidential primary of 1960 would be held.

The situation was delicate. Governor Wesley Powell, a Republican maverick, and the late U. S. Senator Styles Bridges controlled the GOP between them, and their first allegiance was to Vice President Nixon—Powell reportedly because he was hoping lightning might strike him for second place on a Nixon ticket, a political impossibility if the nod were to go to Rockefeller. Clearly, therefore, Rockefeller would not be welcome in the primary.

As a consequence Republican brass was conspicuous by its absence when Rockefeller flew in on a Friday midnight for a football weekend at his alma mater, Dartmouth. But the New York Governor was welcomed warmly and gaily by a group of young Republicans, most of them university students, who staged a torchlight parade at the airport.

On the following morning, Governor Powell performed the courtesy of welcoming Rockefeller to the State Capitol in Concord, but the meeting was more correct than cordial, and after a few minutes of chatting the two parted. Significantly, Powell made no offer to accompany Rockefeller to a press conference the local GOP had set up for him across the street from the Capitol.

It was a press conference in name only. About forty newsmen had covered the Rockefeller-Powell meeting, including a dozen or so correspondents from New York who were traveling with Nelson, but when they got to the hotel, they found all the seats down front taken. They were occupied chiefly by party workers, it appeared, and they arrogated to themselves the right to ask the questions. There was little Rockefeller's press secretaries could do about it, and the visiting press, being unacquainted with the legitimate reporters from the local papers, was in no position to object. But it soon became apparent that the purpose of packing the hall was to set up Rockefeller for needling. And needled he was. He hadn't been hopeful of anything from Governor Powell, but after his enthusiastic airport welcome the night before, he seemed somewhat shocked at the hostility of some of the questions thrown at him. It was doubly disappointing because friends, who were urging Rockefeller to make a run in New Hampshire, had led him to believe that he would find lots of support.

The reception left a lasting impression. Although Rockefeller was cheered by a crowd outside the hotel as he and Mrs. Rockefeller got in their car for a drive up to Hanover to attend the Dartmouth-Holy Cross game, and although he got a warm ovation at Dartmouth, the unaccustomed hostility remained with him. He never alluded to it openly, but it was unquestionably a factor when he came to draft his year-end withdrawal statement.

The people around Rockefeller insisted on calling the New Hampshire trip a "college football weekend," but actually it was a dry run for serious sampling trips that Rockefeller would make around the country in the next few months. Two of these trips would be full-dress campaign efforts in chartered airliners with sixty or so reporters making up the permanent traveling party, and as many more newsmen covering various stops along the line. Advance men fanned out ahead of the barnstorming planes, setting up hotel reservations and communications for the press, lining up motorcades and in general making sure that Rockefeller got plentiful public exposure.

Moving ahead of the Governor also were State Chairman Morhouse and National Committeeman Hinman, whose job it was to corral the moneymen and more powerful politicos for private meetings with Rockefeller. These were the meetings, never publicized, that edged Rockefeller out of the contest.

Before starting out on his major swings, Rockefeller made a two-day trip to Atlantic City and Chicago in late October. It was a disappointing experience. At Atlantic City, addressing the Public Health Association, Rockefeller made a nonpolitical plea for support of a program to provide health insurance against "catastrophic" illness for those who couldn't meet the rising costs of medicine. The reception was warm, but the audience passed on to other matters without touching on his plan.

Rockefeller's excuse for going to Chicago was to speak before the Inland Daily Press Association, but he flew there from Atlantic City, in the twin-engined, luxury Convair he'd bought soon after becoming Governor, a day ahead of time to try to make some political hay. It proved a forlorn hope.

The Cook County Republican organization, when informed of Rockefeller's coming, had set up a reception for him, but when he arrived, trailed by a dozen New York and Washington reporters, no welcoming committee was on hand to greet him. Instead, he was left to his own devices in getting to his hotel, where a disappointing turnout of the Chicago press showed up for his news conference.

At the reception, in a penthouse suite at a lakefront hotel, Rockefeller found himself boxed in. The guests were restricted to party workers—no general invitation had gone out—and Rockefeller didn't even get to make a speech, his activity being confined to shaking hands at the head of a receiving line, with the committee members, almost all men, shuffling past him at the rate of several a minute. As Mrs. Mary Brooks, widow of Senator C. Wayland (Curly) Brooks remarked, the Chicago area was "Nixon country," and the organization simply didn't feel any obligation to go out of its way to give any encouragement to the New York Governor.

Later, Governor William Stratton called on Rockefeller to pay his courtesies, but like other Illinois Republicans he was unenthused.

The Inland Press luncheon the following day was something less than a total success. The editors and publishers greeted Rockefeller enthusiastically, particularly the ladies among them, but unfortunately somewhere along the line his staff had goofed. In a speech designed to intrigue and arouse the interest of the men and women with the most direct pipeline to the Republican rank and file in the all-important Midwest, Rockefeller said not a single word about one of the subjects dearest to their hearts and to the pocketbook nerves of their readers: agriculture.

Instead, Rockefeller designated the six "greatest" areas of our national concern "where problems of gravity confront us," as "foreign policy, defense policy, education, economic growth, labor policy and the crucial area of civil rights and social equalities."

The editors quickly picked him up.

"I didn't notice the farm problem was among your six on the list," came promptly in the question-and-answer period. "Do we understand that you do not consider it among the six most important?"

The question caught Rockefeller with his answers down. He'd been working on a farm speech to be delivered later, but it was still in the study stage and he was totally unprepared to ad-lib in front of this special audience with a large number of farm experts sitting before him. Nor did his recovery repair the omission.

"I consider it [agriculture] a vital and integral part of the economic growth, the same for the industrial and business," he said. "So that I include it as very important in economic growth."

It was an answer that satisfied few. "Well, what do you expect them to know about the farm problem in New York?" one editor muttered sourly at a table near the visiting press.

But in other questioning, the editors showed keen interest in Rockefeller's political plans.

Rockefeller responded almost gaily. Enthusiastic as always, he sensed the quickening stir when the inevitable query, "Are you a candidate for the Presidency?" was put to him, and he lightened the moment as he replied:

"Perhaps I should say I am not now a candidate for the Presidency. I am not a candidate, but I appreciate your asking. I get to feel neglected."

And, of course, he had to say again, as he had been saying since his election and as he would continue to say right down to the convention before he could make it stick: "I would not under any circumstances be a candidate for the Vice-Presidency."

All in all, Rockefeller was satisfied with the outcome of his first meeting with the Midwest editors. As they queued up to shake hands after the meeting, it was clear that they were interested in Rockefeller as a new figure in the national speculation. Rockefeller himself felt that his error in omitting mention of the farm probably would be overcome when he issued his farm plan. But he'd been invited to the luncheon as a curiosity; from the comments after his speech, it was clear that he was being taken seriously. That in itself was an accomplishment considering that Nelson was on his first political trip to what a great many people call the American side of the Hudson River.

But the mood wasn't to endure. That night at a very private meeting at the exclusive Chicago Club, the moneymen gave Rockefeller the word, cold turkey. The commitment to Nixon, he was told, was total, and he could only interfere with local affairs by injecting himself into the situation. The harshness of the rebuff, perhaps more than the rebuff itself, repelled Nelson. He had known in advance that what the *Tribune* calls Chicagoland was Nixon country, but being invited to go away and stay away fell just short of rudeness. Although he never commented on the incident, his subsequent trips bypassed Chicago.

It was chilly on November 11, 1959, when, just before midnight, Nelson Rockefeller and Mrs. Rockefeller boarded a commercial airliner at La Guardia Field for an overnight flight to Los Angeles to begin the first of his campaign-type journeys to find out just what support would be available if he bid openly for the Republican nomination for the Presidency. The Governor was accompanied by a full staff, includng two press secretaries, a stenotypist, speech writers, political experts and about thirty New York and Washington correspondents. The party would shift to a chartered plane on the West Coast, with about forty more reporters joining the press corps.

The flight was an inauspicious start for the campaign tour. With detours to go around storms that built up ahead, and with smog closing in the airport at Los Angeles, the plane, scheduled to land in time to give everyone a few hours sleep, was kept aloft until dawn. When it finally landed it was at Burbank, while the welcoming party, including the band from the Cocoanut Grove (furnished courtesy of Marion Davies), was at the other field. There were delays while buses and cars were conscripted so the new arrivals could show up for their welcome, and at last everybody got together. The band, up all night, was as weary as the passengers who'd piled off the plane, their eyes glued with sleep.

Rockefeller and Mrs. Rockefeller were of course as sleepless as the rest. But neither showed it. Mrs. Rockefeller almost miraculously restored the quiet elegance that is her public personality, and the Governor, with his tremendous ability to bounce back, seemed as fresh as if he'd had a good night's sleep. But the late arrival had upset schedules. Everybody had to start work at once, with time out only for a quick shower and change.

The Republican Party in California, in 1959, as always, was in wild disarray. Crushingly defeated in Governor Edmund G. (Pat) Brown's 1958 sweep, the GOP was leaderless and frustrated. The Conservatives, who would surface to fight Nixon for the nomination for Governor in 1962 behind Joseph Shell, were grouping for a power play to unify the party according to their lights. Former Governor Goodwin Knight, rudely thrust aside in 1958 to make way for U. S. Senator William Knowland's grab for the governorship as a presumed stepping-stone to the Republican nomination for the Presidency—a scheme that was washed out by defeat—was an unpredictable factor on the scene. On the lower levels, the organizations, directionless and confronted with the danger of winding up on the wrong side if they became enmeshed in the bigger struggles, were taking the only protective coloration available to them: enrollment behind Nixon. In the circumstances only a few of the bolder spirits went out of their way to associate themselves with Rockefeller. Conspicuous among them was the politically surefooted minority leader of the State Senate, John McCarthy, of Marin County in the San Francisco Bay area, who would turn up again after the election of 1962 as the first Republican officeholder in the country to press for the Rockefeller for President movement.

As the situation existed in the fall of 1959, however, Rockefeller's position in California was particularly delicate. Only a year before he'd all but kicked Nixon out of New York State, reasoning that if he accepted help from the National Administration he'd have to defend its record, which was precisely what Averell Harriman tried to force on him. Now Rockefeller was making a test run on Nixon's home grounds without so much as a by-your-leave to the Vice President. The foray aroused a certain bitterness among Nixonites who accused Rockefeller of violating the unwritten (and more often than not unhonored) rule that prospective candidates for national nominations wait to be asked into the home states of their rivals. Nixon himself, however, with his usual astuteness, had said in advance that Rockefeller would be welcome.

After his experience in Chicago, Rockefeller was aware that he might run into some rough going in California, particularly in Los Angeles, and, without yielding ground, he carefully defined the purpose of his visit. In the only frankly political speech he delivered in California, he told the Western States Republican Conference at the Hotel Biltmore that one of the prime objectives for every Republican was "to make nomination by the Republican Party in 1960 mean something. That objective is to win next November," he added, "for without victory there is no opportunity to exercise proper leadership."

As for his own role, Rockefeller said he was touring the country as a "toiler in the Republican vineyard.

"It is the responsibility of Republicans anywhere," he said, "to be deeply concerned with the vitality of the Republican Party everywhere. That concern can best be met, that vitality best stimulated, by frank, open competition of ideas openly discussed."

Unfortunately for Rockefeller's purpose at this point, he lacked the publicly recognized credentials to participate in the national dialogue on questions of high policy. As a bright, new, engaging figure on the American scene, who'd bucked the Democratic tide of 1958 to win a tremendous personal election in New York—the one state the Republicans can't win without—he was entitled to a full hearing on the political level. But he'd been away from discussion of world affairs almost since the start of the Cold War. His tour of duty with the Eisenhower Administration had been spent publicly in government reorganization and as Under Secretary of the Department of Health, Education, and Welfare, and in the anonymous role of White House adviser on foreign policy—a role little understood outside close administration circles. And, of course, in his long immersion in state affairs from the time he decided to run for Governor, he'd been under his own self-imposed gag rule. As a consequence, the expertise he'd acquired in and out of government in foreign affairs was largely disregarded by editors and political leaders.

A further limiting factor on Rockefeller's contribution to the "competition of ideas" within the GOP was that he had little to offer. By upbringing, he was morally incapable of taking an extreme position simply to sharpen debate and provide a rallying cry for his followers. And by conviction he followed the internationalist tradition that gained ascendancy in the Eastern wing of the Republican Party with the nomination of the late Wendell Willkie for President back in 1940. Since General Eisenhower owed his nomination for the Presidency largely to the Eastern GOP, and since he embraced most of its tenets, Rockefeller had little chance for maneuver unless he wanted to tackle the President head on.

A case in point was what the Rockefeller people called a "major statement" on foreign policy that Rockefeller delivered on the day of his arrival in California before the World Affairs Council at the Beverly Hilton Hotel in Los Angeles.

A crowd of twenty-six hundred gave Rockefeller a warm welcome at the luncheon which was the curtain raiser of the California trip. But the applause clearly was for the man, not the "major statement." For while many in the crowd unquestionably turned out to see Rockefeller in the flesh, the audience as a group was sufficiently sophisticated in foreign affairs to recognize that while Rockefeller called for "debate" on how to conduct our "quest for peace," his program fell within the classic formula of diplomacy-*cum*-military buildup. He did urge that the United States should "pursue policies striving to enable the Soviet leaders to liquidate the political conflict—the Cold War—that they have imposed upon the world," but he coupled the urging with the warning that the Soviets remained committed, despite Premier Khrushchev's visit to the United States in the early fall, to peace on its own terms, a peace he called totally unacceptable to the West.

As a profession of faith, the statement was lucid; as a political document intended to sharpen debate and stake out a position, it was couched in terms so broad, as Rockefeller himself acknowledged ("I shall have more to say on other occasions about the details of this design for the future"), that debate seemed to be foreclosed. And so it was received. Not even the most loyal of Rockefeller's followers could fashion a rallying cry out of his statement, and the press, generally, found it routine and so treated it.

The Rockefeller people were disappointed with the reaction to the speech, but it was truly of a piece with the way nearly everything turned out in Los Angeles. Later that day, at a reception given by the local Republican organization in connection with the Western States Conference, Rockefeller was introduced standing under a billboard-size picture of Nixon that was the featured decoration of the hall, while coeds drawn from the nearby universities circulated among the drinkers handing out Nixon buttons. It was perfectly clear that the organization wanted no part of the New York Governor.

By contrast, San Francisco, on the following day, seemed a far friendlier place. No special effort was made to provide a showcase for Rockefeller, but the route of his motorcade was drawn to give him a certain public exposure. On the streets the crowds were cordial.

Although the stated purpose of the San Francisco stop was to address a joint luncheon of the Press-Union League and Commonwealth Clubs at the Hotel Sheraton Palace, Rockefeller also was entertained at a reception held in his honor by the Bay area Republican organizations to enable him to meet local leaders. Among those he met was a distant Rockefeller cousin, who assured one and all, firmly and repeatedly, that he was for Nixon first, last and always. Nelson accepted the cousinly defection graciously.

Other politicians were openly friendly. Former Governor Knight turned up to visit Rockefeller at his hotel and former Senator Knowland, as publisher of the Oakland papers, was at the speakers' table at the luncheon Rockefeller addressed. On the whole, the atmosphere was a good deal more relaxed.

In his speech at the joint luncheon, Rockefeller again concerned himself with world affairs, making again many of the points that he'd made on the previous day in Los Angeles. This time, however, there was no expectation that great things would come from the speech. It was written to underline an already stated position and to give Rockefeller an opportunity to present himself at the top of his form to the editors, businessmen and community leaders making up the membership of the clubs. In this it succeeded admirably. The San Francisco listeners had perhaps a keener interest in the political implications of the speech, and the problems it presented for Rockefeller, and weighed in these factors, as the previous day's audience had failed to do.

Pleasant as the day was, on the whole, night had to come, and that night Nelson dined privately at the Pacific Club with the shakers and movers of the Republican Party on the West Coast. Again the word was "No." There were plentiful expressions of interest in Rockefeller and even sympathy for his ambitions, but the advice was "wait 'till next time." The decision to throw the full weight of the financial and business community, as well as the hierarchy of the Republican Party, behind Nixon was too far advanced to admit challenge, Rockefeller was told. The consensus was that he could only hurt himself and the party if he persisted in his effort to offer an alternative that could turn the nomination into a contest. And, he was told, he couldn't win.

It was a peculiarly bitter blow. Rockefeller was not actively soliciting support at the time, it must be emphasized, but he had hoped to find in San Francisco a more open attitude. To find the top leadership as shut against him as in Los Angeles, where he had more or less expected to be frozen out, was an unexpected disappointment.

There was, of course, no trace of the disappointment apparent later that night when the Rockefellers rejoined their touring party to fly to Oregon as the trip continued. The Governor and Mrs. Rockefeller were understandably tired, and Rockefeller had nothing to say about his dinner meeting, but his spirits seemed high as he bantered with reporters.

Oregon was a pure joy for Rockefeller, the campaigner. He had a friend in Oregon, in the person of the attractive young Governor, Mark O. Hatfield, like Rockefeller a surprise winner in 1958, and the independent Hatfield, who would declare for Nixon after Rockefeller publicly resigned his ambition for the nomination, went all out to give the maximum public exposure to the visiting New Yorker. The effort produced the biggest crowds Rockefeller saw on any of his trips.

Saturday, November 14, 1959, dawned clear and cold in Eugene, Oregon. Early risers with the Rockefeller party found the air winy and what the hotel clerk described as an unusual stir of activity in the quiet university town. By 9 o'clock cars were arriving from as far as a hundred miles away, bringing whole families. The big attraction was a special convocation of students, faculty and the public in the University of Oregon gymnasium to hear Governor Rockefeller of New York.

Well before 10 o'clock the gym, which holds 8,500 for a basketball game, was more than half filled, and by the time Rockefeller arrived the crowd had swelled to between 5,000 and 6,000. Before the morning ended, estimates ran as high as 7,500; a spectacular turnout according to veteran Oregon political reporters. As was to be expected, most of the crowd was young, drawn from the undergraduates at the university, but there was a substantial leavening of middle-aged, middle-class couples who'd got up early on a good Saturday for sleeping to drive 150 to 200 miles, round trip, to see Rockefeller.

It was a crowd made to order for Rockefeller. Dominated by the young people, to whom he is always drawn, it was the type of audience that has always brought out his best campaigning talents, and he displayed these talents at the peak of his form. He was warm and friendly. He was patient. And he established that certain rapport he seems to conjure up with all audiences when his interest is passionately involved and his hearers meet him at least halfway. At Eugene, he got a lot better than halfway acceptance.

The speech that morning was inspirational rather than earth-shaking. Rockefeller was concerned with his recurring theme that the young must move into politics if they intend to share in the life of their times and the preservation of the democratic system. None of his points was particularly new. But it was clear to Oregon politicians that Rockefeller had a direct and, possibly, potent appeal to the people the Republicans had to look to for votes. It would be several months before the Oregon GOP would go Nixon.

That night in Salem, Governor Hatfield came within an ace of putting himself publicly in the Rockefeller camp. The young Governor (he was thirty-seven at the time) lent his endorsement to a big public and faculty meeting for Rockefeller at Willamette University, where Hatfield had been associate professor and dean of students before becoming Governor, and with Mrs. Hatfield sat on the speaking platform with Mr. and Mrs. Rockefeller. His introductory remarks were nonpolitical, but warm in their commendation of Rockefeller as a man to watch.

The remarks heartened the Rockefeller people. They regarded Hatfield as representative of the rising generation of attractive young Republicans who would soon be in position to make their weight felt in party councils—the group that Rockefeller was presumed to appeal to most directly. And in this estimate, Hatfield's posture was singularly outstanding. He'd fought a bitter primary to get the Republican nomination for Governor in 1958, and his election, like Rockefeller's, was one of the few Republican bright spots of that year. Coming from the Northwest, his political tradition was liberal enough to fall within the philosophy of the Eastern-internationalist wing of the Republican Party with which Rockefeller was identified. And if Hatfield, as rumored, cherished the hope that he might wind up with second place on a national ticket with an Easterner at its head, the Rockefeller crowd couldn't hold that against him.

For it was Hatfield's graciousness and his willingness to co-operate that made Rockefeller's visit to Oregon the most success-ful part of his West Coast swing. Rockefeller expressed his grati-tude freely.

The Oregon visit, however, was not a total success. A number of leading Republicans were conspicuous by their absence from the public ceremonies, and the Republican Party, as such, made no effort to provide a forum where Rockefeller could meet the rank and file and do his famous handshaking act, the act that had endeared him to voters, even in Democratic strongholds, in New York City—an act that some of his derogatory critics liked to say, with due allowance for hyperbole, was his greatest political asset.

Seattle on the following morning provided a pleasant sur-prise. It was a cold, gray Sunday, with chill winds whipping across the airport as the chartered Rockefeller plane landed. The drive downtown was dreary.

The stop had been scheduled as a quickie. Rockefeller's prin-cipal purpose in going to Washington was to confer with leaders of the badly disorganized Republican state organization. A break-fast for 150 had been set up to give him a chance to meet some of the more influential party leaders. But the breakfast plans soon got out of hand. A week before Rockefeller arrived, the committee had applications for 350 tickets; by the time he actu-ally appeared, 950 tickets had been sold. And nearly every ticket holder showed up despite the weather and the early hour on Sunday morning.

Rockefeller reacted to the turnout with his usual enthusiasm, and at a press conference that followed he sounded exactly like a candidate, while denying as strenuously as he could that he was contemplating making a run for the nomination. However at the private meeting with the top leaders, he got little encourage-ment to enter the field.

The Western swing ended officially that afternoon in Boise, Idaho. Governor Robert E. Smylie, like Hatfield one of the rising Republican figures in the West, was outgoing in his wel-come, and at a downtown reception most of the business leaders of the state turned out to meet Rockefeller. So far as could be determined, Idaho was maintaining a flexible position.

But one incident marred the stopover. At a press conference, Earl Mazo, respected national political correspondent of the *New York Herald Tribune,* who had made the full swing with the party, informed Rockefeller that the Associated Press was carrying a story about the formation of a Nixon for President Club in New York, with a group of top financial figures on the organizing committee.

"Would you expect to become a member of that club?" Mazo asked.

"No," replied Rockefeller, "but I would expect you to."

Mazo, who'd recently published a biography of Nixon, flushed angrily. He interpreted the somewhat flip reply as an attack "on my integrity as a reporter," and he walked angrily out of the room.

The incident came to nothing.

But in retrospect, it was revealing of the strain Rockefeller was under as the first trip ran out. By nature inclined to lean over backward to avoid embarrassing anyone publicly, and particularly reporters with whom his relations are generally cordial, Rockefeller could only have tossed out the uncharacteristic wisecrack under an emotional stress that was not apparent to others at the time. Had the correspondents been better informed at what went on at the private meetings, they might have been better prepared for Rockefeller's snap answer.

On the way home the following day, Rockefeller interrupted his trip to take care of a gubernatorial chore: an address to the New York State AFL-CIO at its annual convention in Buffalo. Somewhat to his surprise he got a standing ovation from the delegates, although most labor unions had actively opposed him in the 1958 election. The ovation was the more surprising because Buffalo was one of the distressed areas in the state, with a large and growing unemployment problem. It was also a harbinger of things to come.

The homecoming was not to good news. The Western swing had proved undeniably that Rockefeller's appeal as a campaigner could cross state lines, but the scope and style of the trip apparently disturbed the powers-that-be in the Republican Party who wanted a quiet convention. Rockefeller got back to find friends and associates openly injecting themselves into the Nixon movement in what seemed to be a rush to stand up and be counted.

This patently was not because of any fear that Rockefeller constituted a present danger to the plans to nominate Nixon. Every national survey that fall showed Nixon with an unbeatable head start on all comers, and Rockefeller himself seemed to agree with this estimate when the matter was put to him at a press conference. The exchange went this way:

> Question: "Governor, such magazines as *U. S. News* and other outfits have recently in nationwide surveys claimed that it looks as though Vice President Nixon all but has the nomination next year locked up. Would you agree with that?"
>
> Rockefeller: "I wouldn't know. I really don't know."
>
> Question: "Do you get any reports from other people you know around the country which indicate otherwise?"
>
> Rockefeller: "Well, I read the piece that you are referring to in the *U. S. News,* and it seems to me that was a pretty reasonable summary of the situation from what I gather."
>
> Question: "Reasonable and accurate?"
>
> Rockefeller: "Well, I am not in a position to know whether it is accurate. You asked me my opinion, and all I can say is that I thought it was a pretty reasonable piece."

Back home from the West Coast, Rockefeller had reason to accept the accuracy of the surveys, particularly as new advices to stay out of the contest poured in on him from many quarters. But he also had evidence that a certain unrest lay beneath the surface unity of the Republican Party, and that, when the opportunity was allowed him, he could arouse the enthusiasm and interest of rank-and-file Republicans, many of whom told him that they were looking for an alternative to Nixon.

He decided to take a couple more looks at the situation.

Before starting his second, and last, major swing, however, Rockefeller made a one-day foray into New England. It was, in some degree, a homecoming. Rockefeller's destination was Providence, Rhode Island, and his grandfather for whom he was named, the late U. S. Senator Nelson Aldrich, had long dominated the Rhode Island Republican Party. As was to be expected, his reception was warm. The best that could be arranged for him was a luncheon, but it brought out a friendly crowd of Aldriches and their connections, and Governor Christopher Del Sesto introduced Rockefeller graciously, although he did not allow his graciousness to obscure the fact that he was not with him.

And later in his private talks with the party leaders and big contributors, the reaction to Rockefeller was decidedly noncommittal. In a showdown, it was indicated, there might be some shifting of position, but nobody wanted a showdown. It was a consensus that Rockefeller was coming to expect.

But that evening, Rockefeller got another demonstration that the people were interested in him and responsive to his call for debate of national issues, even if the party hierarchy was not. Addressing the New England Society of Newspaper Editors, Rockefeller evoked repeated applause with a not-very-original warning that in the struggle with Soviet Communism the West, and particularly the United States, faced the need of proving to the new nations of the world the values of democracy as opposed to the "seemingly bolder, swifter ways of totalitarianism." This, of course, was not new to the editors. What they seemed to feel was new, as their comments indicated, was that the question was being injected into national debate by a man whom most of them regarded (they were polled informally) as an active candidate for the Republican nomination for President. In any event they seemed to welcome Rockefeller's stand.

On the morning of December 12, 1959, a salesman bound for Cleveland on a nonscheduled flight wandered into an airplane standing on the apron at the Eastern Air Lines hangar at La Guardia Field, New York. Half an hour later, with the plane airborne, the salesman began to realize something was wrong.

This was no ordinary nonscheduled flight. The passengers wandered far too freely up and down the aisle, bantering with each other and swapping insults. Up front, a small group of men, huddled in deep conversation, was left strictly alone. Here and there a portable typewriter tapped.

The luckless salesman had somehow boarded a chartered plane taking Nelson Rockefeller, his staff and a retinue of about fifty political correspondents on his second major swing around the country. The first stop was South Bend, Indiana.

The small foul-up of the lost salesman was quickly straightened out, but the incident was a portent of the snafus that would follow. None would be major; all would be annoying.

Rockefeller stepped from his plane when it landed in South Bend right into the middle of a raging fight in the Indiana Republican Party. He'd been invited to help draw a crowd to a GOP fund-raising dinner on the Notre Dame campus, and he drew guests from all over northern Indiana. But he could hardly have anticipated that the Republicans, split in several directions with the major bloc committed to Nixon, would fight a skirmish during his visit.

That was precisely what happened. United States Senator Homer Capehart, deeply involved in a fight with the state administration, latched onto Rockefeller as a rallying figure and promptly began telling the traveling reporters that he could deliver half the Indiana delegation to Rockefeller for President anytime Rockefeller wanted to declare. It was a rather anomalous situation. Capehart's identification was with the Midwestern rather than the Eastern wing of the Republican Party, and as a Senatorial colleague of Nixon, his sudden espousal of Rockefeller seemed somehow out of character.

Capehart's claim, of course, was never put to the test. But he found a ready audience in the visiting press that night, and Rockefeller apparently felt he was being crowded. For at the dinner he went out of his way to emphasize he wasn't in the race for the nomination. He would soon have to make a decision on his personal political future, he said, but he was not in Indiana to promote his possible candidacy. He went on:

All this is absolutely secondary in my political life, to the overriding consideration that brings me here tonight and that is taking me all over this wonderful land. That consideration is the vitality of the Republican Party and its approach to the great issues of the day.

If I can help to stir up fresh interest in the Republican Party—the Grand Old Party that has given America such giants as Abe Lincoln, Teddy Roosevelt and Dwight Eisenhower—and if I can help the Republican Party to keep its sights trained firmly on the future while the Democrats fritter their time on internal quarrels and nostalgia for those twenty years in the Thirties and Forties, my time will have been well spent, whatever else might occur.

For as a politician, I am dedicated—as I know you are— to one proposition: the Republican Party can, must and will win in 1960.

It was not exactly the kind of talk to cheer the Nixonites. In the fall of 1959 there was a certain amount of "Nixon can't win" talk in the GOP, and, although Rockefeller would later disassociate himself strenuously from this attitude, his reminder that he was a "card-carrying Republican from one of the most Republican states in the Union, measured in terms of victory" was not particularly encouraging to those whose ambitions were involved elsewhere.

Call it political inexperience, call it poor staff work, or whatever, the Indiana experience never should have happened. Rockefeller's problem in the fall of 1959 was to establish his credentials as a Republican with the GOP leaders of the country and to dispel the myth that he was a political dilettante out to claim the Presidential nomination by virtue of his great wealth. Allowing himself to get caught in a savage intraparty row that wasn't remotely of his own making did nothing to accomplish those ends; on the contrary it armed his critics with what they gleefully called an example of his political amateurishness to beat him over the head with.

Unhappy though the outcome was, the South Bend incident proved a fitting curtain raiser for Rockefeller's sortie into the

Mid- and Southwest. In the week that followed, Rockefeller, constantly on the move, would manage to avoid getting tangled up in local battles, but he would get no more encouragement to run for President than he got in Indiana. And, as on his West Coast trip, frequent demonstrations that he could bring out and interest people wherever he went would count for nothing in shaping the attitudes of the controllers of the GOP.

St. Louis was a case in point. More than nine hundred people, well-dressed and obviously well-heeled, gave Rockefeller a warm, even effusive welcome, at a Sunday afternoon reception—described by local political leaders as the biggest turnout in several years— but the top Missouri Republicans could see only Nixon. And like most other top Republicans, they wanted no contest at any level.

Minnesota was a double disappointment. Although many prominent Minnesotans told Rockefeller privately and reporters off the record that they preferred the New Yorker to Nixon, none was bold enough to stand up and be counted. "Our hands are tied," one Congressman explained to a group of correspondents. "The big boys have decided they want Nixon, and we have to go along if we want to survive."

The second disappointment came when Rockefeller presented his farm program before the Minneapolis Junior Chamber of Commerce at the Hotel Leamington. Rockefeller and his staff had been working on the speech for several months, and, since being twitted about overlooking the farm problem by the Inland Press editors in Chicago back in October, Rockefeller had been counting on the presentation to make a big splash. It was wishful thinking.

Only a radical new policy could have produced the reaction Rockefeller wanted, and he was in no position to come up with such a program. His boldest proposal was for doubling the acreage going into the soil bank, which he coupled with a plan to speed up the transition of low-income, inefficient farmers from the land to industry through job training and education. Since the sentimental appeal of the farm problem is based on preservation of the small farm, and since the small farmer jealously guards the right to mismanage his land, the Rockefeller program had little political sex appeal.

From Minneapolis, Rockefeller moved on to Wisconsin where the official Republican organization openly displayed its hostility to him in Milwaukee while he got private assurances at Green Bay from a group of the larger contributors to the GOP that he could count on them for support if he would declare himself. It was the only time on any of his cross-country trips, as Rockefeller was to acknowledge long afterward, that any sizable segment of a state's financial and business community expressed sympathy for his candidacy and a willingness to take on a fight on his behalf if necessary.

There was sound reason for the official Wisconsin Republican attitude toward Rockefeller. Commitment to Nixon by the party leaders was deep, but the evidence indicated that the rank and file would gladly look elsewhere. The Milwaukee organization came up against this when it scheduled a luncheon, as a minimum courtesy, for Rockefeller on December 15, 1959. The luncheon was no more than announced before the luncheon committee was swamped with fifteen hundred applications for tickets. Unwilling to sponsor such an outpouring, the ticket list was limited to members of the Milwaukee GOP committee, holding down the audience to under three hundred. And three months later, a survey by the *Wall Street Journal* showed that only one Wisconsin Republican in seven wanted Nixon.

At the time of his visit, Milwaukee's interest in Rockefeller also was demonstrated by the overflow crowd that packed Memorial Hall to hear him urge on the World Affairs Council that the United States needed to rethink its foreign policy. In liberal Wisconsin, the speech was well-received.

After Wisconsin came the Southwest—Oklahoma City, Dallas and Houston. He was received with the traditional hospitality in the three cities, and at Dallas the World Affairs Council turned out a capacity crowd at a luncheon to hear him call for a "common market" of the Americas to bolster Latin-American growth. But the political intelligence he got from private talks was all discouraging. In fact, the pleasantest thing that happened to him on this leg of the trip was that Speaker of the House Sam Rayburn made a special trip to the Sheraton-Dallas Hotel to welcome Rockefeller to Texas.

"Nelson and I go back a long time," said Mr. Sam. "I just wanted him to know that here in Texas he has friends."

Rockefeller enjoyed the meeting, but having Democratic friends in Texas was exactly no help to him at that stage.

The following morning, Rockefeller flew from Houston to Miami where early winter vacationists, many of them from New York, gave him a cheerful reception.

And the trip ended as it began, with a minor snafu. Rockefeller left the chartered propeller plane at Miami to catch a jet for New York. But the jet developed hydraulic trouble, and for five long hours Rockefeller sat it out on the airstrip while repairs were made. The reporters flew out on schedule; Rockefeller was several hours behind them.

18

The Gage Declined

NELSON ROCKEFELLER is not an introspective man. He likes to say he puts his regrets behind him and goes on to the future because there is no point in wasting time over past mistakes. Yet there is a very good chance that he will live out his life regretting the statement he issued on December 26, 1959, taking himself out of the contest, which he'd never publicly entered, for the Republican nomination for President. In the hindsight of the close election of 1960, friends and critics agreed that Rockefeller may have thrown away his "one best chance" of becoming President of the United States in that 700-word statement.

The decision to quit before he got started was a painful one for Rockefeller. Barnstorming across the country with a full campaign complement of reporters in the week before Christmas, he'd looked, acted and been received by the general public as a candidate for President, when he got a chance to present himself. He'd left the traveling correspondents with the conviction that he would declare himself in an announcement of his political plans around the first of the New Year. On that assurance, the political writers had scattered to their homes.

But that Saturday in Albany the wheels abruptly began turning. There were no correspondents in the pressroom when Dick Amper, Rockefeller's press secretary, and his staff arrived in the late morning to start preparing an important announcement. By the time the mimeograph machines started rolling, most of the correspondents permanently assigned to Albany had been hunted down and summoned to the Capitol. Amper, working the long-distance phones, notified other selected correspondents around the country to be ready for a major statement at 1 P.M. The writers in turn alerted their news desks. Even before the statement was issued, some radio stations were jumping the gun, forecasting that Rockefeller would declare himself a candidate.

The assumption seemed safe enough. Since Rockefeller's upset election as Governor of New York in November, 1958, he'd been considered the only Republican with the political sex appeal to oppose Richard M. Nixon for the nomination. For months, Rockefeller had been calling for a bolder Republican policy as essential to win the Presidency in 1960. And only Rockefeller could propel the party toward this bolder program. Of course, he crossed up the early guessers.

When the withdrawal statement was distributed, Rockefeller himself was not available for comment and the few high Republicans who were privy to his plans had gone underground to get away from reporters.

The statement, a remarkable political document by any standard, was handed out to stand by itself. It said:

> I have come to a definite decision with respect to my candidacy for the Republican nomination for the Presidency. I have done so after long and serious reflection. And my decision has been dictated by clear and sharp convictions.

These convictions bear upon the two political roles that prescribe my responsibilities. The first of these is the position of Governor of New York State. This is an office and an honor plainly commanding my full respect and utterly deserving of my faithful service.

The second role that I must serve is that of any American, namely: responsible citizenship on the national scene. And this responsibility assumes a particularly keen and explicit form when our nation confronts issues and challenges of truly historic size and seriousness.

If I were not profoundly concerned with these issues, I would have no reason to be in public life in any capacity.

I have had to weigh, however, and to decide how best to express this concern. This question has largely inspired the several trips I have recently made through the country. For only by meeting and talking with many citizens of many states could I form a reasoned conclusion as to how I may best serve both the State of New York and the nation.

These trips have made it clear to me, as I believe they have to others, that the great majority of those who will control the Republican Convention stand opposed to any contest for the nomination. Therefore any quest of the nomination on my part would entail a massive struggle—in primary elections throughout the nation—demanding so greatly of my time and energy that it would make impossible the fulfillment of my obligations as Governor of New York.

My conclusion, therefore, is that I am not, and shall not be, a candidate for nomination for the Presidency.

This decision is definite and final.

By this decision, and my intended course of action, I deeply believe that I can best serve the needs of both Party and Country.

As to my Party: I am a Republican—seriously concerned about the future vigor and purpose of my party. I believe that we live in an age that challenges representative government and the two-party system that is its American expression. In such an age, neither of our great parties can hope to meet the issues and opportunities of the future merely with the devices and programs of the past. The vitality—the sense of realism and the sense of purpose—of so great an institution as the Republican Party is, therefore, quite truly a matter of national interest and national need. To the invigorating of this Party's spirit, and to the clarifying of its purposes and policies, all of us who are Republicans should devote our thoughts and energies. In this spirit, I expect to support the nominees, as well as the program, of the Party in 1960.

As to our Country: the national and world issues before us, I deeply believe, hold omen of both menace and hope, both danger and opportunity. We all know the range of these issues: world policies, military defenses, economic growth, educational excellence, racial relations, social needs, public morals. Not one of these spheres tolerates complacence toward the future. Every one of them invites scrutiny. Such a scrutiny must be full and foresighted. For such a time as this calls for a profound and continuous act of national self-examination.

I shall contribute all I can to this political act. I shall speak with full freedom and vigor on these issues that confront our nation and the world.

To all those who have urged upon me a different course with respect to candidacy, I am deeply grateful. I hope and trust they will respect my decision and its reasons.

Quite obviously I shall not at any time entertain any thought of accepting nomination to the Vice Presidency, even if the honor were offered, for this would clearly run counter to all the considerations inspiring my present decision.

I hope my friends will respect this absolutely definite resolve.

I believe I have chosen the right course.

I shall do all in my power, as citizen and as Governor, to make it a creative and constructive one.

The decision created an uproar, not only with the press and general public, but among Republican leaders. The statement was one of the best-guarded secrets of the Rockefeller administration, and only a few top men in the GOP, among them State Chairman Judson Morhouse and National Committeeman George Hinman, had been given advance notice. The rest learned of it through the newspapers.

The surprise decision, and the almost furtive way it was rushed out in the middle of a holiday weekend, provoked wide speculation, most of it on the side of fantasy. The most strenuously promoted story was that the Wall Street financial community, solidly lined up for Nixon at that time, had brought pressure on Rockefeller's brothers to get him out of the contest with a promise that they would be for him later if he'd be a good boy in 1960. Although the idea of pressuring the Rockefellers was ridiculous, on the face of it the story persisted for several months.

There was also a general feeling that Rockefeller's retreat from a fight because certain unnamed people didn't want a contest in the Republican Party was "uncharacteristic" in view of the way he had disregarded all informed advice in making his run for Governor of New York against Averell Harriman.

The situations, of course, were not analogous. In 1958, Rockefeller had everything to gain and nothing to lose in his run for the governorship. No Rockefeller ever had been elected to public office and it was the stated opinion of most political seers, Thomas E. Dewey among them, that no Rockefeller could be elected. Nelson therefore could take a chance without materially altering his status. Even if defeated for Governor, he would still have been in position to exert a measure of influence in the Republican Party and to return to appointive office if he so desired.

By late 1959 all this was changed. In little over a year, Rockefeller had vaulted into a position of national power that could be seriously compromised if he should come off second best in a contest with the Republican leadership. The stakes were too high for him to go for broke.

There was also the matter, sedulously underplayed at the time, that the Republican nomination didn't shape up as the most precious political bauble late in 1959. The election of 1956 had proved that President Eisenhower couldn't translate his popularity into votes for the GOP, and the big Democratic sweep of 1958 seemed a portent that the Democrats would return to power in 1960. It would be several months before Republican hopes would rise on the evidence that the Democrats would have to nominate John F. Kennedy, a Catholic, for President or tear themselves apart. And by that time it would be too late for the Republicans who put unity above all else in 1959 to reconsider their position and their candidate.

Yet almost as soon as the statement was issued, it became apparent that Rockefeller was unhappy about it. Although he used the phrase "definite and final" to underline his withdrawal, he showed keen interest in newspaper observations that his statement had carefully omitted any mention of a draft. Flying to Albany in his private Convair on the Sunday the papers carried his statement, he commented to the reporters still traveling with him that he found the draft suggestions "extremely interesting."

In the next couple of weeks, Rockefeller would play down the draft talk, but in May, long after it was too late for it to mean anything, he would announce his availability if a draft movement were organized. He maintained this position right down to convention time.

But that was for the future after Rockefeller realized just what kind of a box he'd squeezed himself into by giving up before he had at least a position of strength that would give weight to his pronouncements. It was a lesson dearly learned.

Meanwhile, the question of why Rockefeller thought it necessary to bow out of contention was a matter of political debate. Professional politicians simply refused to believe his repeated statement that he acted on what he believed to be the best interests of the party. Such reasoning to them was naïveté. According to standard political practice, Rockefeller should at least have exacted a promise of consideration for his ideas before giving Nixon a clear field.

But all the evidence attests to his sincerity. Although Rockefeller was referring to himself as a politician by late 1959, he was far from being as politically sophisticated as he imagined. As a wealthy man, he had inside experience of the power structure of the national Republican Party and how it impressed its wishes on the organization. What he failed to realize was that this power could be exerted only when expressed in general concepts; that on the organization level, where the direct concern is winning office, a popular figure could exert a counterpressure that Big Money would have to deal with.

Nearly three years later in a long interview at his Pocantico Hills home, Rockefeller acknowledged that his withdrawal was a political mistake of the first magnitude.

"I didn't know," he said. "I'd been in politics what, about a year I guess, and here I was with everybody against me. Everyone I talked to told me I didn't have a chance and that I could only ruin everything."

Rockefeller said the warnings and the polls that, almost without exception showed Nixon in an unbeatable position, had a profound bearing on his decision. "I didn't run for Governor to become a party wrecker," he said. "I couldn't see how I could go ahead with everybody against me."

Another real concern, Rockefeller said, was that if he left the state to campaign in the primaries his tax and other programs would be cut back in the generally conservative Legislature. "I put a lot into that program," he said, "and I wanted to be on hand to make sure we followed through. I thought going around campaigning in the primaries might set back everything I'd tried to do."

Reminded that other governors had successfully campaigned for presidential nominations while in the Executive Mansion without sacrificing their programs, Rockefeller conceded that his judgment on this point possibly might have been a mistake. "I was up against something new," he said.

As for the withdrawal statement, Rockefeller said it was far from as sudden as it seemed. Actually, he said, he'd just about made up his mind after his first swing out to the West Coast in November that 1960 wasn't his year, but went through with his other travels to convince himself.

"We had perhaps ten meetings about it in November and December," he said.

The writing of the withdrawal statement was a long-drawn-out task. The major part of it was turned over to Emmet Hughes, onetime Eisenhower speech writer and later head of the Rockefeller family public relations setup, but many people were consulted, including Frank Jamieson, who was just out of the hospital after lung surgery and was already dying. Others consulted included Wallace Harrison and John Lockwood.

"But I made up my own mind," Rockefeller said. "I listened to what the others had to say and I talked it over with my family. But it was my decision. A lot of people had to be considered, but in the last analysis it was up to me."

Whether, in a showdown, Rockefeller could have wrested the nomination from Nixon and gone on to win against President Kennedy—and many professed to believe after the election that he could have—will always remain a question.

And to Rockefeller the decision to bow out may be a cause of lasting regret unless fate gives him another chance.

19

....

A Time of Troubles

THE YEAR 1960 was a political "time of troubles" for Governor Rockefeller from New Year's through Election Day. Unhappy at the start over his own decision to take himself out of presidential consideration, he soon found that the painful withdrawal had done exactly nothing to put him in the good graces of those who would "control the Republican convention." Nobody, it seemed, would take his statement at face value. Perhaps because he so pointedly avoided mentioning Richard M. Nixon in his December 26th announcement, the professionals waited for him to drop the other shoe. Suspicion deepened rather than faded.

His troubles began right in Albany.

Even before Rockefeller rose at the joint session of the Legislature on January 6th to deliver his annual message, the word was out in the Capitol that several Republican county chairmen were going to declare immediately for Nixon for the Presidential nomination and were looking for allies. By the time the Governor sat down, the report had spread through the chamber and reached the press row.

That Nixonites around the state, and there were many, would press for a declaration in his favor was to be expected. But anything that looked like an organized move to jump the gun might kick off a bandwagon rush that would render New York powerless at the convention. As a matter of party discipline alone, premature commitment had to be blocked.

Stopping it was a routine political exercise. Responsible Republican leaders told the Nixonites pointedly, and as firmly as the occasion required, that New York could best serve itself by remaining uncommitted until after the convention delegates were elected in the June primary. All signs of an organized bolt disappeared.

In itself, the incident was insignificant. But later it was seized on by Rockefeller's critics as the basis of a charge that he was scheming in some devious fashion early in January to "blitz" the convention. This same kind of distrust attached to almost every move he made.

Yet Rockefeller could have done no less without abandoning his position as leader of the New York State Republican Party. And since he is an intelligent man, he was also aware that an uncommitted delegation would be a handy thing to have if Nixon faltered. But there was no sign in January that Nixon would falter, and, of course, he didn't until after his nomination.

Another "plot" charged against Rockefeller in those preconvention months was that he resigned the contest for the Republican nomination at a time when it looked like any Democrat could win, but put himself back in the picture when GOP chances rose after Senator John F. Kennedy's sweep of the primaries confronted the Democrats with the presumed alternatives of nominating Kennedy, a Catholic, and losing on the 1928 pattern, or rejecting Kennedy and losing the Catholics and the election on the 1924 pattern. The charge doesn't bear scrutiny. Even conceding that he hoped against hope late in the spring when he said he would accept a "genuine" draft, it is a matter of record that he made no effort to win delegates. And since when can hoping be equated with scheming?

There can be no doubt that Rockefeller's troubles in 1960 stemmed, at least in part, from the death on January 30th of his friend, confidant and public relations chief, Frank Jamieson. It was a grievous personal loss. For twenty years the two men had worked in tandem, in good going and bad, fighting out their disagreements man to man. "Let's see what Frankie thinks," was a phrase constantly on Nelson's lips, and when the two were separated they checked with each other several times a day by long-distance telephone.

To some observers, Jamieson was the Svengali of Rockefeller's political career. The assessment couldn't have been more inaccurate. Jamieson, who coupled his immense public relations skills with a sure, sensitive touch in politics, actively opposed Nelson's decision to run for Governor in 1958, sensing the Democratic tide that was running strong across the nation as shown in the polls. It was a sound judgment, as proved by the election returns, and neither Jamieson nor the polls could be faulted for failing to anticipate that Rockefeller's unsuspected campaigning talents and a series of fumbles by the Democrats would make New York an exception.

It was a measure of the confidence and respect between the two men that Rockefeller, after overruling Jamieson's more sophisticated political judgment, turned around and placed his political future in Jamie's hands. In the ensuing, brilliantly conceived and executed campaign, it was Jamieson who called the shots, and what he vetoed stayed vetoed, even when the idea originated with Nelson.

Jamieson's death, therefore, was a tremendously unsettling factor for Rockefeller at a critical point in his life. And the dislocation was compounded when less than two weeks later a heart attack killed 44-year-old Dick Amper, whom Jamieson had picked and trained to be Nelson's press secretary. Although Amper had nothing like Jamieson's authority with Rockefeller, or those around the Governor, for that matter, he did represent a continuity of a sort. The two deaths precipitated a public relations crisis.

Rockefeller's prompt promotion of Amper's assistant, Robert L. McManus, to press secretary raised new difficulties. McManus, formerly on the staff of Democratic Governor Harriman, was a brother of a Democratic county chairman, and Republicans in the State Capitol balked at sitting in leadership meetings with him. Eventually, the situation was worked out, but in the immediate period there was considerable stress.

Whether the most skilled public relations could have taken the heat off Rockefeller is moot. The presidential primary season was on, and there were a great many people anxious to involve Rockefeller in one primary contest or another. Some of these efforts were based on the sincere conviction that Rockefeller offered the best hope for the Republican Party and the country; in others it was apparent that local political fights were the real motives. But in no case did the official GOP leadership in any of the sixteen states holding some form of presidential primaries join in inviting him to enter. The less the committed men of the Republican hierarchy heard of Nelson Rockefeller the better it suited them, and, while they remained suspicious, it clearly served their purpose to accept his December 26th statement that he would not run in the primaries as binding and final.

It was a trying time for Rockefeller. The national Republican leadership seemed to be pretending he wasn't there, while carefully scrutinizing everything he did. For his part, Rockefeller lived up to both the spirit and the letter of his withdrawal. Early in January, he refused to allow his name to be entered in the New Hampshire primary—which is important chiefly because it is the first in the nation and presumably carries some bandwagon value—when a group of friends began circulating petitions in his behalf. And on March 2nd, he wrote the Secretary of State in Oregon asking to have his name removed from the primary ballot.

Moreover, he refused all out-of-state invitations for the four-month period from January through April—except for a single trip to campaign for a friend in Pennsylvania—although after the Legislature adjourned in March he could have freed himself to travel without in any way affecting the performance of his duties as Governor. When, in late March, a suggestion was put to him that there were still a couple of primaries he could file in, he merely referred to his December 26th statement. In keeping with this policy of sticking to his knitting in Albany, he also refrained from commenting on national affairs. His only major statement on world affairs was in an article he wrote for the April isssue of the quarterly review, *Foreign Affairs,* in which he discussed in broad, philosophic terms the goals America should set herself in the confrontation with Communism. The article avoided specifics, but restated the Rockefeller thesis, which he'd pressed so strenuously while a White House assistant, that we must deal from strength in any negotiations. He also urged the West to re-examine its aid program to counter the economic offensive the Soviets were waging selectively in the nations on the periphery of the Red-bloc countries. Not even the most rabid partisan could classify the article as political.

In all other respects, Rockefeller conducted himself as a sophomore Governor intent on putting through his legislative program (which he did with very little difficulty, passing his budget unchanged and about 90 percent of his other major proposals) and determined to live up to the compact implied in his withdrawal statement. Privately he watched national politics closely, hoping, no doubt, for some break that would cause the Republican bosses—a word he never used—to reexamine their adamancy against him as a presidential aspirant. His public posture, however, was correct to a degree that was frustrating to well-wishers. They argued, with considerable plausibility, that Rockefeller was fencing himself out of any effective role in party affairs by sidelining himself so completely. The pressure was considerable.

Rockefeller acknowledged as much on March 15th when he put out a second supplement to his December 26th statement—

the first had been issued two days after the original announcement to reiterate that he would not run for Vice President. In the second supplement, Rockefeller called attention to his pledge to "support the nominees as well as the program" of the Republican Party in 1960 and again expressed himself as "seriously concerned" about the party's future.

"I have made no further statement, publicly or privately, on the subject," the second supplement went on. "That was my position then, and it is my position now . . .

"In the December 26th statement, I also said that, 'I shall speak with full freedom and vigor on these issues that confront our nation and the world.' When the legislative session is over, I expect to do so."

That was as far as he would go, and it pleased no one. For his friends it was too little; his critics interpreted it as the loosening of the other shoe.

As it failed to satisfy friend or foe, so the supplementary statement failed signally to achieve what was, to Rockefeller's mind, its paramount purpose: to stimulate a national debate that would enable the Republican Party to assume a policy posture fitted to the requirements of the 1960's. This purpose was always central to Rockefeller's intentions, but he had as little luck getting people to credit his sincerity as he had convincing them that he wouldn't run for Vice President. This obduracy puzzled and offended him; first because he honestly believed the debate was needed to define an American policy of initiative against Communism, and, second, because he was too new to practical politics to realize that public cynicism would attach to all his statements so long as anyone believed he might be lusting after the presidential nomination.

Whether Vice President Nixon recognized the March 15th statement as a challenge doesn't matter. He was, in any event, in no position to speak up. He was a part of the Administration which even then was preparing for the ill-fated Paris Summit Conference and had been part of that Administration for eight years. He couldn't suddenly produce a set of different ideas on how to run things. Besides as the front-runner for the nomination, with no declared opposition in sight, it was his best bet, according to the political book, to avoid anything that even hinted of controversy if he could.

Rockefeller was not insensible of Nixon's difficulties. But the Governor considered that it was entirely within the ground rules to keep up his pressure for a preconvention debate to define positions that would be written into the Republican Party platform. And it was in keeping with these same ground rules early in April that Rockefeller publicly "deplored" a "Nixon can't win" statement circulated to the Republican National Committee.

"This statement," said Rockefeller's spokesman, "was drafted and distributed without the authorization or knowledge of Governor Rockefeller and without the authorization or knowledge of any one associated with Governor Rockefeller, personally, politically, or officially."

Had Richard Nixon responded either to the implied challenge or to Rockefeller's swift and generous disavowal of the "Nixon can't win" movement, the head-on confrontation between the two that ended in Nixon's humiliating "surrender" in the Republican platform fight might have been averted and the postconvention bitterness ameliorated. For, as Nelson said repeatedly in the preconvention period, the positions of the two were close enough to be reconciled if they sat down to work them out. And, considering the narrowness of John F. Kennedy's victory, even the outcome of the election might have been changed.

But the Vice President chose instead to give Nelson the same silent treatment he was getting from most of the GOP top echelon of leadership. As he sat in Albany, signing or vetoing the twelve hundred or so bills left on his desk when the Legislature adjourned, Rockefeller couldn't help but feel that he was being boxed in; that there would be no debate of what he considered the desperately urgent questions of foreign policy and defense unless he himself forced the issue.

Yet he continued to play the game according to the rules as he understood them. While what seemed to be an inspired chorus of statements rose from Republican leaders around the country calling for "Rockefeller for Vice President," he remained in Albany, flying to Pennsylvania toward the end of April to campaign for his friend and college classmate Herman Schneebeli in a special election in the "safe" Republican 17th Congressional District. He also spoke out on foreign policy for the first time in months in an address to the World Affairs Council in Philadelphia, but the only thing political attaching to his talk was a reiteration at the inevitable press conference that he was not a candidate for the Presidency or any other office.

As April merged into May, the tempo quickened. On May 1st, the Vice President told Washington reporters "off the record" that he wanted Rockefeller for Vice President, and a couple of days later Nixon stepped up the heat in New York by saying for quotation that there was "tremendous support" for Rockefeller for a place on the national ticket.

Rockefeller was understandably offended. "Did he say what place?" he asked snappishly later that day when Nixon's New York remark was quoted to him at an Albany press conference.

"Do you assume he meant the Presidency when he spoke about a place on his ticket for you?" was the follow-up question.

"I didn't see the statement."

It was Rockefeller's first public display of annoyance with the Vice President, and, although he quickly softened it by saying, "Dick Nixon is a very good friend of mine," the surprise was not that he should show a flash of irritation but that it was so long in coming. For months Rockefeller's political leadership of the New York State Republican Party had been under siege by Nixon forces; allies of the Vice President had trumpeted for a Nixon-Rockefeller ticket with the idea of putting Nelson on the spot, and now, without troubling to pick up a phone, Nixon was adding to the pressure in Rockefeller's home state. The patience of Job, after all, had its limitations.

And from this point on the personal relationship between Nixon and Rockefeller deteriorated. Not that it had ever been close. The "friendship" of which both men spoke was never more than a kind of political respect that developed out of working together toward common goals. Even when Rockefeller was part of the Eisenhower Administration and living in Washington, the two never met socially except at official functions. After Nelson left Washington, they rarely met at all.

No sooner had Rockefeller got through saying that he wouldn't take the vice-presidential nomination "no matter who might ask, or under any circumstances," than new pressure was turned on. Senator Thruston B. Morton, of Kentucky, chairman of the Republican National Committee, formally invited Rockefeller to be temporary chairman and keynoter of the Republican National Convention, or, alternatively, permanent chairman. In either role, the New York Governor would have been effectively gagged.

Before Rockefeller could answer, his father died on May 10th and Nelson dropped politics for a few days. The loss was a heavy one. Nelson and his father often seemed to be at cross-purposes, but John D., Jr., encouraged and was proud of his son's political career.

But politics and the world took no pause. By the time Rockefeller got around to rejecting Morton's invitation, events had overtaken and passed him. Once again his leadership in New York was under a Nixonite attack, this time a threat so serious it could have wrecked his political base and left him voiceless, so to speak, in the climactic weeks leading up to the Republican National Convention.

The threat came from the so-called Taft country in upstate New York where rural county chairmen were straining at the restraint imposed on them to remain uncommitted until after the June primary. The chosen battleground was a fund-raising dinner of the Republican organization run by Congressman John Taber, famous for his budget cutting, in the sprawling 36th Congressional District. Taber, an outspoken Nixon man, had invited the Vice President as guest of honor. Rockefeller, although the leader of the party in the state, was conspicuously omitted from the guest list, a snub that was not lost on him.

Even as Rockefeller turned down Morton's offer of the convention posts on May 14th, writing that he would stay away from the convention because "my mere attendance . . . could be misconstrued by the delegates" as a back-door bid for the nomination for Vice President, which he was again refusing, reports circulated that there would be a mass bolt to Nixon at the Taber dinner.

This was far more serious than the movement that had been quashed back in January. Leonard W. Hall, who'd been steamrollered out of the gubernatorial nomination by Rockefeller in 1958, was now running Nixon's campaign, with particular attention to New York, and it was conceded that he had the backing of enough county chairmen to command perhaps as many as thirty delegates to the convention in a showdown. If any such bloc declared for Nixon at the Taber dinner, it would be tantamount to repudiation of Rockefeller as party leader.

State Chairman Morhouse, trying to keep the troops in line, threw a block at the bolt by expressing the opinion that Rockefeller's position was shifting and he might now accept a draft. It was the best Morhouse could do under the circumstances. On the surface nothing had changed, and he couldn't go charging in warning against change. But the reaction was nil. The Nixon forces apparently didn't get the message until Rockefeller himself let the Republican State Committee know that he was open to a draft. Once again the New York delegation was frozen.

This sequence is important because a theory was later developed that Rockefeller seized on the national embarrassment over the U–2 spy incident as an opportunity to reactivate his presidential ambitions. The theory was both indefensible and insulting. The record shows that Rockefeller never did anything to encourage the draft; that the "campaign staff" he'd assembled in 1959 and dismantled after his withdrawal was never reassembled, and that even his draft availability was never publicly announced but was "leaked" from the state committee meeting by others.

Long afterward Rockefeller said, perhaps with the extra realism of retrospect, "I knew there would never be a draft, but I had to do something to make them listen to me." It is quite possible that in his secret heart he may have Walter Mitty-ed a delegate stampede in the surcharged preconvention atmosphere, but if he did, he never tried to make the daydream come true.

The theory was insulting because it dismissed out of hand

Rockefeller's sincere, and, indeed, passionate concern for the American position in the fearful confrontation with Communism that Nikita Khrushchev forced on the world as the result of the U–2 affair. This concern, Rockefeller felt, required him to put before the GOP high command and the country, in the most forceful terms possible, his views, developed out of firsthand experience, on what he considered the dire need for a sweeping defense buildup and a more effective foreign policy that would forestall Red aggression. For this was a period, remember, when U. S. intelligence sources were estimating that the Soviets had achieved a missile-firing superiority over the West that would endure for a minimum of three or more years.

It is in this context that Rockefeller's course in May, 1960, must be examined. From May 5th, when Khrushchev announced the shooting down of Francis Gary Powers, a Central Intelligence Agency spy pilot, in his U–2 reconnaissance plane deep in Russian territory, Rockefeller watched with dismay the almost incredible mishandling of the situation by the Administration. Our denial that there ever was a spy was exposed as a lie before the world when Khrushchev produced Powers and his confession. And we fumbled repeatedly as the Soviet dictator brilliantly and brutally exploited the incident to wreck the Paris Summit Conference, and insult President Eisenhower, whom Khrushchev publicly called a "hypocrite" and "liar." The President's humiliation in Paris at what was to have been the crowning international conference of his eight years in the White House was painfully disturbing to Rockefeller.

He said as much on May 23rd when he broke his five-month silence on national and world affairs. "We have reason to be proud of the dignity and integrity of the President," Nelson declared as he called on Republicans and Democrats to put aside partisan debate to make "the act of national re-examination" of our policies "an act of realism, an act of renewed and reasoned dedication." In a statement issued from Albany, he said:

I fervently hope that the Democratic Party, in its proper desire to get at the facts, will not engage in any shallow partisan effort to assign all error to its adversaries, all wisdom to itself . . .

I hope—no less fervently for being a Republican—that Republicans will not try to disguise the present situation for equally partisan reasons. For it would be false and frivolous—and ultimately damaging to both nation and party—to dismiss sober criticism of specific American conduct as a peril to national unity.

This was a strong challenge to an Administration already reeling from its own fumbles and Khrushchev's gleeful, unrelenting and savage pressure, and Rockefeller did nothing to soften it by listing "a few facts essential to serious analysis [that] are, already, clear enough." He declared:

> One—the failure of the Paris Conference—in the wake of the implacable aggressiveness of the Soviet Premier and in spite of the admirable dignity of the President—places in serious question some of the illusions, as well as the procedures, that led to the summit itself.
>
> Two—the crudity of Soviet conduct gives neither reason nor excuse for denying that some aspects of American conduct, immediately prior to the conference, demand examination of their purpose and prudence.
>
> Three—we know that the cost of recent events will be borne not only by ourselves and the Soviet Union but also by our allies throughout the world, now sure to suffer harsher Soviet pressure, hence now more than ever anxious to see us display honest sense of proportion and calm sense of purpose.

Rockefeller was not so naïve as to underestimate the political impact of this spelling out of the blunders of an Administration controlled by his party. He fully realized, as he told those around him, that no one was going to thank him. But his sense of crisis was urgent, and, from his own experience in the State Department, he had little hope that anything meaningful could be accomplished without the goad of political pressure. It was his purpose to explode the question into the open and shatter what he considered the dangerous complacency of the Republican Party.

Yet Rockefeller, who would be proved a prophet in the coming weeks as the Communist-directed mobs rose around the world—in Tokyo to bar a goodwill visit by the President of the United States, in Korea and Turkey to assault Western-oriented governments supported by the American Administration—made no effort to capitalize personally on the situation. On the contrary, after issuing his call he refrained from any follow-up to give the party time to reflect.

Exactly nothing happened. In the next two weeks it was borne in on Rockefeller that, unless he took positive action, his voice would go unheeded. While he waited, Rockefeller carefully reviewed his own position on the problems facing the country, refining the list and settling on the points he felt it mandatory to develop before the convention in July. Working closely with Emmet Hughes, Nelson roughed out a series of speeches to be delivered if the GOP leadership continued to stand pat.

Meanwhile Rockefeller stayed close to New York. He made one out-of-state trip, flying to North Dakota on June 3rd–4th to campaign for John Davis in the special election for U. S. Senator. The invitation had been extended by Senator Morton, as national chairman, and the North Dakota State Republican Committee, several weeks earlier, and Rockefeller avoided bringing his rather one-sided dialogue with the national leadership into his speeches.

In his only significant North Dakota address, he urged the stockpiling of farm surpluses in strategically located areas around the country to feed the people in case of nuclear war. He noted that a year's stockpile would take nearly half the wheat surplus and "turn a present liability into a great national asset." Nobody, apparently, listened except the North Dakota farm audience.

Back in New York it now was unmistakably clear that Vice President Nixon and his advisers were going to continue the silent treatment of Rockefeller. Although the Democrats were in ferment over foreign policy, with Adlai Stevenson once again being talked up as a possible nominee, the Republicans ignored the Rockefeller challenge on the highest levels, while on the lower echelons there was only condemnation of the New York Governor for rocking the boat with the convention only weeks away. The time had come for action.

The course Rockefeller chose was so politically dangerous that most of his closest advisers were against it, fearing the very great possibility of failure. Time and again Rockefeller had been told by the proprietors of the Republican Party to be a good boy in 1960 and they'd look more kindly on his ambitions the next time around. Now he was mounting a frontal assault on their chosen nominee on the battleground of issues which the high command would prefer to settle quietly in a convention committee. "If you go through with this," Rockefeller was told by one Republican leader, "you could sink yourself permanently." The Governor brushed aside the advice.

"I couldn't wait any longer," he explained after the election. "The convention was too close."

On June 8th, he moved on two levels. While he met the executive committee of the New York State Republican Committee at the Hotel Roosevelt in New York to announce his intention of heading the state delegation to the national convention, his Albany office put out a blockbuster statement directly challenging the Vice President and "the new spokesmen of the Republican Party" to "declare now . . . what they believe and what they propose to meet the great matters before the nation." Rockefeller said:

> "The vitality and integrity of the Republican Party, at so critical a time as the present, become matters of national concern. Without a two-party system that works with candor and courage, the American Republic—the very processes of democratic government—cannot work responsibly. Without the Republican Party displaying such candor and courage, the two-party system cannot work creatively . . .
>
> "I am deeply convinced, and deeply concerned, that those now assuming control of the Republican Party have

failed to make clear where this party is heading and where it proposes to lead the nation.

"Now is the time to face and weigh these facts."

The facts were such, Rockefeller said, that he couldn't "pretend to believe that the Republican Party" had fulfilled its duty of providing "an assurance—and a strategy—of national purpose" for the conduct of the nation.

"I know it is unconventional on the political scene to mention lacks or lapses in one's own party," he went on. "But the times we live in are not conventional. And the scene we must view is not simply one of partisan politics, but the politics—perhaps the destiny—of all the world."

But Rockefeller didn't rest at a challenge. After carefully trying to absolve the President—("No attack or abuse from any quarter can diminish—it can only dramatize—the dignity and the integrity of the leadership that President Eisenhower has given to both nation and party")—Rockefeller undertook to list "a number of problems, concrete and crucial, on which the Republican party—and any of its leaders—must state their stands." The listing, upon examination, amounted to an indictment of the major policies followed by the Eisenhower Administration.

Rockefeller started with the premise—wounding to the Administration which was being belabored with similar charges by Senator John F. Kennedy on his way to the Democratic nomination—that the U. S. position in the world was "dramatically weaker" than at the end of World War II and that only drastic means would stop the decline. He found the United States unprepared, despite the huge defense budget, to meet the "physical danger" of nuclear war, and totally unready to fight brush wars with conventional weapons. The Soviets, he said, outclassed us in missiles, could blast our strategic bombers on the ground and had little to fear from our Polaris submarines, then building.

He called for increasing defense spending by $3 billion a year, plus another $500 million for civil defense, reorganization of "our whole government structure" with emphasis on a "more tightly organized Department of Defense," and increased pressure for "adequate and formal international inspection and control of arms."

Domestically, he said, the United States needed to step up its growth rate by at least 50 percent, revise taxes to encourage investment, end labor featherbedding, institute compulsory arbitration for strikes "endangering the national welfare," speed up desegregation on all fronts, provide Federal aid to education and develop a medical insurance program under the "proven" system of Social Security.

"There remain less than two months before the Republican Party assembles in convention to set its course and to choose its leaders," Rockefeller said. "This time must be spent in one way: In placing the facts before the people and in summoning the people to the great endeavors that these facts demand . . . The path of great leadership does not lie along the top of a fence.

"Is the party ready?" That was the raw meat of the Rockefeller challenge.

It was a gallant and daring undertaking. Rockefeller stood alone before the nation as the "conscience" of the Republican Party, demanding that its preordained nominee for President break with the Administration he had served for eight years and chart a course repugnant to his commit.ed delegates, to President Eisenhower, on whom he leaned so heavily, and to the proprietors of the GOP.

Rockefeller was ill-armored for the contest. He had no delegates; his control of the New York delegation was at best shaky and, unquestionably, would have broken in a showdown; his announced availability for a draft, perhaps because it came so late, had evoked little enthusiasm; and the following he'd picked up in 1959 had made other accommodations after his withdrawal statement. Against him the Vice President held all the power of the Republican Party, control of the apparatus of the convention and the prestige of the President.

But Rockefeller had in his arsenal one weapon more potent than the party professionals realized: ideas. To millions of Americans, of both parties, shuddering under the clanking of Khrushchev's hydrogen bombs in far-off, but missile-close, Moscow, and watching Fidel Castro, who'd been put in power with the Eisenhower Administration's blessing, seize American properties as he moved Cuba, just ninety miles offshore, into the Communist bloc, Rockefeller seemed to be calling for action to relieve the intolerable suspense of waiting.

To Vice President Nixon it was, at long last, a challenge that could not be ignored. It was directed at him personally as "the leading Republican candidate for the presidential nomination." It implied criticism of the Eisenhower Administration that he could not let stand. If he let it go unanswered, the press, which Nixon always distrusted, would start repeating and spreading the challenge.

But Nixon was playing it cool. Rather than dignify the Rockefeller challenge by replying under a newsworthy Washington dateline, he shifted the scene to Camden, New Jersey, where he was to address a dinner for a local Congressman. Late on the afternoon of June 9th, as political reporters scrambled into town from New York and Washington, the television network crews from Philadelphia set up their cameras and lights in the main ballroom of the Walt Whitman Hotel for a press conference. About fifty newsmen were on hand.

The Vice President arrived about six o'clock, nearly forty-five minutes late, and apparently was surprised to find so large a press corps assembled. He was relaxed, however, and, in keeping with the low key of his attitude, there was no prepared statement. His manner indicated that this was merely a routine exercise in public relations.

He simply couldn't understand, he said, what Rockefeller was talking about. His position, Nixon said, was known to everybody; as Congressman and Senator his votes were in the record; as Vice President he had taken his stand on nearly every question facing the country. Few men in public life, he said, had declared themselves so many times in so many places on so many questions of high importance.

As for the issues staked out by Rockefeller in his challenge, Nixon said, they represented differences in degree and approach rather than fundamental splits. These were matters to be threshed out by the platform committee, which would come up with the right solutions. He left the impression that he felt Rockefeller was being crowded by overzealous supporters into a position he never sought. But, if it would make the Governor happy, he said, he'd be glad to answer his questions on television.

Rockefeller read the statement as it came off the wires and fired up his mimeograph machines in Albany. He was unable, he said, "to reconcile the contradictory responses" of Nixon and his supporters.

"The Vice President insists today," Rockefeller commented, "that he has spoken his views on all national issues in great detail. But his supporters simultaneously insist that he has been perfectly correct in not stating his views . . .

"I reiterate my firm conviction that the people of this country are entitled to receive from the Vice President no less than a clear, candid statement of his views on the emerging problems that challenge, as never before, the security and well-being of the American people—such as the problems listed in my statement yesterday. Certainly the Republican Party and its delegates are entitled to this statement now, and not after the Republican convention."

Rockefeller spurned the television discussion curtly.

"He does not need me to interrogate him on television," he said. "Once the Vice President has made his position clear on the specific issues . . . I shall be glad to debate these issues with him."

With this exchange, Rockefeller dropped all pretense that he was seeking debate with unspecified leaders. From now on it was Rockefeller versus Nixon, man to man. The drama, such as it was, of their conflict would color the remaining weeks before the Republican convention. But it would be a curiously one-sided performance so far as the public was concerned; to some inside the Republican Party it would be a "rule or ruin" fight by a disappointed hopeful; to others, more sophisticated, it would be a power struggle to shape the party. Few would credit Rockefeller with seeking what he always claimed was his paramount goal: a debate that would shift American policy from the passivity of reacting to the Reds to seizure of the initiative in the Cold War.

For Nixon would not and did not debate. Barring a miracle, he had the nomination locked up. Controversy was the last thing he wanted. For seven and a half years he'd been pointing for the prize that was almost within his grasp, and he could do himself no good in an intraparty fight. Once again his attitude was that Rockefeller wasn't there.

Rockefeller plugged ahead, but there were a number of obstacles. Months earlier his strategists, not knowing what June might bring, had decided to keep his schedule open for that month. Now June was here, and the only speaking dates he had were within the state, and, at the very time when it would best have served his purpose to be facing large forums around the country, no new invitations were coming in. Furthermore, with nobody answering him back, the press was more interested in the doings of the always colorful Democrats who seemed to be getting set for a tremendous brawl.

If Rockefeller felt at times like a man talking in a rain barrel—and he has admitted he did—he nevertheless shirked no opportunity to speak his piece. To startled Rotarians at lunch in Binghamton, New York, he outlined an involved government reorganization program calling for the creation of a First Secretary who would rank Cabinet officers and perform, in general, the functions of a prime minister. To Young Republicans expecting a pep talk in New York City, he presented a comprehensive program for unity in the Western Hemisphere. At a Baptist Convention in Buffalo, he put forward a strong civil rights program going far beyond anything the Eisenhower Administration ever countenanced. From Albany came a series of what his staff nicknamed "white papers," spelling out his position on arms control, automation, economic growth and like matters. He testified before a Senate subcommittee in Washington to urge reorganization of the Defense Department. He fought at the Governors' Conference at Glacier Park, Montana, for a strong Federal civil defense program.

It was an assault carried on under intermittent harassment.

Rockefeller and Mrs. Rockefeller arrived at the Governors' Conference in Glacier Park late in June, for example, to be confronted with a round robin signed by all Republican governors, pledging them to support Nixon for the nomination. Nelson got out of that, easily enough, by pointing out that he was chairman of an uncommitted delegation and couldn't endorse anyone. He also tweaked the GOP noses by teaming up with Democratic Governor G. Mennen Williams of Michigan in drafting a health insurance report keyed to Social Security payments, a program the National Administration adamantly opposed.

Yet Rockefeller's campaign in the six weeks from June 8th, when he issued his challenge, to July 18th, when the Republican Platform Committee opened hearings in Chicago, was truly a virtuoso performance. Powered only by ideas, he became in that period a force in his party that the regulars would have to deal with. He won no delegates in that assault; he never got within striking distance of the nomination; but he stood forth as the leader of a whole army of independent Republicans who cared nothing for the machinery of politics but whose votes would be desperately needed in the populous, internationally oriented states of the industrial Northeast. And by the time the focus shifted to the platform committee, the regulars and their man Nixon were looking ahead to voters rather than delegates.

But Rockefeller's political position was both exposed and ambiguous when he flew to Washington on July 1st to testify at a Senate hearing in support of his government reorganization plan. His appearance had been scheduled before he started his cannonading to redefine the Republican position, and there was no question of propriety, because he possessed substantial credentials as an expert on government reorganization, having headed the President's Advisory Committee for five years. But the Republican regulars bitterly resented his taking a proposed platform plank before a Senate committee controlled by Democrats, before the platform was written.

And his *sub rosa* blessing of a national Draft Rockefeller movement that blossomed two days earlier in San Francisco had again stirred up suspicions that he would use his millions in a last desperate effort to blitz the convention as Wendell Willkie had blitzed the 1940 convention in Philadelphia.

The hardiness of this suspicion, which endured until the New York delegation caucused in Chicago and declared for Nixon, must be put down to the American folk belief that the Republicans never turn away a man who is rich enough. Certainly the analogy between Rockefeller, 1960, and Willkie, 1940, was so imperfect as to be meaningless. Willkie's blitz was as patiently and meticulously planned as a major invasion. For two years, he'd been lining up support around the country. The convention he faced was open to deadlock with several possible candidates in the wings. When the button was pushed for the assault, the telegrams that went out to switch the delegates' votes were sent from Wall Street. Rockefeller in 1960, on the other hand, had no committed delegates (it remains doubtful that he could have held New York solid), he'd discouraged earlier attempts to line up citizen support outside the regular organization and leagued against him were the same potent financial interests that twenty years earlier had imposed Willkie on the convention.

The Draft Rockefeller movement itself lived out its short, unhappy life in a kind of limbo. William Brinton, a young San Francisco lawyer, who'd set up a National Citizens Committee for Rockefeller in 1959, flew to New York late in June while Rockefeller was in Montana and got a go-ahead from the Governor's aides to organize the committee on his own. The go-ahead amounted to little more than a promise that the committee wouldn't be publicly repudiated. Neither then nor later, Rockefeller has repeatedly insisted, was any Rockefeller money put into the project.

Nor were the draft committee leaders ever taken into Rockefeller's confidence. Liaison between the drafters and the Rockefeller staff was so slight as to be tenuous, and Rockefeller's own specialist on citizen committees, Oren Root, Jr., a veteran of the Citizens for Willkie, conspicuously stayed aloof from the Brinton crowd. The drafters, in fact, were still carrying their banners and shouting their slogans after all the decisions had been made.

At its peak, the committee claimed to control 275 convention votes, a highly suspect figure, since it undoubtedly included all of New York's 96, and from a mathematical standpoint the Brinton operation was never a convention factor.

Nevertheless it was not without impact. In two major advertising efforts in twenty-nine important newspapers and on national TV, it focused attention on the nationwide interest in Rockefeller and what he stood for. And, although the volunteers never got a chance to engage in political battle, they perhaps rate an assist for spotlighting the sentiment in the country for Rockefeller's ideas and thus helping prepare the convention for the platform he would give it.

The volunteers also provided a spot of color for a convention that shaped up as drab and lifeless as the Republican performance in San Francisco in 1956 when President Eisenhower was nominated for the second term. Setting up headquarters in the Conrad Hilton Hotel and the Blackstone Theatre, across the street, on July 18th, they filled Chicago hotel lobbies for a week with pretty girls distributing buttons and literature, and from time to time marched their bands around. The delegates, who knew very well they were being managed, appeared to relish the trappings of a convention since the decisions apparently were foreclosed.

But Rockefeller waged his deadly serious political fight far from these pleasant excitements. From July 1st on, it was apparent that if he failed to impose his ideas on the platform committee, he would be exiled from the party councils for a long time to come. But he also faced the problem of getting his way without being euchred into running for Vice President.

This called for high skill in political tightrope walking. It was the consensus of the regular Republicans that a Nixon-Rockefeller ticket, with Nixon on top, of course, would be nearly unbeatable. And being realists, they were quite willing, if that would shut him up, to go along with many of the things that Rockefeller wanted in the platform, which they regarded, in any circumstances, as an empty exercise in rhetoric. But this was precisely what Rockefeller wouldn't countenance. He was under no

illusions that a platform alone would bring a metamorphosis in
the character of the men controlling the party, but he fully realized that any "deal" for what he considered important would
destroy the statement of purpose he was after.

Came now the days of testing. Early in July, Charles H.
Percy, chairman of the Republican Platform Committee, who
had spent more than a year trying to draw up a statement of Republican philosophy, called on Rockefeller in New York with
a preliminary draft of the platform he would submit to the full
platform committee in Chicago. For three and a half hours in
Rockefeller's office on the second floor of 22 West 55th Street,
the two men went over the draft line by line, paragraph by paragraph. Occasionally Rockefeller called in an aide to get an expert
or legal opinion on definitions.

Rockefeller had a high regard for the brilliant young Percy,
who at forty was president of Bell and Howell. Although picked
by Nixon a year or so before for the task of defining the GOP
philosophy and gravitating naturally from that job to the platform committee, he was not identified with either wing of the
party. The platform he proposed to offer was framed to touch all
bases, and it was acceptable to Nixon and President Eisenhower.
Rockefeller found it seriously wanting. He saw the flames of
crisis around the world; the preliminary draft, to his view, ignored the crisis.

On July 9th, in a "Dear Chuck," letter, Rockefeller put his
rejection in writing. He appreciated, he said, "the long, thought-
ful and candid exchange of views we had the other day," but he
insisted the issues were so grave that the party must state them
with "vigor and force" if it hoped "to serve the nation or itself."

"The Republicans cannot offer the people, in the year 1960,
a document that fails to honor the intelligence of the American
people, to heed the facts of life in the world, or to meet the
challenges plainly before all free men," Rockefeller wrote. "This
would be no way to serve the country. Nor, incidentally, would
it be any way to win a national election."

In an accompanying memorandum, the New York Governor
made it clear that facing the facts and meeting the challlenges

called, among other things, for an arms buildup far beyond anything President Eisenhower ever advocated, a civil rights plank
so tough that, inescapably, it implied criticism of the Administration for not doing enough, and soaring programs for North
Atlantic and Western Hemisphere unity. He still wanted reorganization of the national government and of the Defense Department, with all officers above the rank of brigadier removed
from their separate services into an interservice command corps,
an immediate resumption of underground nuclear testing which
had been abandoned by the Eisenhower Administration in an
informal moratorium (to be broken by the Soviets in the following year) and strong action for Federal aid to education.

In brief, what Rockefeller wanted was nothing less than a
total rewrite of the preliminary draft. He would "welcome discussion" of "honest differences," but, although he made no
threats, it was plain that he wasn't going to give up very much.

But Percy, who achieved what many considered a remarkable
consensus in reconciling Republican differences over a long year
of work, wasn't disposed to write a new platform draft on Nelson
Rockefeller's say-so. He neither spurned nor approved the Rockefeller demands, but he had had a great deal of experience in
the unrewarding task of trying to write sentences that would
please, say, Barry Goldwater, of Arizona, and Jacob K. Javits, of
New York, and he knew what lay ahead. The matter was put
over for the meeting of the platform committee in Chicago.

In the meantime, Rockefeller stuck close to Albany in the
tradition of New York governors intimately involved in national
conventions. He backed up his civil rights proposals with action
by promulgating by executive order a Fair Practices Code for
state employes. And he watched the Democratic antics in Los
Angeles on television as Senator John F. Kennedy, who took the
primary route that Nelson spurned, bent his party bosses to his
will. It must have been wry watching. For the proprietors of the
Democratic Party had wanted no part of Kennedy in 1959, as
the proprietors of the Republican Party had wanted no part of
Rockefeller. But Kennedy, by boldness, had won what he wanted,
while Rockefeller, who prides himself on his boldness, had

thrown away his opportunity. Possibly, also, he watched the rout of the Adlai Stevenson volunteers as their last-minute draft failed.

The headquarters hotel of the New York delegation at the Republican National Convention was the Sheraton Towers, hard by the *Chicago Tribune*. When the Rockefeller vanguard arrived on Sunday, July 17th, they ran head on into a convention of dancing masters who were having so much fun winding up their meeting that they were reluctant to give up their rooms. Gradually, by dint of persuasion, they were moved out and space cleared. But early-arriving reporters had to double up overnight.

To the press and to those delegates who got a chance to view it close up, the Sheraton Towers layout looked exactly like a campaign command headquarters. One wing of the hotel was reserved for the Governor's party and staff, at a cost of $1,000 a day, a special switchboard was installed with connections to the rooms of all the principal New York delegates, and outside trunks were set up for swift communication with New York and with the convention headquarters in the Conrad Hilton. Elevator timetables were juggled to provide direct and frequent service to the tower offices where the key people worked. Two large rooms were set aside for the working press on a floor at a discreet remove from the staff quarters.

The staff that moved in was easily the biggest of any delegation at the convention. Besides the press secretaries, speech writers and researchers, there were stenographers, typists, mimeograph machine operators. There was Rockefeller's personal stenotypist, who accompanies him everywhere, and there were switchboard operators. There was a staff photographer and a movie cameraman. By the time the convention opened, experts were shuttling back and forth from New York almost on a commuter schedule.

On Monday, July 18th, while the staff was still settling in, Rockefeller flew to Chicago for a two-day visit, the stated purpose of which was to testify on the following day before the Republican Platform Committee, and he showed considerable irritation with newspaper stories describing his headquarters setup. It was "absolutely not correct," he said, that his switch-board had six trunk lines to New York.

"I have an office, and I have lines in the hotel to members, the key members of our staff and delegation," he said. "It seems to me it is the only intelligent thing to do, if you are head of a delegation you have to keep in touch with them, if you are going to lead them. Otherwise you have to follow them."

The big staff layout, however, intrigued the press. When Rockefeller faced about 150 newsmen that afternoon at a press conference in the Conrad Hilton Hotel, at least 90 percent of the questions revolved around his possible candidacy for Vice President or as a draft candidate.

Almost, it seemed, Rockefeller's long fight to impose his principles on the Republican Platform Committee was being downgraded as an empty exercise rather than the deadly serious struggle it was. The oversight was understandable. One week before the convention opened, no one, it appeared, realized that the shaping of the platform would be the critical political controversy of the Republican session. On the contrary, as Rockefeller faced the cameras and microphones that Monday afternoon, the chief emphasis of the press was on pinning Rockefeller down to what he would consider a "genuine" draft. He finally settled for a "consensus of the majority of the delegates of the convention which would make 666 or more votes which is what is needed for nomination.

"That," he added, "would be my idea of a genuine draft."

This amounted to acknowledgment that the draft movement was already marked for demise, but, instead of focusing attention on the platform fight, it served merely to shift the questioning to Rockefeller and his possible nomination for the Vice-Presidency. Often as he had said that he wouldn't consider the second place under any circumstances, he was again led through the rigamarole of restating his position. This meaningless exercise would continue.

And Rockefeller himself signally failed to convey the sense of urgency he felt about the Republican platform. He obscured his deep conviction that the GOP must come out strongly on civil rights and for vastly increased defense spending, as well as other issues, by repeatedly insisting that he expected the Percy committee to come up with a "platform which we Republicans and the people of this country will feel reflects both a recognition of the issues and tangible concrete suggestions and methods for achieving their solution."

These certainly were not fighting words. Newsmen, long conditioned to the view that platforms are written to be thrown away, could hardly be blamed for concentrating on other things.

Nor for that matter did the Republican Platform Committee itself give any sign that it recognized a crisis aborning. Although Percy and his key aids were still working feverishly on compromises that would satisfy Rockefeller, the full platform committee heard Rockefeller testify the next day without excitement. Only four questions, none of them very probing, were asked after he read his prepared statement, and his resubmission of his policy views, as set forth in his letter to Percy earlier, as a Republican Party centennial memorandum to the committee, got only passing attention. Yet the issue had been joined.

After Rockefeller returned to Albany that afternoon, his chief spokesman on the platform committee, New York State Assembly Speaker Joseph F. Carlino, began stating the Rockefeller points more forcefully. As the days passed, mutterings were heard that New York would go to the floor with the platform issues unless its views were listened to. Percy redoubled efforts to find wording that would be acceptable to Rockefeller and the committee.

Still the air of crisis was missing. The platform subcommittees worked on as though Rockefeller hadn't spoken.

Friday, Rockefeller called for a showdown. In his office in the State Capitol in Albany, his press secretary, Bob McManus, put out a brief statement laying down the challenge.

"The Governor," the statement said, "has been keeping in touch with all developments on shaping the platform through the Governor's staff in Chicago specifically assigned to this task. . . . He is deeply concerned that the reports reaching him clearly indicate that the drafts on a number of matters—including national defense, foreign policy and some critical domestic issues—are still seriously lacking in strength and specifics.

"These matters are among the most important in the whole platform.

"The Governor is convinced that vigorous and forthright positions in all these areas—and in the particularly crucial case of civil rights—are vital both for the nation and the Republican Party."

This was the point of no return for Rockefeller. For more than six months, ever since his December 26th statement acknowledging that the controllers of the Republican Party wanted no part of him, Rockefeller had been moving toward this confrontation. What national support he commanded attached to the ideas he stood for. Both politically and as a matter of principle, he had to follow through. His personal political risk was enormous. If he failed to achieve a substantial part of what he wanted, he faced the possibility that his own state delegation would bolt, leaving him discredited before the country.

He was not, however, entirely without cards. The proprietors of the Republican Party wanted above all things to avoid a floor fight that might endanger their control of the convention by stirring up quiescent bitterness. And the Rockefeller viewpoint had wide support among nonorganization Republicans whose money and votes would be essential to any chance of election.

But in the showdown, help came from an entirely unexpected quarter—Richard M. Nixon.

For Nelson Rockefeller, the Republican presidential convention of 1960 ended, for all practical purposes, as dawn grayed the skies over New York on Saturday, July 23rd, two days before the gavel pounded down to call the delegates to order for the opening session at the Stockyards in Chicago, nearly nine hundred miles away.

Around three o'clock that morning in Rockefeller's triplex apartment high above Fifth Avenue, Rockefeller and Richard M. Nixon put the final period to their celebrated and explosive agreement to rewrite the all-but-drafted Republican platform to cover fourteen hard specifics demanded by Rockefeller. Implicit in the agreement, although it was never so stated, was an understanding that if Nixon could deliver an acceptable platform within these terms, Rockefeller would take himself out of the convention. But, significantly, the Governor reserved his draft status and delayed the caucus of the New York delegation pending adoption of the final draft. He also reserved the right to stage a floor fight if Nixon failed on any significant section of the platform.

The agreement, known variously as the Pact of Fifth Avenue and the Fourteen Points, came as close as anything could have to splitting that disciplined convention wide open. Conservatives, led by their hero, Senator Barry Goldwater, of Arizona, screamed "surrender," and Goldwater impetuously charged that the pact was Rockefeller's price for agreeing to take second place on the national ticket—a wild stab that fell of its own weight within several hours.

Although the Fourteen Points contained strong meat for a convention apparently pointed toward preserving the North-South conservative alliance which had given President Eisenhower six Southern states, it was the manner in which the Nixon-Rockefeller alliance was forged, in secret negotiations far from the convention scene, on the initiative of Nixon who had things locked up, that most outraged the delegates when the pact became known. In the instant bitterness that swept Chicago, Nixon, who'd played a lone hand with Rockefeller, was damned as savagely as Rockefeller himself.

But cursing was the only outlet the delegates could find in their frustration. No political realist on that weekend in Chicago could conceive of any nominee except Nixon. The web of alliances that put him in control was so tightly woven that it could be torn only by destroying the fabric of the party. As the candidate-designate he was entitled, by tradition, to a platform of his liking. Only President Eisenhower, vacationing in Newport, Rhode Island, could upset the schedule, and, although Ike fumed over the secret negotiations, of which he was informed only belatedly, Nixon in the end would placate him.

Nixon could do no less. He initiated the talk that led to the

Pact of Fifth Avenue, and once embarked on the course there was no turning back.

It was a break undreamed of by the Rockefeller people. After the Governor put out his Friday statement rejecting the key planks of the proposed platform, their position was extremely exposed. The convention was in the hands of the Nixon forces; the platform was shaping up according to a draft approved by Eisenhower and Nixon; and, while they bravely threatened floor fights for principle, their arsenal was the limited one of ideas, and the risk was very real that they would be ridden down and discredited in an open test of strength.

So when Rockefeller got a call that afternoon from former U. S. Attorney General Herbert Brownell, saying Nixon wanted to come up to New York for a private meeting, the Governor was both jubilant and cautious. No one had foreseen anything like this, and the principal Rockefeller advisers were manning the command post in Chicago, keeping up what pressure they could on Chairman Charles Percy and the platform committee. Rockefeller temporized, and then started working the long-distance phones.

In Chicago, the Rockefeller platform interests were being managed by State Chairman L. Judson Morhouse, Lieutenant Governor Malcolm Wilson, George Hinman, national committee, and Emmet Hughes, who was now Rockefeller's principal writer. They were deeply suspicious of the overture, but Rockefeller was out on a limb, and what could he lose?

However the conditions laid down were harsh. Nixon would have to phone Rockefeller in person and ask for the meeting; it would be held in Rockefeller's apartment; Rockefeller would control the news release. The Vice President accepted everything. But the mistrust continued. Early the next morning when rumors of the meeting leaked in Chicago, Rockefeller people angrily accused the Nixonites of jumping the gun on the release.

Actually, Nixon lived up to his part of the bargain meticulously. The Chicago leak, it was later shown, came from the platform committee, which was keyed into the negotiations by long-distance telephone. Some of Nixon's own people at the

Blackstone Hotel actually first got news of the meeting from the reporters who angrily accused them of suppressing it.

Nixon flew to New York with one aide for the meeting which started with a quiet dinner in the Rockefeller apartment at Fifth Avenue and 61st Street. "He came to ask me to run for Vice President," Rockefeller said sometime afterward, "and that's all we talked about at first." It was a prolonged talk. Although Rockefeller had been saying almost daily for months that nothing in the world would induce him to take second place on the national ticket, Nixon apparently couldn't accept the idea that any man could really turn down the offer he was making. (In his own case, of course, he'd fought hard, and with a certain ruthlessness, to win second place, and it was to him still a big prize.)

"I convinced him at last," Rockefeller said, "but it took a lot of doing."

By that time, however, Rockefeller was ready to talk platform. His Chicago staff had distilled out of his various position papers a memorandum of minimum demands, and he handed it to the Vice President to read.

As Rockefeller recalled it later, Nixon accepted most of his proposals without question, raising few substantive questions. Through the night, Chuck Percy was consulted frequently.

It was the wording that prolonged the meeting into the early hours of Saturday morning. For more than three and a half hours, with a twenty-minute interruption around one o'clock in the morning (New York time) when a switchboard operator went home and pulled down all connections, the phrasing of the Fourteen Points was worked out over a long-distance telephone hookup linking the platform committee and Rockefeller's command post in Chicago with Nixon and Rockefeller in New York.

Unfortunately the original copy of the memorandum Rockefeller handed Nixon no longer exists. It became a working paper as the night wore on, and the commas were shifted and the phrases turned around, and exact comparison with the Pact of Fifth Avenue as Rockefeller issued it at five o'clock that morning is not possible.

The document released by Rockefeller in New York, Washington and Chicago, however, contained nothing that Rockefeller hadn't been saying for months, although it embraced a number of points that Nixon had been steering clear of, proof incontrovertible that Rockefeller had his way.

For the Fourteen Points, divided, for convenience, into seven on foreign policy and national defense, and seven on domestic affairs, sounded loud and clear Rockefeller's cry that the country and the world faced in the 1960's an emergency that could not be dealt with in terms of the past. And there wasn't so much as a nod for the accomplishments of the Eisenhower Administration in which Nixon had served for nearly eight years.

The foreign-policy section opened with an acknowledgment that "the growing vigor and aggressiveness of Communism demands new and profound effort and action in all areas of American life"—an only slightly oblique rephrasing of Rockefeller's theme that U. S. prestige was slipping in the world because the initiative had passed to the Soviet Union.

It further went on to press for such Rockefeller programs as the creation of Free World defense confederations, resumption of underground nuclear testing, vastly expanded missiles research and bigger and better defense spending. Although Rockefeller dropped the precise spending increases of $3 billion for the military and $500 million for civil defense, he insisted on a declaration that "there must be no price ceiling on America's security." The concession was made because Eisenhower was easily antagonized by any criticism of his defense planning.

Before the final version of the defense plank was written, Rockefeller's phrasing was further altered out of deference to Ike, but his point that spending would have to be increased in the face of growing threat was retained.

On the domestic front, Rockefeller, who claimed impressive qualifications as an expert on government reorganization, got Nixon's backing for creation by law of high-ranking aides to the President to coordinate security and international affairs, and in national planning, as well as for stepping up the growth rate, key-ing medical care for the aged to a contributory system (which meant Social Security by Rockefeller's definition) and for expanded rights for labor and Federal grants for school construction. But his principal concern was domestic civil rights, in which he insisted that Nixon endorse the "objectives of the sit-in demonstrators" in the South and join in denouncing discrimination in voting and housing, schools and jobs. In the long run, the endorsement of the sit-in demonstrators was deleted, but the platform contained what Rockefeller accepted as the strongest civil rights plank ever written by the Republican Party.

Nevertheless, although all these were Rockefeller causes, Nixon's agreement to them was far from being the abject surrender Barry Goldwater and others called it. When he set up his meeting with Rockefeller, Nixon was already looking beyond the convention to the election. His gaze had shifted from the delegates to the voters, and the Pact of Fifth Avenue represented for him his declaration of independence as a candidate as much as it represented a direct bid for the independent vote without which he couldn't hope to contest John F. Kennedy for the Presidency. After all, what chance would Nixon have of carrying New York, which has no majority but only a bewildering assortment of minorities of varying sizes, if he quarreled with New York's Governor on civil rights? And the country at large, still alarmed by Soviet Premier Khrushchev's wrecking of the Summit Conference, was demonstrably in a mood for stronger Federal policies.

That in the election showdown Nixon bumbled away whatever advantage there was in the strong civil rights program by trying to keep both North and South happy on the segregation issue in no way alters the fact that in the bargain he struck on Fifth Avenue, without the aid or knowledge of his advisers, he made distinct gains in staking out a campaign position for himself that he was already being compelled toward by hard political necessity without any essential sacrifices. Whether a different posture would have served him better, considering the narrow margin of his defeat, is beside the point. At Rockefeller's apartment, Nixon was dealing with the realities of July, not the imponderables of November. In this view, his so-called surrender was anything but that.

As for how much the Vice President "humiliated" himself, that would appear to be a matter of attitudes. Certainly he violated a number of political shibboleths by soliciting the meeting with Rockefeller and giving him what amounted to a free hand in writing the Pact of Fifth Avenue. But this type of direct action was in character for Nixon (and Rockefeller, it may be added), always a loner when the chips are down. On balance, therefore, it would appear the only "humiliation" was felt by the fanatical anti-Rockefeller people who feared the New York Governor.

None of which detracts from the important political advance the Pact of Fifth Avenue represented for Rockefeller. Friday afternoon he'd been in very real danger of a devastating setback. By 3:30 the next morning, when Nixon left his apartment to fly back to Washington after nearly eight hours of talk, Rockefeller's convention role was secure. After months of dogged, seemingly hopeless struggle, he was on the point of moving the Republican Party in the direction he considered vital to the party and the country.

This was victory, a heady, exciting recovery from a grave danger, and Rockefeller well knew it. When he flew back to Chicago early that Saturday afternoon, after only a couple of hours sleep, he was relaxed and confident. The early editions of the afternoon papers and the radio were carrying storm warnings of the conservative assault to be made on the Fourteen Points, but Rockefeller, although following all developments closely, already was moving into position one step back from the firing line. Later that day, in his second press conference in a week at the Conrad Hilton, he strengthened this impression.

He declared there was a "very good chance" that the Fourteen Points would be written into the platform without a floor fight, minimized Nixon's "concessions" ("I think this is a question of honest people sitting down trying to find common ground relating to their thinking on these important questions"), flatly denied Barry Goldwater's charge that he'd made a deal to accept the vice-presidential nomination, and repeated again that he would not run for Vice President even if asked by President Eisenhower. He allowed himself only a single display of ruffled feelings when asked whether he was "actually offered" the nomination for Vice President by Nixon.

"The answer is," Rockefeller said, "we had a full and free discussion of the whole question and it covered all ranges of the problem."

"What does that mean?" he was asked.

"Next question," snapped Rockefeller.

It was the only moment he tightened up, although the transcript shows he got some rather obvious needling, and for the most part the press conference went so smoothly that one reporter remarked as it broke up, "Hell, he's playing elder statesman without waiting to be a statesman."

It was a stance dictated by the situation. When the conservative storm broke in all fury on Sunday morning, it was clear that Rockefeller was cast as the villain of the piece. Nixon, it is true, was cursed fervidly by some conservatives, but more in pity than anger. The not-very-complimentary theme was that Nixon somehow was a victim of political blackmail by Rockefeller. Just how this could have been accomplished, considering Nixon's grip on the convention, was never spelled out.

In this atmosphere, it was only common sense for Rockefeller to stay out of the fray. The key battle would be fought in the platform committee, and the Nixonites were in solid control of the committee. Obviously the Vice President was the one to undertake to switch the votes; anything Rockefeller attempted would only stir up more bitterness.

The storm raged through Sunday night. Subcommittee chairmen rushed their reports to the press without waiting to submit them to the full committee. All approved sections of the platform were ordered made public by Thruston Morton, the national chairman. The cries against Rockefeller increased in bitterness. But there was nothing Rockefeller could do except keep an eye on things. Part of the time, Sunday afternoon, he spent with the

Draft Rockefeller volunteers in the Blackstone Theatre, thanking them for their support, but neither encouraging nor discouraging the movement.

By Monday morning a lot of the noise had gone out of the conservative uproar. Nixon flew in from Washington to take command, and the word quickly got around that the savage infighting was hurting the party. In hour after hour of man-to-man negotiations in his suite in the Blackstone Hotel, Nixon slowly switched enough votes—and arranged abstentions where switches were unobtainable—to establish his control of the platform committee.

Then methodically he began putting through planks covered by the Fourteen Points. Once, when he showed signs of wanting to water down the defense spending section to make it more palatable to President Eisenhower, the Rockefeller people nudged him with the threat of a floor fight, but otherwise it was a Nixon show all the way. By the time he assembled the full platform committee on Tuesday, he was in control with a platform acceptable to both Rockefeller and Eisenhower.

Although Rockefeller declared himself "personally disappointed" that endorsement of the Southern sit-in demonstrators "did not express as strong a moral position" as he would have liked, he accepted the committee version. And he very promptly moved to commit the New York delegation to Nixon.

One last convention chore remained for Rockefeller. Although he'd refused either to nominate or second the nomination of Nixon while the New York delegation was officially uncommitted, he agreed to introduce him to the convention on Thursday, July 28th, in a gesture of unity at the closing session.

The speech in the Stockyards Auditorium, while the nation looked on via television, was in the "man who" tradition, and Rockefeller played it out to the end, winding up with:

"He is the man who will succeed Dwight D. Eisenhower next January—Richard E. Nixon."

The wrong middle initial drew a gasp from the Stockyards audience, but Rockefeller sat down without realizing his mistake. Later, however, he made amends. When his introductory speech was printed in Rockefeller's published papers, Nixon's correct middle initial was inserted. Deadpan!

Rockefeller rushed back to New York from the convention, and within three days had set up a special 1960 campaign committee to begin electioneering at once for Nixon and Henry Cabot Lodge, whom Nixon had picked as his running mate. The special committee was headed by a close ally, Lyle W. Hornbeck, secretary of the state committee, and before its first week was out it was already deep in a survey to determine where its efforts would do the most good.

Although Rockefeller believed his primary responsibility was to try to keep New York, which he'd carried so big in 1958, in the Republican column, he'd also put himself at the disposal of the Republican National Committee and Nixon's strategists for assignments in other states at their discretion. They made extensive use of him. Before settling down in October to concentrate on New York, which was also electing a State Legislature, Rockefeller campaigned for Nixon-Lodge in California, Delaware, Ohio, Minnesota and Michigan on a grueling schedule that began shortly after Labor Day and took up most of the rest of September.

The New York campaign was doomed from the outset. For some reason, Nixon never aroused any great enthusiasm, even among Republicans, in New York. For six months, he'd been trailing Kennedy in most reputable polls in the state, and, as the campaign went into October, it became apparent to most observers that the question was not whether Kennedy would carry New York, but by how much.

Rockefeller, who relies heavily on polls, was well acquainted with the odds, but he campaigned with a kind of quiet frenzy as if single-handedly he could swing the state.

In the last six weeks before Election Day, a new urgency entered the campaigning. In a state with a population estimated at 38-percent Catholic, and with the polls uniformly indicating Kennedy, Republican legislators upstate, by tradition safe in their jobs, abruptly started calling for help. Rockefeller responded by traveling the state tirelessly on a bone-wearying schedule that wore out the people around him and even sapped his tremendous energy, although he never let it slow him down. Unquestionably, the intensified late drive saved the Legislature for the GOP, but the Nixon cause was beyond help.

On November 8th, John F. Kennedy carried New York by a margin of 383,666 votes over Richard M. Nixon, as he won the Presidency by a nationwide margin of 112,000 popular votes and an electoral count of 303 to 219, with 15 more ballots going to Senator Harry F. Byrd, of Virginia, in a "plague on both your houses" protest by segregationists from Alabama, Mississippi and Oklahoma.

And on November 9th, Rockefeller woke to find that political pundits around the country were second-guessing, with remarkable unanimity, that he would have knocked off Kennedy's ears as the Republican nominee.

20

Personal Crises

SINCE THE ORIGINAL John D. Rockefeller was first labeled the "richest man in the world," the American people have always accorded a unique position to the Rockefellers. Whether in hate as when John D. was damned as the preeminent robber of the robber barons, or in respect and affection in the latter years as the wide-ranging Rockefeller philanthropies changed the image of the Rockefellers as the times changed, they have always been a family apart. No other family has ever been so identified with the nation, not only here but around the world. No other has ever come so close to royal status in a determinedly egalitarian society. No other has so stirred the national imagination.

Small wonder, then, that the divorce of the Nelson Rockefellers sent a shock of dismay across the country and around the
world. This was far more than the divorce of two private persons.
And though the Governor even then was the leading prospect
for the Republican nomination in 1964, it had a special significance beyond its direct political importance in affecting Nelson's
chances of becoming President. For the 31-year marriage of the
Nelson Rockefellers in a society of commonplace divorce had
seemed to many an affirmation of old-fashioned standards that,
although more honored, perhaps, in the breach than in the ob-
servance, still represented the highest morality. That devoted,
successful parents of five children, devout in their churchgoing
and their dedication to good works, should abruptly part was a
deeply disturbing thought.

It is not the purpose here to write the inside story of the
Rockefeller divorce. That has been attempted *ad nauseam* by the
tabloids and the gossip columnists, by self-styled respectable newspapers and radio-TV chatterers, by magazines of all types, ranging from the stuffiest of the newsweeklies to the girly publications
that print in the shadow of blackmail. With energy worthy of a
more commendable goal, all have sought out scandal in the life
of Nelson Rockefeller, meaty, sexy scandal, tying him up with
one or more other women in the interest of circulation and en-
larged listening audiences.

Nothing came of the unrelenting search. Rumors there were,
many of them malicious and some baldly invented, as in the case
of the press agent who got considerable mileage for a movie
glamor girl long past her best days by planting items that she
was about to marry Rockefeller and then issuing demure denials
in his client's name. This got so threadbare it became ludicrous,
but the planted items kept popping up periodically for more
than a year. Mildly amusing as such gambits were, other rumors,
widely circulated on the New York-Washington-Philadelphia
cocktail party circuits, were considerably more vicious. But the
press, restrained by the laws of libel and a dearth of hard facts,
had to curb its eagerness to print them. It wasn't until more than
a year after the Rockefeller divorce became final that the news-

papers openly speculated whether the Governor would marry Mrs. Margaretta Fitler Murphy whose name had been linked with his in the gossip and, by innuendo, in the gossip columns.

This was all in the future, however, when the long torment of the separation and divorce began early in 1961.

When it all began nobody—probably not even the Rockefellers themselves—could say. But when fire swept the Executive Mansion in Albany in the early hours of March 3, 1961, it was disclosed, after the Governor led his wife to safety down a fire ladder, that they were occupying separate suites in the sprawling mansion. And later that day, Mrs. Rockefeller returned to New York, never to return again to Albany and never to appear publicly again with Nelson, although they preserved the amenities two weeks later at the wedding of their younger daughter, Mary, twin of the ill-fated Michael, and Ensign William Strawbridge.

But no one suspected a separation. Sometime after Mary's wedding, Mrs. Rockefeller entered the hospital for minor surgery, and in the coming months her absence went unremarked on the assumption that she was taking things easy. This view prevailed even late in June when other governors' wives at the Governors' Conference in Honolulu expressed disappointment that she was not at Rockefeller's side.

Rockefeller himself, of course, played it straight. In the early part of 1961, he was engaged in a serious reassessment of his political position. Never so naïve about politics as his critics charged—after all he was a Rockefeller and had rather a keen appreciation of the power structure of the major parties—his perspectives nevertheless had broadened considerably in 1960. His successful fight to rewrite the Republican platform had shown him at firsthand that the leadership control of the party was not nearly so pervasive as he'd believed in December, 1959, when he'd put aside his ambitions in the face of Big Money opposition. And the example of John F. Kennedy, who'd bent a reluctant Democratic Party leadership to his will by use of the primaries, was not lost on him. In the aftermath of the presidential election that the experts kept saying he might have won, he was taking a long, hard look at his future.

At the same time he sharpened his political skills. The new insights into the manipulation of power he'd gained in the previous year now came into play. He didn't put aside the long-term view that had characterized his political approach, but he showed a keener awareness of the professional officeholders' necessary concern with problems on the basis of immediacy even when immediate solutions might seem to run counter to eventual goals. As a consequence, his relations with the Legislature were perhaps the smoothest of his first term. His legislative program was enacted without substantial amendment. And with the passage of a temporary 10-percent cut in income taxes, some of the wounds inflicted by his 1959 tax rise were healed.

Up to this period Rockefeller had thought of politics in the sophisticated frame of reference of his class. He was accustomed to the belief that Big Money and Big Business usually got just about the programs they wanted over the long run, regardless of temporary setbacks or even the individuals involved. There was nothing in his experience to alter that. Even his own nomination for Governor when he entered politics at the top was largely an assertion of the power of money. Certainly without his money, Nelson Rockefeller never could have steamrollered the 1958 state convention.

This viewpoint is tenable for the political scientist and philosopher; it is downright dangerous for the practicing politician. It overlooks the fact that the management of party politics in the United States is almost exclusively a middle-class business, and this includes very definitely labor leaders, regardless of their origin, who presume to speak for the working classes. These operating echelons, however much they may subscribe to the overall goals of the top 1 or 2 percent of the power structure—and subscribe they do in the main, for isn't great wealth, after all, a high desideratum in American folklore?—of necessity run the party organizations on an *ad hoc* basis. From the precinct level up, they must put private ambition first and the good of the party second, if they are to survive. But collectively they have the power of ultimate decision within certain limits if their private ambitions can be harnessed to a single cause.

It was his acceptance of this other facet of power that changed Nelson Rockefeller from a talented amateur to a professional politician. By the spring of 1961, he was thinking like a professional politician, and his use of the instruments of power was rapidly developing.

Paradoxically, it was just as his political perspectives broadened that Rockefeller came as close as one of his optimistic temperament could to despairing of his political future. Although the Rockefeller separation was still a secret, known only to the family and very close intimates, Nelson faced up late that spring to the possibility that divorce would drive him out of public life.

He said nothing, of course. But in late May when I talked to him about writing this book, he tried to discourage the idea. "I don't know if I'd go ahead with it if I were you," he told me. "Something may happen to take me out of the picture."

Months later, soon after the announcement of the separation and impending divorce, Rockefeller recalled the May conversation as we flew home across the Atlantic from the fruitless search for his missing son, Michael, in Dutch New Guinea.

"When we first talked about the book, I tried to warn you about this," he said, referring to the divorce. "But I couldn't say anything then."

Although we'd talked many times that summer and fall, about the book, his life and other matters, this was my first insight into the doubts that assailed him. Looking back, however, many things that had seemed out of order fell into place.

All that spring, Rockefeller had seemed something less than his usual, impetuous self. Once his official duties in Albany were wound up with the conclusion of the thirty-day bill-signing period after the adjournment of the Legislature, his pace seemed to slow down. Pictures taken at the time show him tired and drawn. He dutifully attended to his ceremonial chores and made the expected rounds of the fund-raising dinners. But while he responded to enthusiasm as if by reflex action, a certain impatience, a sort of "let's get this over with" attitude seemed to grip him.

This was, perhaps, best shown by his performance at the Governors' Conference held June 25th to the 28th that year in Honolulu. The conference is a ceremonial junket at which the governors get together to size each other up, discuss their mutual problems in terms so general that no one can be offended and have a good time at a plush resort. But it is also a superb show-case for a governor seeking a national audience. In 1959 at Puerto Rico and in 1960 at Glacier Park, Montana, Rockefeller had made the news and the headlines. The ninety or so reporters who made the trip out to Honolulu from the mainland for the 1961 meeting looked to him for a repeat as the only likely presidential prospect among the chief executives of the states. About all he had to do was speak and his words would be printed.

Piquancy was added to the situation by the presence of the astute John M. Bailey, Democratic National Chairman, whose mission it was to thwart any attempt by Rockefeller to use the conference for a national buildup. Any direct clash between the two would be hard news everywhere in the country.

Nothing happened. As usual, Rockefeller had brought a large retinue with him to the conference, and as usual his news conference drew the biggest crowd of reporters at the meeting. But he made very little news. And he held only the single press conference, staying away from reporters most of the time.

Even when Bailey began operating, Rockefeller refused to accept the challenge. It is the practice of the Governors' Conference to alternate the chairmanship between Democrats and Republicans, and 1961 was a Republican year. By custom, Rockefeller was the logical GOP candidate. But Bailey lined up the Democrats, who outnumbered the Republican governors by two to one at the conference as well as nationally, and sent word to the Republicans that Rockefeller was unacceptable. Nelson acted as if he couldn't have cared less. And when the Republicans, unable to get a chairman from among those in Honolulu, decided to put up the unpredictable Wesley Powell, of New Hampshire, an open foe of Rockefeller, the New York Governor went along without a murmur. That proved later to be a mistake. When the governors next met at Hershey, Pennsylvania, in 1962, Powell used his chairmanship to give Rockefeller a rough time just as Nelson was about to plunge into his campaign for reelection.

At Honolulu, however, Rockefeller's chief affirmative action was to get his Republican colleagues to sign a round robin calling for adoption of a strong civil rights resolution. Even on this he didn't follow through. Quite the contrary, he went along without comment after the Southern Democratic governors rewrote the resolution into a meaningless "all men are brothers" declaration.

Sitting on the terrace of the Royal Hawaiian Hotel overlooking Waikiki Beach after the vote, he commented, "Nobody here wants to go into anything too deeply. At least they've passed something called a civil rights resolution. A fight wouldn't have changed anything."

It was a singularly uncharacteristic remark, but it was oddly in character with Rockefeller's attitude toward the entire conference. He seemed impatient to get it over with and, in fact, left the final dinner early to rush to a plane for a flight back to New York with no stopover en route. His stated reason for the big hurry was that he wanted to get back for a Republican dinner on Long Island. It was apparent, however, that he also was glad to get away from the conference.

Back in New York, his marital problem still unresolved, and still unknown to the public, Rockefeller soon found a political situation to absorb all his energies: the New York City mayoralty election. It led him directly into an adventure in kingmaking.

It was from the outset a forlorn undertaking, even though superficially feasible. In that summer of 1961, the Democrats were in serious disarray. Fired up by the money of their most respected elder statesman, former Senator and Governor Herbert H. Lehman, and with the persuasive backing of the late Mrs. Eleanor Roosevelt, reform elements were locked in a death struggle with the "bosses"—with Tammany leader Carmine G. De Sapio as the number one target—and Mayor Wagner, a product of the Democratic machine, casting himself on the side of the "angels" in his bid for a third term. The struggle was savage, with the machine organization putting up State Comptroller Arthur

Levitt, the only Democrat to win a statewide election against the Rockefeller sweep of 1958, in a primary fight. Other rows were in progress in all five boroughs. Such was the bitterness that it seemed the Democrats would be so fragmented by Election Day, whatever the outcome of the primary fights, that the Republican candidate would have only to be on the voting machines to win.

To Rockefeller this looked like an opportunity. In his spectacular election of 1958, he'd held the combined Democratic-Liberal plurality against him to 309,000 votes against Mayor Wagner's margin of more than 920,000 votes a year earlier. If a Republican Mayor could be elected in 1961, Rockefeller could reasonably hope to carry the city in 1962.

And if Rockefeller could carry New York City, something no Republican governor has accomplished, his position in 1964 would be immeasurably stronger, particularly considering that the presidential election of 1960 was won in the big cities. It was a long gamble, but the stakes were attractive.

Against the counsels of his advisers, who warned him that logic has no connection with New York City politics, Rockefeller decided to put his cash and his prestige on the line in an all-out effort to elect a Republican Mayor. The difficulties soon proved to be enormous. The candidate considered most likely to have a chance, if any Republican had a chance, was U. S. Senator Jacob K. Javits. Javits, after going through the motions of thinking things over, flatly refused to run, being unwilling to risk his prestige in what he very obviously considered a lost cause. Efforts to resuscitate the old Fusion movement that kept Mayor F. H. LaGuardia in office for twelve years failed dismally.

In the end, Rockefeller had to fall back on his own Attorney General, Louis J. Lefkowitz as the candidate. It was a choice that slotted the election into a narrow, partisan pattern—and doomed Rockefeller's hopes. Lefkowitz, a product of the Lower East Side, had come up through the Manhattan Republican organization, which as the "loyal opposition" had got the crumbs of the spoils from Tammany Hall's munificent municipal table, and enjoyed almost no standing with New York City voters. Lefkowitz himself, although a Rockefeller "liberal" as a state officer, had, as a party regular, frequently clashed with elements within the GOP that looked to Senator Javits for leadership before Rockefeller came on the scene.

Nothing could deter Rockefeller from going ahead. Although advised to stay out of the campaign directly to avoid involving his own prestige, he insisted on going all out. He made walking tours with Lefkowitz until he was footsore. He addressed rallies and he used television lavishly.

No Republican Governor ever involved himself so completely in a New York mayoralty election. And Rockefeller moved the whole GOP with him. Veteran publicity agents and researchers were detached from the Republican State Committee and the various state departments, and sent to New York to give Lefkowitz a staff large enough to handle a state campaign. Spending reached an all-time high for a Republican campaign for Mayor, the estimate running between $750,000 and a million—precise figures are impossible to obtain because of the number of overlapping committees that handled the money. How much of this came from Rockefeller himself cannot be pinned down.

But on Election Day, Mayor Wagner won handily by a plurality of just over 400,000 votes over Lefkowitz, a respectable margin considering that Lawrence E. Gerosa, who was kicked off the Democratic ticket by Wagner, ran independently for Mayor and siphoned off 340,000 votes.

As a matter of strict bookkeeping, this was a major political defeat for Rockefeller. In the long run, however, it cost him nothing, except the money he spent. When he ran for reelection the following year, he made a better race in New York City than in his spectacular first showing in 1958. And the municipal campaign provided him with a laboratory for testing his skill in operating directly in the arena of party politics rather than at the gentlemanly remove of his past experience.

More importantly, the heavy involvement in the election carried him through a period of severe personal stress, a lonely time beset with doubts. Nelson spent most of that summer and fall of 1961 in the apartment at 810 Fifth Avenue, cut off from his normal social life because he couldn't accept invitations without revealing the still-secret separation. Politics and work were the only outlets for his energies.

There was no sign of stress in the family when the breakup of the marriage was announced to the world on November 17, 1961, in a terse, four-paragraph statement that was the first and last comment ever made by the Rockefellers on their divorce. Timed to catch the Saturday morning papers of November 18th—with their comparatively limited circulations as compared to weekdays—the announcement came out of the office of the Rockefeller Brothers in Room 5600 at 30 Rockefeller Center just before 6 o'clock in the evening. The statement said:

> It was announced today that Governor and Mrs. Nelson A. Rockefeller have arrived at an agreement of legal separation.
>
> It is anticipated that the terms of the agreement will be incorporated into a subsequent decree of divorce.
>
> Governor and Mrs. Rockefeller were married in 1930. They have five adult children.
>
> There has been an agreed property settlement and Mrs. Rockefeller will continue to have a New York apartment at 810 Fifth Ave. The Governor will reside at the Executive Mansion in Albany and in New York temporarily at the apartment of his brother, Laurance S. Rockefeller.

The carefully calculated timing of the announcement was of course wasted effort. This was too great a human-interest story to be held down. Except for Winthrop, whose expensive divorce from Bobo Sears was considered a youthful exuberance, the Rockefeller brothers were widely admired exemplars of what American husbands should be. Nelson, in particular, was identified in the public mind as a family man par excellence. Since he'd entered politics more than three years earlier, his role as father had been repeatedly stressed. That such a family could break up was inexplicable.

That weekend the press was concerned chiefly with the political implications of the divorce. What effect would it have on

Nelson's position as the man most likely to be the Republican nominee for President in 1964? Could he even be reelected in New York, with its large Catholic population? Would he remain in politics at all?

No answers were forthcoming. The Rockefellers themselves couldn't be found. Mrs. Rockefeller was at the white frame home they'd shared on the Pocantico Hills estate (eventually she was awarded the right of possession in the separation), and Nelson was at his stepmother's place on the estate, the old John D., Jr. home. Their isolation from the questing reporters was complete.

The newspapers on Sunday were filled with speculation about what divorce would do to Rockefeller's political future. The comment followed a patttern that would be repeated with curious fidelity later after Nelson married Mrs. Murphy: those who liked Rockefeller called divorce a private matter and said it would have no effect; those opposed to him forecast that his career was ended.

And then tragedy struck and crowded the divorce story inside the papers: the Governor's youngest son, Michael, was reported missing and presumed lost in far-off Netherlands New Guinea.

Nelson was lunching with the David Rockefellers early on Sunday afternoon when the first call came from the Dutch officials at Hollandia. The transmission was scratchy. Atmospherics somewhere in the western Pacific were scrambling radio communications, never too good at best, and only about one word in three came through by radiotelephone. The message when pieced together was ominous. Michael was missing, missing at sea off the New Guinea coast.

For hours that was all the Rockefellers knew, a single grim, appalling fact for an already tormented family. As the afternoon wore on, scraps of information came in by cable and phone, from The Hague, from the Netherlands Embassy in Washington and from the news services. Most of it was contradictory. Out of the welter, however, there was the slimmest of hopes. Although the Dutch were deeply pessimistic, they had no proof that Michael was dead. Nelson decided to fly to the scene. If big decisions had to be made, he wanted to be on hand to make them, not half a world away at the mercy of an off-again, on-again communications system that might delay vital messages for hours. Mary Strawbridge, as Michael's twin, would go along.

The Rockefeller organization moves with frightening efficiency to achieve its objectives, but even so it takes time to set up a trip half around the world. It was midnight when Rockefeller and his daughter boarded a commercial jet airliner at Idlewild Airport on the first leg of the flight to New Guinea, and the Governor was fretting with impatience. By this time his party had grown to include Robert McManus, his press secretary; State Police Captain Edward Galvin, his bodyguard; Berent Friele, an old friend and expert on New Guinea who would brief him during the transcontinental flight on what to expect, and Robert Gardner, of the Peabody Institute at Harvard, who'd been the leader of an archeological expedition to New Guinea, with Michael as a member of his staff, earlier in the year.

Hatless as usual, but with his hands thrust deep in his topcoat pockets, Rockefeller paced up and down the first-class section of the airliner as the final good-byes were said—David Rockefeller and several members of the family had come to the airport to see the Governor and Mary off. Nelson waved off the stewardesses as each in turn offered to take his coat. He was tightly wound up, but lines of fatigue already were apparent.

As the last visitors departed and the light flashed, "Buckle Seat Belts," he dropped into the chair next to mine, still in his topcoat, and caught up the straps. I'd greeted him as we came aboard, and now I murmured a few words of sympathy. He thanked me absentmindedly, but he obviously was only half-listening.

"A sweet boy," he said. "He was a very sweet boy."

That "was" at the very start of the long trip was something of a shocker.

As the plane rose toward cruising altitude, some of the tension seemed to go out of Rockefeller. When the seat belt light blinked out, he muttered, "At last it's warming up in here" (I hadn't noted any chill), and got up, shrugging out of his topcoat. For the next couple of hours he was busy: talking with the experts, going over plans with McManus and Galvin and sitting with Mary until she dozed off.

Then, while others catnapped in the dimmed cabin, Rockefeller again settled in the chair beside me and picked up where he'd left off as if there'd never been a break. It was a soliloquy rather than a conversation. After the long, stressful day, he'd seemed to be summing up his impressions in order to formulate them more precisely in his own mind.

"I'm a realist," he said. "I pride myself on being a realist. You can't go behind the facts. I don't think we've got a chance, not any kind of a chance, of finding him."

That explained the "was" of his earlier remarks but why, then, this long and frantic journey across the world to rush into heartbreak if there was no hope?

Nelson's "realism" was perhaps insulation for his hurt. Michael shared many of his father's interests, including a passion for primitive art, and it was, in fact, because he wanted to bring back specimens for the Museum of Primitive Art, headed by the Governor, that he'd remained in New Guinea after the Peabody expedition returned to the United States for a final trip in the jungle.

The flight went on. There was the change of planes at San Francisco and a layover of several hours in Honolulu while Pan American Airways freed a jet airliner for a charter flight to remote Wake Island. At each stop, and as more reporters joined the trip, it became quietly evident that there would be a moratorium on questions about the pending divorce. The moratorium endured everywhere Rockefeller went—and the trip went completely around the world—and for several days after his return to New York.

At Wake Island, the Rockefeller party and the ever-growing press entourage boarded a KLM jet for Biak, and there changed again for a beat-up Dakota (the old reliable DC-3) for the last leg of the journey. At every stop along the way, Rockefeller got new reports, and each report was more somber than the last. The rescue at sea of Rene Wassing, a Dutch anthropologist and museum expert, who was Mike's guide and adviser, raised hopes briefly, only to bring deeper gloom when he reported that he'd last seen Mike more than twenty-four hours earlier far out in the Arafura Sea, making a desperate attempt to swim through shark-infested waters to the distant shore. Wassing, a weak swimmer, saved his own life by staying with the craft.

At Hollandia, on the northern edge of New Guinea, Dutch Governor P. J. Plateel waited with the first full report of the disaster and the grimmest conclusion. Michael, he told Rockefeller sorrowfully, unquestionably was dead. In the opinion of Dutch experts, the only men who knew anything of the area except for the native Papuans, his body would never be recovered, nor would it ever be known whether he drowned on the long swim or was torn to pieces by the sharks that patrol the waters of the Arafura Sea or the crocodiles that guard its river mouths. If by a miracle he'd reached shore, the cruel jungle had claimed him.

Recital of the bare facts was chilling. Michael and Rene Wassing, planning a long stay in a primitive section of the Asmat jungle rarely visited by white men, set out from Agats, a tiny Dutch administrative post and mission, on the north branch of the Eilanden River, intending to sail down to the Arafura Sea, follow the coast southeast along the shore to the lower mouth of the river and then go upriver to trade with the far-inland natives who never ventured close to the settled areas. Their craft was a jury-rigged catamaran, made by lashing together two flat-bottomed native canoes, planking them over with rough boards and raising an awning against the tropical sun. It was powered with an outboard motor. Such craft are in fairly common use on New Guinea's rivers because of their freight-carrying capacity, and Michael and Wassing, intending to skirt along the shoreline once they reached the sea, needed substantial supplies and trading materials for the protracted stay in the jungle they'd planned as a windup to the expedition. Two Papuans, long experienced in jungle lore, accompanied them as guides and bearers.

The improvised catamaran rode low in the water and handled clumsily, but seemed to be seaworthy. The downriver voyage was uneventful. But as the heavy-laden craft swept out of the lee of the shore into the Arafura Sea, it began lumbering badly. The lashings shifted in the buffeting, and the canoes that served as floats began to ship water. Two miles off the mouth of the river, the craft lost headway completely and the strong current took over, driving it relentlessly to the open water. The Papuan guide-bearers, fearing immediate disaster, plunged overboard to swim back to shore. It took them six hours, by their later reckoning, to reach land, and another eleven hours to fight their way through the jungle back to Agats.

Michael and Wassing remained aboard the catamaran, trying to tighten up the lashings and shift cargo to gain steerageway. But as they drifted farther out to sea, the waves turned unexpectedly choppy, and in the pitching and tossing the helpless craft tipped over. It was now a raft rather than a boat. Through the long night, they clung to the planking.

At dawn, Michael decided to try to swim to the shore which, as later tests proved, was at least eleven and may have been as much as fifteen or sixteen miles away. He lashed himself to two reserve gasoline cans, which he proposed to use as floats, and struck out. Wassing, clinging to the wreckage of the catamaran, lying low in the water, watched him for a few hundred yards and then lost sight of him in the choppy seas.

He was never seen again.

This was the report the Dutch officials gave Rockefeller and Mary at Hollandia. The Dutch started their search a few hours before they called the Governor at Pocantico Hills on Sunday and, now, two-and-a-half days later, despite continuous crisscrossing of the area, there wasn't the slightest trace of Michael. Wassing had been spotted from the air and picked up, twenty-four miles at sea, after a second night spent clinging to a life raft dropped from a plane, and had been brought ashore with the full report. The Dutch consensus was: hopeless.

Now, if ever, was the time to turn back. Realistically there was nothing ahead but more heartbreak. The practicing realist, however, is rarely as firm as he thinks when his emotions are involved. Some of the Dutch experts expressed surprise that the bright-red cans Mike had been using as floats hadn't been sighted. On the blank surface of the rarely traveled Arafura Sea—the natives never ventured more than a mile or so offshore, and shipping was almost nonexistent—the splashes of color should have been instantly visible from the air. It was just possible that Michael might have swum into a shore-curling eddy and been washed up on land under the trees that grow right down to the waterline. It was the wildest sort of chance, but Rockefeller, faced with accepting the full implications of his "realism" and abandoning the journey or putting his faith in a "miracle," opted for the miracle. Back he went to the chartered Dakota.

The plane by this time was jammed. Television newsmen, lugging their hundreds of pounds of equipment, had been waiting at Hollandia for the Rockefeller party, and all were trying to get aboard. With the Stanley Mountains to be topped and five hundred miles of flying over jungle ahead, the TV men were forced to leave some of their gear behind for a later flight, but on takeoff every seat was taken. Bob McManus exacted a promise that no pictures would be taken inside the plane.

Even from the air, the Asmat is a stinking, fetid jungle, cut up by hundreds of nameless streams and dotted with seemingly endless morasses of swamp. From an altitude of less than a thousand feet, it is steaming, cruel and lifeless. Natives there may be below, but there are no clearings. Nothing moves except when a vagrant breeze stirs an occasional treetop in the matted green that hides the earth. As the plane bored southward, silence settled on its sweltering passengers. Dismay showed in the expression of Mary Strawbridge as from time to time she turned her binoculars on the terrain. Rockefeller was grim. How could anyone, how, specifically, could a 23-year-old youth survive alone down there even if he reached shore? It was a brutal, factual underlining of the Dutch pessimism.

And so the flight continued down the center of the Asmat to Merauke, which is tucked away in the southeast corner of West New Guinea. On hand to greet the party were a couple of hundred natives and a score of Australian newsmen who'd flown in by their own charter from Port Moresby. Not that the natives

knew who Rockefeller was or why he was coming, but there was
a lot going on for that part of the world, and the natives turn
out for any excitement.

Having seen the jungle in all its cruelty on the flight southward, Rockefeller decided, without leaving the airstrip at Merauke, that he wanted to view the actual area where Mike was
lost, perhaps in the forlorn hope that it would be less forbidding.
While the plane was refueled, he and Mary conferred in the open
shed that served as a waiting room with the Dutch district commissioner, F. R. J. Eibrink Jansen, who was in direct charge of
the search. He could offer no reason for new hope. All reports
were negative.

Nor did the search flight help. Once over the Arafura Sea,
the Dakota dropped down to 250 feet above the water, and from
that altitude the jungle was, if anything, more menacing than
when seen from higher up. Still more appalling were the mud-
banks, stretching from the sliver of sand where the trees over-
hung the shoreline from a mile and a half to five miles out in
the sea. No swimmer coming in at low tide could cross that mud,
pocked with craters, unaided, according to the jungle experts.
Occasionally, through the glasses, a crocodile could be spotted
near one of the many streams and inlets that cut up the coast.

For four hours the flight continued, ranging north to the
mouth of the upper branch of the Eilanden River, where the
disaster began, and inland on the lower branch to Atsj, which
was Michael's destination on the fateful trip. Nothing was to
be seen except a few canoes and small craft patroling along the
shore and, far out at sea, mere dots against the sinking sun, the
search planes crosspatching the endless waters. As night came
down, the Dakota returned to the Merauke airstrip.

Rockefeller and his daughter stayed while in Merauke at the
home of District Commissioner Jansen, while the American press
was quartered in the eight-room government hotel, about two
hundred yards away, packed four to a room and sharing a shower
room that ran for thirty minutes or less, usually less, at 6:30 in
the morning. The Australians were put up in the Dutch Army
barracks.

Once each day, Rockefeller walked the two hundred yards from Jansen's modest home to the hotel for a press conference. Although the temperature was around one hundred and the humidity so heavy you could pour the air, he somehow managed to look cool. At his first meeting with the reporters, he announced his decision to leave the search to the experts. "They know what to look for; I would only take up space in the plane," he explained. His only excursion out of Merauke was a flight to Pirimapoen, a jungle outpost, where Dutch missionaries organized their native sources to help in the search.

The daily press conferences—"briefings" perhaps would be more accurate—yielded only a dreary series of reports on continuing failure. By Friday the word was passed that Rockefeller would start home on Sunday.

Then came the only hopeful break of the journey. A search plane, crisscrossing the Arafura Sea, had spotted an oil can. A naval vessel was dispatched to pick it up. The departure plans were canceled. But the find proved inconclusive. When the oil can reached Merauke Sunday evening, there was no way of identifying it as one of those Michael used as a float. Dutch officials said they were 99 percent sure it was what they were looking for, but they couldn't prove it. After another day of waiting, Rockefeller turned homeward.

Mary Strawbridge dropped off at Manila to visit her husband, Billy, then an ensign on the troop transport *Noble,* who had a few days' leave. Rockefeller flew westward toward home via Amsterdam. With Mary gone, his exhaustion seemed to catch up with him. The very inactivity he forced on himself by his decision to leave the actual searching to the experts had tensed him up. For the first part of the thirty-hour trip, he dozed frequently. The weariness didn't last long.

At stopovers along the way, he strolled around the airports, unrecognized most of the time.

The divorce was very much on his mind as he flew home, but he talked around it rather than about it, speculating on the problems he'd face in the 1962 election and what his prospects were of carrying New York City. It seemed a little ambitious even to think about with a divorce looming, but he was patently sincere.

Rockefeller landed back at Idlewild Airport in New York a little after 9 o'clock on November 29th. On hand to greet him were his brother, David; his sons, Rodman and Steven, and Steven's wife, Anne Marie, a number of state officials—and two hundred newsmen. Bone-weary though he was, he faced the television lights and the reporters immediately in the "briefing" room of the VIP section at the airport.

It was an odd press conference. Not a single question was asked and no reporter spoke except Russell Porter, of *The New York Times,* who extended "the sympathy of the press." Rockefeller spoke without notes under obvious emotional strain, his voice low-pitched. It was a situation made for pathos, but he talked with a simple dignity that showed him at his very best. His moving tribute to his missing son impressed even the most cynical.

"I would just like to say a word about Michael himself," he said. "Ever since he was little, he has been very aware of people, their feelings, their thoughts. He is a person who has always loved people and has always been loved by people. He has a tremendous enthusiasm and drive, love of life. He has always loved beauty in people, beauty in nature and beauty in art, whether it is in painting or sculpture, and has been quite an artist himself.

"I think it is fair to say that he was never happier than he has been out there for some seven or eight months."

Rockefeller drove from the airport to Pocantico Hills where he gathered his children together with his estranged wife to tell them all he knew about Michael.

On December 21st, in Albany, Rockefeller announced the search for Michael had been officially closed. Some months later a permanent exhibition of materials he'd gathered in New Guinea was opened at the Museum of Primitive Art. It remains as his memorial.

Rockefeller's return to New York ended the moratorium on discussion of the divorce. Having indulged in the unaccustomed canons of good taste so long as the tragedy of Michael's disappearance filled the headlines, the gossip columnists, as if triggered, now began what was almost a concerted campaign. Nor were the columnists alone in the search. Responsible reporters, who normally wouldn't be asked to touch such a story, were detached from their regular assignments by even the most respectable newspapers to run down rumors.

Rockefeller's office put out a curt statement, "The Governor does not comment on rumors," and that became his stance. He stuck by it despite all efforts to needle him into a denial or comment that would open the way for publishing the rumors.

By mid-December, however, the sophisticated gossip had zeroed in on one woman: Mrs. Margaretta "Happy" Murphy, a vibrant, outgoing Philadelphia Main Liner who'd worked for Rockefeller as a campaign volunteer in 1958 and as a member of his staff until May, 1961. Nearly twenty years younger than the Governor, Mrs. Murphy, whose husband was Dr. James Slater Murphy, a microbiologist who worked for the Rockefeller Institute, moved in the intimate Rockefeller circle. The Murphys had a country home in Tarrytown, New York, adjoining the Rockefellers' Pocantico Hills barony, on land they'd bought from the Rockefellers in the early 1950's, and a summer place near the Rockefeller summer home at Seal Harbor on Mount Desert Island. As a girl, Happy had spent all her summers there.

As a member of Rockefeller's staff, she worked in his converted brownstone offices in Manhattan. At the 1960 Republican Convention, she was very much on the scene in the large staff that Rockefeller took with him to Chicago.

Although Mrs. Murphy became the second Mrs. Nelson A. Rockefeller in May, 1963, the press handled the gossip about her gingerly in the winter of 1961–1962. A Hearst gossip first printed her name in early December in a "blind" item, saying merely, "The most discussed lady wherever socialites gather is a Mrs. Murphy." Lady Jeanne Campbell, writing in the London *Evening Standard,* carried it a step further, writing, "People are beginning to compare her [Mrs. Murphy] to the Duchess of Windsor when she was plain Mrs. Simpson," recalling the British constitutional crisis of a generation ago when King Edward VIII abdicated his throne for "the woman I love"—the Baltimore divorcée Wallis Simpson. Even the newsmagazines worked in background stories about Mrs. Murphy without explaining their significance.

Rockefeller, who wasn't about to abdicate anything, faced out the gossip, rumors and speculation with surface good humor, whatever dismay he felt privately. But in early 1962, a great many Republicans were deeply worried about the effect of the gossip on the state elections coming up in the fall. After a Paris newspaper put out a wild story that Mrs. Murphy had moved there to get a divorce (she was in Bermuda with her husband and children at the time), indirect suggestions were made to Rockefeller that he make some gesture or statement to shut off the rumor mill.

Rockefeller stated: "I'm not going to answer rumors, and I'm not going to discuss my private life. There's nothing more to say."

Time was working on his side. The newspapers turned to other things. The gossip staled in repetition. The Republican fears quieted, but did not die.

Mrs. Rockefeller established residence in Reno, Nevada, on February 1, 1962. On March 16th, the divorce was granted on the grounds of mental cruelty after an eight-minute hearing behind closed doors. The papers were sealed.

Through all this, Rockefeller was running furiously for re-election. While other Republicans worried about the effect of the divorce on the state ticket in the November election, the people closest to Rockefeller aimed at lifting his plurality to between 750,000 and 1,000,000. And despite the failure of his adventure in kingmaking in the 1961 mayoralty election, he personally never quite gave up on his hope that somehow he would manage to carry New York City on his second time out. If in his most private moments he ever considered the possibility of losing, he kept his doubts to himself. Publicly his posture was always that of the confident man, and he kept saying he'd be happy with a "plurality of one."

Politically he moved with what some party leaders considered almost indecent haste. In 1958, he'd left organization politics to State Chairman L. Judson Morhouse. But early in 1962, he turned to William L. Pfeiffer, a former state chairman and effective Republican money-raiser, and put him in charge with the title of preconvention manager. It was a meaningless title. No Republican in his right mind was likely to oppose Rockefeller at the state convention. But the title gave Pfeiffer an excuse to get an early start. Rockefeller also made his peace with Leonard W. Hall, the former national chairman and Nixon campaigner, who agreed to serve as consultant. Long before the nominations were placed before the convention, the electioneering was rolling in high gear.

The Legislature of 1962 gave Rockefeller no trouble. His program was tailored to keep peace in the Republican Party and to avoid stirring up opposition outside the party. Since the program was drafted in consultation with the legislative leaders, and with the election very specifically in mind, it sailed to passage over the *pro forma* "nays" of the Democrats. Needless to say, it was a program concerned more with housekeeping than with breaking new ground.

As the summer drew on, it became apparent that the Rockefeller political luck would hold again. In 1958, the Democrats paved the way for Rockefeller's landslide victory by nearly tearing their party apart in the fight over the nomination for United States Senator. Now, in 1962, the Democrats, still bitterly divided although Mayor Wagner had emerged as state leader by reason of his primary and election victories of 1961, seemed to be headed for another donnybrook. It never quite came to that, but it might as well have for all the unity the Democrats were able to show.

Their problem was the old one of finding a candidate. State Comptroller Arthur Levitt, the only Democrat with proved ability to carry the state, proof given when he withstood the 1958 Rockefeller sweep, was ineligible for the top spot because he'd had the effrontery to run against Mayor Wagner in the primary. Wagner, however, interposed no objection to Levitt for reelection as Comptroller.

But if not Levitt, who? James A. Farley, Franklin D. Roosevelt's Postmaster General and former Democratic National Chairman, wanted the nomination, but his generation of leaders was fading and he had no more than the sentimental backing of a few upstaters. No other "name" Democrat relished the idea of taking on Rockefeller, divorce or no. In the void, District Attorney Frank D. O'Connor, of Queens County in New York City, Congressman Samuel S. Stratton, of Schenectady, and Howard Samuel, a millionaire industrialist from Canandaigua, set up separate shops and began competing for delegates.

Then Mayor Wagner emerged from a White House conference with the suggestion that it would be just dandy if the Democrats nominated United States Attorney Robert Morgenthau, of the Southern District of New York. A poll showed, Wagner said, that Morgenthau was the only possible winner. The argument offered was that Morgenthau would bring back the Jewish vote that strayed to Rockefeller in 1958 and that, as the son of Henry Morgenthau, Jr., President Roosevelt's Secretary of the Treasury, he would have a claim on the loyalties of the old New Dealers. Furthermore, Morgenthau was a friend of United States Attorney General Robert F. Kennedy and President Kennedy. (The friendship was proved after Morgenthau's defeat in a most unusual political maneuver when he was reappointed U. S. Attorney, a post he'd been required by the Hatch Act to resign.)

A colorless personality against the vitality of Rockefeller, hampered by disunity in his party and lack of funds, and working with a state chairman whose only previous experience had been on the county level, Morgenthau never really had a chance. He nevertheless fought a hard fight, and in the closing days of the campaign stung Rockefeller with a charge that the Governor had a secret plan to raise income taxes after the election. Rockefeller was goaded by the charge into making a pledge, "I will not raise taxes," that returned to bedevil him in 1963.

Morgenthau's nomination was a signal for the Democrats to try to turn the state election into a curtain raiser for a possible Rockefeller-Kennedy contest in 1964, but Rockefeller anticipated the strategy. Even before the conventions met, Rockefeller reverted to his tactics of 1958, limiting his campaign to state issues. In 1958, he'd been unwilling to defend the foreign policy of the Eisenhower Administration; in 1962, he stuck to state issues in an attempt to keep President Kennedy, whose popularity had been rising in the polls since his narrow victory over Richard M. Nixon, out of the campaign. Unquestionably, although it is not measurable, this stance aided Rockefeller when Democratic prestige zoomed just before Election Day because of Kennedy's firm handling of the Cuban missile crisis.

The campaign, as Rockefeller waged it, was almost a replica of 1958. Once again, he patroled the boardwalk in Coney Island, strolled along the Lower East Side, drew a large crowd in Manhattan's garment district and dominated the news. As the vote neared, Pfeiffer, his campaign manager, predicted victory by a plurality of 750,000 to 1,000,000 votes.

On November 6th, Rockefeller was reelected by a margin of 529,000, a drop of more than 40,000 from his 1958 showing. He was the low winner on the Republican ticket, U. S. Senator Jacob K. Javits having rolled up a plurality of nearly a million and Attorney General Louis Lefkowitz coming in strongly with an edge of more than 700,000. Only John P. Lomenzo, who was defeated for Comptroller by Levitt, made a poorer showing.

21

•••

The Second Election

By NATURE, politicians are an optimistic breed. Only the most hopeful of men would voluntarily submit their careers and ambitions to the unpredictable whims of the electorate. It follows, therefore, that front-runners are prone to two besetting sins. Either they dream impossible dreams, battening on every scrap of what seems to be good news, or they sink into complacency as Thomas E. Dewey did in 1948, and begin picking their cabinets while the election slips away from them.

In the 1962 election, Nelson Rockefeller was the front-runner all the way. Already the man to beat for the Republican presidential nomination in 1964, Rockefeller went into his campaign for reelection knowing full well that a landslide victory would make his position vis-à-vis the presidential nod nearly impregnable. With this prospect before him, he worked harder even than in 1958. The signs seemed to augur well. Labor, which usually plumped for the Democratic candidate, was sitting out the election officially, and Rockefeller picked up a substantial union following. A high registration, later proved overloaded with carry-over voters from the 1960 presidential election, who habitually ignore all other elections, pointed to a heavy gain in the vote in Republican "country." Secretly, Rockefeller hoped against hope right up to Election Day to pull off the near miracle of carrying New York City.

Carrying New York by 500,000-plus votes for the second time was a considerable political achievement for Rockefeller, given the special circumstances of the election. And those circumstances included the fact that the two Republicans who ran ahead of him—Senator Javits and State Attorney General Lefkowitz—had "setups" for opponents. Javits's opponent was James B. Donovan, a politically unknown Brooklyn lawyer, chiefly famed at the time for negotiating the release of the U-2 pilot Francis Gary Powers from a Soviet prison; Lefkowitz ran against Manhattan Borough President Edward Dudley, the first Negro ever nominated for statewide office by a major party, who had no previous exposure north of the New York City line.

Aside from the breaks Javits and Lefkowitz got, the Republicans had a rough time in the election. They'd gone to the polls confident of greatly increasing their strength in the Legislature, and emerged with the State Senate unchanged and a net gain of only one seat in the Assembly—and that a traditional Republican seat in Syracuse that had been thrown away, so to speak, in 1960 as an aftermath of the fight over the Rockefeller tax rise program of 1959. In Congress, they'd fared even worse. In the special session of 1961, the Legislature reapportioned the Congressional districts to reduce the number of seats from 43 to 41 as required by the 1960 census, and had sedulously gerrymandered the new districts to provide a 25 to 16 edge for the GOP in the Congressional delegation. On Election Day, however, the

Democrats upset the calculations by winning four of the "safe" Republican seats.

The underlying Democratic strength in New York, the strength that gave the state to John F. Kennedy in 1960 and safely returned Mayor Wagner for his third term in 1961, was clearly apparent. Surmounting this strength, plus the specific obstacles of his divorce, a lingering resentment over his tax program, and an all-out campaign from the Far Right to destroy him, to win the state by more than half a million was proof of Rockefeller's grip on potent New York, even though his plurality was diminished. He soon came to accept it as such.

For analysis of the returns showed several pluses not apparent in the bald arithmetic of the count. First and foremost in Catholic New York—estimates of the Catholic population are 35 to 38 percent—there was no firm evidence that his divorce was a decisive factor, one way or the other, a finding having an important bearing on his national availability. It was true he lost Erie County, with its high concentration of Catholics (58 percent of the population), by around 36,000 against a 65,000-vote victory edge in 1958, but the divorce issue was not clear there because the county, an economically distressed area, was plagued with high unemployment, a condition which normally runs against the ins.

And the Erie County defection was very nearly offset by Rockefeller's strong run in New York City. He didn't carry the city, but he cut the Democratic margin against him, losing by only 205,000 votes. This was significant, in national calculations, because President Kennedy won New York State in 1960 only by piling up a plurality of close to 800,000 inside the city limits.

Moreover, Rockefeller scored a point that was not lost on Republicans nationally by facing up to the challenge of the Far Right. The Conservative Party of New York was put together in 1962 for the avowed purpose of defeating Rockefeller and Senator Javits, with the hope that defeat would bring about realignment of the Republican Party leadership. The right-wingers nominated David H. Jaquith, a 65-year-old industrialist from Syracuse, for Governor.

Although the Conservatives proved far from adroit—their first nominee to oppose Senator Javits withdrew publicly rather than accept the support of the John Birch Society—the official Republican leadership and many officeholders took a dim view of them having a place on the ballot. The reasoning was that a Conservative line would open a refuge for any protest vote that might develop—over Rockefeller's divorce, or his tax policy, or even from disappointed Nixonites of 1960. Since New York law requires twelve thousand petitions for nominations for statewide office, with at least fifty from each of the sixty-two counties, for a new party, elaborate plans were made to challenge the Conservative positions county by county in an effort to knock the party off the ballot. Whether the effort would have led to anything is moot because the test never came.

Rockefeller made the decision on his own. Those Republicans in favor of fighting the Conservative Party in the courts estimated that the new grouping would poll upward of 250,000 votes, a damaging loss to the GOP if the estimates were accurate. Rockefeller never agreed with the figures. Samplings he had made indicated a far smaller Conservative tally than the pros expected. Knowing that sooner or later he would have to accept the challenge of the ultras, whose votes could never be his in any case, Rockefeller chose to fight it out in the election. It was a bold decision—and it paid off.

For the Conservative Party was never a factor in the election. It polled only 141,877 votes for Jaquith, its candidate for Governor, but the chief significance of that figure was its exposure of the weakness of the Far Right in New York State. The message was heard loud and clear across the country.

All in all, therefore, the election buttressed Rockefeller's position for his move toward the Presidency. He didn't get the spectacular assist he'd hoped for, but he came out of the election stronger than he went into it, and he couldn't reasonably ask for anything more.

And while Rockefeller firmed up his New York base on that Election Day, across the country, Richard M. Nixon, starting his political comeback as a candidate for Governor against the Democratic incumbent Edmund G. (Pat) Brown in California, got himself clobbered. This second defeat, coupled with his extraordinary and bitter valedictory to the press when he at last conceded the election, seemed to seal Nixon's withdrawal from politics.

At any event, by the weekend after election, Rockefeller stood alone as the probable 1964 nominee. Off to the right, far off, was Senator Barry Goldwater, but he was strenuously denying any White House ambitions, and even those who admired him and greatly liked what he preached conceded that his chances were remote. The two most attractive Republican newcomers to make the national scene in the November 6th election—Governors-elect William Scranton of Pennsylvania and George Romney of Michigan—were not present threats.

Almost, it seemed, events were conspiring to thrust the nomination on Rockefeller, willy-nilly, at a time when President Kennedy, fresh from facing down the Soviet missile threat in Cuba, looked entirely unbeatable. Warily, Nelson evaded efforts to goad him into a premature commitment. It was too early to talk about candidates, he insisted: the proper concern of Republicans was the rebuilding of a unified party. It was to be his theme for the next several months.

In the meantime, serious trouble broke out on the home front. Right after Election Day, Manhattan District Attorney Frank S. Hogan began presenting to a grand jury evidence gathered in an eighteen-month-long investigation of corruption and suspected bribery in the Republican-dominated State Liquor Authority. Such investigations are not new in New York. Since the State Liquor Authority was set up after the repeal of Prohibition to control licensing of liquor stores and bars, as well as the liquor industry generally, periodic inquiries have been the rule rather than the exception. Usually politically motivated, they explode in a rash of headlines, expose some lower-level graft and fade away.

The Hogan investigation was different. Five times elected District Attorney with the support of both major parties, Hogan has managed to maintain a nonpolitical stance despite the fact that he was the unsuccessful candidate for U. S. Senator in 1958. His inquiry could not be brushed off as another partisan attack.

Nor could his facts. An ever-cautious man, Hogan prepared his case meticulously before taking it to the grand jury. And when he made his move, he struck hard at the higher echelons. The fallout scarred the Rockefeller administration's reputation for probity, the more so because under the statute of limitations, Hogan investigated only events since Rockefeller began his first term.

Nelson felt betrayed. Although there was never any thought that he condoned or even knew of the shenanigans in the Liquor Authority, the main targets of the inquiry were one of his associates and two of his appointees. Before November was out, he fired Martin C. Epstein, whom he'd appointed chairman of the Liquor Authority on the recommendation of the Republican organization, for refusing to sign a waiver of immunity, as required under New York's public officers law, when called before the grand jury.

That was but a curtain raiser. The indictment of a Chicago promoter on a charge of paying a $50,000 bribe to a Liquor Authority official to get a license for the Playboy Club in Manhattan lifted the investigation out of the ruck of ordinary scandals and into the national headlines. And this was followed by the abrupt resignation of State Republican Chairman L. Judson Morhouse, a member of Rockefeller's inner political circle, when the grand jury started breathing down his neck. Morhouse later quit a $17,500 job as a member of the State Thruway Authority rather than waive immunity before the grand jury. Subsequently it was disclosed that he got $18,000 in legal fees for advising the Playboy Club on license problems.

Nor was this all. By early spring a judge of the Court of Claims, appointed by Rockefeller out of a Manhattan West Side Republican clubhouse, claimed immunity before the grand jury, and the Governor felt impelled to call on the Chief Judge of the Court of Appeals to start ouster proceedings. Osterman was removed from the bench some months later.

Rockefeller watched the growing scandal with dismay. He'd

prided himself on the honesty and efficiency of his administration, but the Hogan inquiry left that image tarnished. The Governor, who'd spurned a suggestion that he supersede the DA's investigation and appoint a special prosecutor since a state agency was involved, promised Hogan his cooperation and instructed the Liquor Authority that there were to be no reprisals against complaining licensees.

It was precisely while Hogan was exploding his bombshells in New York that a storm of trouble blew up for Rockefeller in Albany. When the Legislature convened in January, 1963, the Republican Party was badly fragmented. The leadership control, exercised so faithfully in behalf of Rockefeller programs for four years, was showing signs of wear. Tax-conscious legislators whose hearts belonged to Nixon and Goldwater, although their votes had gone to Rockefeller, apparently feared the electorate back home more than a Governor whose denials never quite covered up the presidential gleam in his eye. The first successful revolt against Rockefeller was underway.

The showdown came over license fees. In 1959, Rockefeller easily stifled an abortive tax revolt by adroit manipulation of patronage coupled with a judicious application of party discipline. In 1963, both weapons were blunted. The resignation of Morhouse from the state chairmanship had shut off the normal channel of communication between the Governor on the one hand and legislators and the county chairmen on the other. Moreover, Rockefeller made a telling semantic contribution to his own discomfiture.

In the 1962 campaign, Rockefeller pledged flatly that there would be no tax increase. Undoubtedly, he was sincere. When it came time to make up the budget, however, he was confronted with the hard choice of sacrificing pay-as-you-go financing, the very foundation of his claim to fiscal integrity, or finding new revenues. Politically, he couldn't abandon pay-as-you-go. It was a slogan too often relied on, both in New York and nationally, to underline his claims of a business administration, to be put aside. New taxes it had to be.

But the administration was pledged not to increase taxes.

Somebody came up with the thought that the Motor Vehicle Tax, carried under that title in every budget since New York adopted the executive budget, really represented fees for licenses and registration. Rockefeller bought the idea. When the budget came out, it called for increased "fees" for automobiles and liquor licenses.

As much as anything else, this word juggling defeated Rockefeller. The Democrats cheerfully hooted, "A tax is a tax is a tax even when you call it a fee." Around the Capitol, a standard gag was, "Have you paid your income fees?" Upstate editorialists (New York City was blacked out by the newspaper strike) took a dim view of the verbal gymnastics. Rockefeller himself got nowhere trying to defend the change as a more exact definition. And the rebellious Republicans made "fees" their battle cry.

In the end, Rockefeller had to abandon the boost in Motor Vehicle Fees—the title was retained—scale down the liquor fee increases and submit to a slash of about $40 million in his budget.

This was not too great a change in his program, but the retreat was disorderly, and neither the party unity nor Rockefeller's image benefited. However, the damage was local and presumably would fade swiftly.

Then Rockefeller remarried, and every slightest bit of trouble he had was dragged out for national examination as the press, politicians and the clergy reevaluated his political posture.

The marriage came as a shock even to Rockefeller's closest political aides. By the time she got her quiet divorce from Dr. James S. Murphy on April 1, 1963, in Idaho, the gossip about Rockefeller and Mrs. Margaretta Fitler Murphy had largely died away, and even the columnists had stopped keeping tabs on her.

For nearly three weeks after the divorce was granted, it remained a secret, but at last the story was "leaked" to a New York paper by Dr. Murphy's lawyer. At once all the gossip revived, with many embellishments. And now the press, which had never before directly tackled the subject, put the question bluntly to Rockefeller: Would he marry Mrs. Murphy?

"No comment," said Rockefeller. He said it over and over again for two weeks with a smile. But the smile wore thin. Everywhere he turned, reporters popped up. The pressure began to tell. And the gossip got wilder and wilder with no facts to restrain it.

At noon on Saturday, May 4th, Happy Murphy and Rockefeller were married at the home of Nelson's brother, Laurance, on the family estate at Pocantico Hills. The bride was thirty-six; the bridegroom, fifty-four. The only Rockefellers present, besides Laurance and his wife, were the Governor's stepmother (his father had remarried in 1951) and his son, Rodman, and his wife. The first Mrs. Nelson Rockefeller spent the day at the estate of his older brother, John D., III, in Virginia.

The new Mrs. Rockefeller, like the first, was an heiress in her own right. And like the first Mrs. Rockefeller, the bride claimed a distinguished ancestry, numbering among her great-grandfathers General George Gordon Meade, commander of the Union forces at the Battle of Gettysburg, and among her ancestors further back, Jonathan Dickinson, founder and first president of Princeton University. Through her father, the late William Wonderly Fitler, Jr., the bride was descended from Edwin H. Fitler, onetime Mayor of Philadelphia.

The wedding, of course, was private, being announced by the Office of the Rockefeller Brothers in Manhattan in midafternoon on Saturday, and the Governor and his bride spent their wedding night at Pocantico Hills in the Victorian mansion built originally for the first John D. Rockefeller, which Nelson took over as his home after his divorce.

The next morning at Idlewild Airport, Rockefeller presented his bride to the press at an informal news conference, carefully coaching her to obey the commands of the photographers. While the flashbulbs popped, the reporters met a slender, wholesome-looking young matron, with great flashing eyes, who might have been ten years younger than her acknowledged age. Understandably, she was nervous, but she seemed to enjoy her first exposure to the massed press.

The newlyweds flew by commercial jet airliner to Caracas en route to Rockefeller's Monte Sacro estate in the Chirgua Valley of Venezuela where they spent their honeymoon.

The remarriage injected a totally new factor into national

political calculations, and all aspects of it were carefully examined by both politicians and the clergy. The political comment divided, as might be expected, according to whether the speaker was for or against Rockefeller as the 1964 nominee. The pro Rockefeller people took the view, generally, of New York's new Republican State Chairman Fred A. Young, who proclaimed that he would work for Nelson for the nomination and that the remarriage would help rather than hurt him. Those favoring other candidates were inclined to predict that he'd ruined himself politically.

Neither position was susceptible of proof, short of a primary contest or an actual test at the convention. But one immediate effect of the remarriage was a sharp increase in the interest in possible dark horses for the nomination if a weakened Rockefeller should deadlock the convention with Senator Barry Goldwater. The first beneficiary of this interest was Michigan's Governor George Romney, who already had a quiet boomlet going for him, although he was going through the motions of disclaiming any ambition to do more than make a good record in Michigan.

Ambiguous as the political comment was, there was no ambiguity in the reaction of the clergy. The Presbyterian minister who married Rockefeller and Happy, the Reverend Marshall L. Smith, pastor of the Union Church of Pocantico Hills, where the Rockefellers worshiped, got his wrist slapped for performing the ceremony for a recently divorced woman without getting the approval of his superiors, even though he was acting as pastor of a Union church.

In the first week after the marriage, a number of clergymen of the three major faiths rushed into print with their condemnations, moving Dr. Eugene Carson Blake, chief executive officer of the United Presbyterian Church, to interpose an objection. He called on his fellow clergymen to curb their "excitement," reminding them drily that "both inside and outside" their own flocks there were deep divisions on the "moral and social question" of divorce. Thereafter the clerical "excitement" faded.

Rockefeller and his bride were honeymooning in Venezuela at the height of the ministerial attacks, but when he returned to

Albany early in June, he refused to be drawn into a rebuttal, although he was deeply wounded by some of the comments. Criticisms of his remarriage, he said, were "very understandable."

"One has to see life and the problems of life from other people's point of view," he told a news conference in Albany exactly one month after the marriage. "I think love and understanding are the two greatest forces, and if we have that, then we can understand how people feel, regardless of the situation."

With the pride of a man in love, Rockefeller introduced his new wife to the Albany press corps at a private reception later that day in the Executive Mansion, and that night she made her public bow as First Lady of the state at a civic dinner in an Albany hotel. She scored handsomely in both appearances as she was to score a few days later at a meeting of Republican women in Rockland County.

Her greatest triumph came, however, when she was presented nationally at the annual Governors' Conference in Miami Beach, Florida, in July. The governors' wives, middle-aged in the main and figuring to be a critical audience, accepted her as a member of the club, apparently without reservation.

In the meantime, Rockefeller, who'd fallen from front-runner for the Republican nomination for President to a weak second to Senator Barry Goldwater in the immediate aftermath of the marriage, began to move back into the national political scene. It was a move long planned. At no time had Rockefeller resigned his presidential ambitions, and, while his slump in the national polls after his remarriage was sharper than he expected, he held to his timetable even though some observers were inclined to write him off as a contender.

Rockefeller's first offensive came in mid-July when he blasted the "radical right" that was grouping behind Senator Goldwater, and warned the Arizona Senator to cut his connection with this bloc or risk destroying the Republican Party. The blast was strong stuff. The Goldwater boom was so strong by early July that a countervailing, but leaderless, "Stop Goldwater" movement was beginning to surface, particularly in the Northeast. By seizing the initiative, Rockefeller reestablished himself as spokesman for the international wing of his party.

He followed up the attack on the radical right by brilliantly exploiting the Democratic division on civil rights at the Governors' Conference in Florida. Day after day, he won the headlines as the Democratic majority blocked his efforts to bring a strong civil rights resolution to the floor for a record vote. In the end, the Democrats abolished the resolutions committee, killing all pending resolutions, and the Republicans, unified behind the New York Governor, welded themselves into a caucus to exert state influence in the national deliberations of their party. The caucus had been a Rockefeller project as far back as 1961.

And Rockefeller was off and running again for the Republican nomination in 1964; a contender that no one could dismiss lightly in view of the power behind him and his commitment, freely pledged by New York's National Committeeman George Hinman, that he would carry the fight all the way to the convention floor.

22

A Political Credo

WHATEVER THE POLITICAL OBSTACLES he has created for himself, Nelson Rockefeller is now a force the Republican Party must deal with as the nation moves into the quadrennial exercise of electing a President. The gallant fight he made for principle in the writing of the 1960 platform won him a following of influential and articulate, nonorganization Republicans whose support is absolutely vital to the preservation of the Republican Party, to say nothing of its chances of mounting an effective campaign.

Moreover, alone among the leading Republican possibilities, Rockefeller has long experience in dealing with the country's problems, national and international, in the domestic fields of education and health, in the state-level problems of urban dislocation and local government. As Coordinator of Inter-American Affairs, as Assistant Secretary of State at the birth of the United Nations, as a White House specialist on world problems and as Governor of New York he has compiled a record that, for better or worse, defines his position strongly and unambiguously.

Out of this background, Rockefeller has evolved his philosophy as a Republican. He sees himself as a catalyst, rather than as an innovator, whose function is to develop a consensus that the Republican Party can offer to the nation as a distinctive alternative to the Democratic trend. This consensus, in his view, already exists in Republican beliefs in basic regard for the worth of the individual, in support of free enterprise in a world of encroaching government expansion, in belief in fiscal integrity (translated as budget-balancing), in support for limitation of the role of the central government, in the demand for wider dissemination of the facts of the country's programs, and in the demand for a coherent, forceful and continuing foreign policy.

The problem for the Republicans, as Rockefeller sees it, is to reach agreement on how to achieve these goals within the framework of the Republican organization.

The keystone of Rockefeller's political credo is a passionate dedication to "our belief in the worth and dignity of the individual"—a phrase he uses so often that his critics dismiss it as a slogan. It is anything but a slogan to Rockefeller. In 1960, he was willing to risk political destruction by taking a strong civil rights plank to the floor of the Republican convention, if necessary, and in the intervening years his position has not changed.

"We have certain responsibilities that transcend political advantages," he has said, "and one of them is certainly in the field of human rights . . . we have got to do what is right and, following that, take the consequences as far as the political side is concerned."

As Governor of New York, Rockefeller has clung steadfastly to this principle, often colliding head-on with the conservative, upstate wing of his party in the Legislature. But he has fought, successfully, to broaden the statutes against discrimination in housing, schooling and employment; he has beefed up the state enforcement machinery by creating a civil rights bureau in the Attorney General's office.

This concern with civil rights, which translates in this day and age into "Negro rights," isn't something new with Rockefeller. He is fond of recalling that his great-grandparents cooperated with the Underground Railway that smuggled fugitive slaves through Ohio to freedom in Canada in the pre-Civil War period, and he frequently notes that his grandfather, the first John D. Rockefeller, was deeply concerned and contributed importantly to the cause of Negro education in the South in the post-Reconstruction period, an activity that the Rockefellers of his own generation still pursue. Nelson's concern was deeply rooted long before the ferment of the 1960's raised the issue to critical importance.

In Rockefeller's thinking, civil rights and what he likes to refer to as "human rights" are indissolubly linked. He has pressed unrelentingly for state and national legislation against discrimination because he takes the position that it is morally wrong. But he has also insisted that individual dignity can't be achieved simply through rights legislation. The free enterprise system, he insists, must provide an economic climate in which opportunity is open to everyone capable of taking care of himself. This means, as he sees it, that the economic growth rate, here and everywhere in the Free World, must be geared not only to meet the needs of an expanding population but high enough to raise the general standard of living to the point where all will have a stake in preserving free enterprise.

It is within the framework of these concepts that Rockefeller evolved his political credo and fashioned his record. And that record shows rather impressively that his dedication to human dignity has not been mere lip service.

At the outset of his career, as a young executive of Rockefeller Center in the 1930's, Nelson helped formulate a labor relations policy that has kept that huge real-estate enterprise free of labor trouble ever since. It was a farsighted formulation for the times. Labor was coming of age in the 1930's, under the impetus of the Wagner Act, and many industries—notably the automobile, steel and rubber—fought long and bitter battles against unionization. (Who can forget the sitdown strikes?) The acceptance by the Rockefellers of labor's right to organize was an important psychological factor in shaping the thinking of many employers.

"I felt," Rockefeller has said, "and I still feel that employers and employees have to recognize they are mutually dependent on each other."

In South America, both as Coordinator of Inter-American Affairs and as a businessman, Rockefeller made it a practice to enlist the support of labor if possible when launching new projects, although this consultation sometimes distressed local business and political interests. In the Mexican redevelopment program, for example, no provision was made for labor representation on the official commission for political reasons, but Rockefeller by unofficial personal intercession got the two major union organizations to accept the projects. Without this cooperation, the redevelopment program might have foundered instead of providing a framework for that nation's strong postwar economic recovery.

As Governor of New York, Rockefeller has not been conspicuously prolabor. But his record was such in his first term that in 1962, for the first time since the rise of the New Deal, organized labor failed to endorse the Democratic candidate for Governor. As a consequence, Rockefeller went into his second election with the strongest labor support of any Republican gubernatorial candidate in modern times—support which was a definite factor in running up his second half-million plus plurality.

Education has always been a preoccupation of the Rockefellers, and Nelson has made it a particular province of his own. Perhaps because he found formal study difficult, he puts a very high (some say exaggerated) value on academic achievement, selecting his associates, in government and business, in part on the basis of their educational accomplishments. But he is a firm devotee to the idea that a good basic education is the surest way to help more people achieve their individual dignity. As Under Secretary of Health, Education, and Welfare, he was an early advocate of Federal aid to public schools, accurately forecasting the educational crisis of the 1960's. He helped develop the Eisenhower Administration program for school aid—a program that bogged down in Congressional politics as all school aid bills have since—and fought for it even after transferring from HEW to the White House.

As Governor, Rockefeller has more than doubled New York State's contribution of aid to the public schools, raising it to more than $1 billion a year. He has vastly expanded the state university program, with the goal of doubling its capacity in this decade, and he has instituted a student grant program, providing state contributions of $100 to $300 a year to undergraduates and $400 to $800 to graduate students attending colleges in New York State.

Although he regards education as a good per se, Rockefeller also emphasizes that this country can't afford to fall behind in equipping its youth to master the high skills that will be required by the sophisticated automation now being introduced in almost every field. The future of the unschooled, he has warned, in setting up state programs to persuade high-school dropouts to return to their classes, is likely to be grim in a world in which complicated machines can perform more efficiently the drudgery now falling on the unskilled.

It has, nevertheless, been largely because of the expanded, and vital, spending for schools that Rockefeller's fiscal policies as Governor of New York have been called into question. When Rockefeller instituted pay-as-you-go state budgeting on the strength of the spectacular success of his tax reform program of 1959, it was calculated that, given a constant ratio between spending for state purposes (road building, the maintenance of highways, mental hospitals, state forests and parks, the state university and state police, and similar direct state functions) and for local assistance, revenues would be sufficient over the period of a decade to maintain the tax structure. But it was impossible to sustain the ratio. Local communities, particularly the school districts, were unable to find the money to keep going from their limited resources, and the state was forced to increase its contributions. This led to a proliferation of state-created "authorities" to finance a variety of programs without adding directly to state debt, and the resort to these authorities gave rise to charges of "financial gimmickry" (a phrase used by the staid *New York Times*) in Rockefeller's fiscal policy.

The merit of these charges can be properly assessed only by experts. What the record showed was that under Rockefeller the state has reported a surplus in the operation of all his budgets, the state debt has been cut by $85 million and the state credit rating is top drawer.

"I promised to restore the financial integrity of the state," said Rockefeller, "and we have done so by pay-as-you-go. Government spending must be geared to revenue if we are to have a sound economy."

The criticism of his fiscal policies irks Rockefeller. He considers it unrealistic to expect any significant reduction in public spending at a time when an explosively expanding population is straining public facilities to the utmost. But he believes that the economic growth rate can be sharply increased to yield the needed revenues and leave room for tax cuts. That, he says, has been his program in New York, but New York alone can't make much headway unless the national growth rate is accelerated. Failure to produce such acceleration has provoked some of his sharpest criticism not only of the Kennedy Administration but of the Eisenhower Administration before it.

For, Rockefeller holds, failure to achieve and maintain a high growth rate puts a severe limit on our capacity to lead the Free World in the struggle against Communism. And it is in this struggle, Rockefeller says, that America finds her mission in the second half of the twentieth century.

It is precisely in the discussion of this mission that Rockefeller has made his most imaginative contribution to the dialogue on Whither America. In the Godkin lectures, which he delivered at Harvard University in February, 1962, Rockefeller proposed the application of the Federal idea, as embodied in the U. S.

Constitution, to the Free World in order to provide a stable political structure within which the newly emerged countries would find a refuge from Communist pressure while achieving true statehood. He said:

> The ultimate challenge of Communist imperialism is its promise to fill the political vacuum in world order created by the collapse of old empires and the failure of anything else to take their place. Such a vacuum is as abhorrent to politics as to nature. And Communism offers a design—a cruel design—for world order . . . It seeks to create the illusion that a Communist world order will be more secure, more rational, and more geared to the realities of modern life, science, and technology than any other structure, past or present.

It was Rockefeller's thesis that the United States never faced up to this "ultimate challenge" of Communism. Diverted by the strains of meeting one crisis after another as they arose around the world, he held, the nation never developed a coherent foreign policy that extended the hope of stability to the underdeveloped and new nations as an alternative to the monolith of totalitarianism. He advanced the idea of federalism as pointing "a direction in which free men can begin to think, to act, and—in the case of the United States particularly—to lead.

"No nation today," he warned, "can defend its freedom, or fulfill the needs and aspirations of its own people from within its own borders or through its own resources alone."

Rockefeller distilled his soaring concept of Free World federalism out of his long experience and study of the U. S. role in international affairs. As far back as 1945 as an Assistant Secretary of State, he'd anticipated the need of regional defense and economic groupings under the United Nations Charter and had fought strenuously, against stern Russian opposition, to win approval for the Western Hemisphere Alliance that grew out of the Act of Chapultepec. Later he proposed a common market of the Americas, which would have constituted a kind of economic federalism. The market is still unrealized.

Throughout the postwar period, Rockefeller's principal concern has been that the nation never adopted a clear position in foreign affairs that neither friend nor foe could misinterpret.

"As each crisis confronted us," he said, "we rose magnificently and, even, gallantly to the needs of the moment. Then when the danger was passed we settled back to drift."

The drift disturbs Rockefeller profoundly. It has led deplorably, he feels, to *de facto* acceptance by the United States of the Soviet thesis that the proper way to manage the world is for the United States and Russia, as the two great powers, to settle all major questions between themselves, handing the rest of the world a *fait accompli* in their decisions. The effect, Rockefeller says, has been to weaken the national prestige and to undermine faith in the regional defense associations this country has sponsored, notably in the Southeast Asia crisis. Every time the United States meets a Soviet threat head-on as a two-power crisis, he believes, the other nations of the West are deprived of the sense of sovereignty. He says:

> We must handle our conduct in the Cold War in such a way as to give full faith and credit to the efforts of our allies in meeting the problems impinging directly on the areas of their immediate concern. If we do less, the governments we are trying hardest to help find themselves exposed to intolerable pressures from nationalist elements within their own countries which parrot the Communist line of American imperialism.

Furthermore, Rockefeller says, running foreign policy on an *ad hoc* basis has been extremely costly to the Free World, meaning the United States chiefly, in the financial and military burdens it has imposed. Lofty though his concept of Free World federalism is, he distills it, through the alchemy of his personal pragmatism, as pointing the way to the very practical goal of shifting a large part of the foreign aid load to the private sector of the economy.

In the long term, it is Rockefeller's view, the erection of a stable political system to shelter our allies among the emerging and underdeveloped nations will tremendously advance the cause of freedom by unleashing "the creative possibilities of free enterprise as an economic catalyst in the Free World.

"We haven't begun to use the magnificent tools we have evolved out of long experience with free enterprise," he says.

Rockefeller gives full credit to the generosity of the massive government-to-government aid the United States has distributed since the end of World War II and to the spectacular advances that have been made. But, he argues, while such aid must, of necessity, be continued for many years, the recruitment of the private capital in the aided countries—capital that now frequently seeks refuge abroad because of political instability at home—could produce the kind of economic growth that would lift the standard of living faster than any government program could hope. He says:

> In South America we proved that when we introduced supermarkets in Venezuela. At the start, we had to import 85 percent of all our foodstuffs. Now 85 percent of what is handled in the supermarkets, both our own and our competitors', is locally produced. Local agriculture found new markets when we set up an effective distribution system, and local capital found reason to stay at home.

This kind of development, which deeply involves local interests, makes a contribution to political stability as well as economic growth, Rockefeller says, and indicates a field so far neglected. The problem of getting such projects started, he says, could be solved by government loans where outside private capital couldn't be found, but the cost would be held down because once any program begins to show a profit local interests would move in, as they moved in when Rockefeller's International Basic Economy Corporation showed the way with its supermarkets in Venezuela.

The heart of the matter, Rockefeller says, is that only by getting other nations to help themselves can we weld a free world strong enough to support the growth of democracy.

This wedding of the practical and the idealistic that characterizes Rockefeller's thinking on foreign policy, as it marks his record on civil rights, is the hallmark of his political philosophy. He can be as partisan as the next Republican in criticizing the Democratic Party and its policies, but his principal emphasis is always on the future.

The world we have to save, he says, is the world we live in; not the world of our fathers.

Bedford Hills, N. Y.